THE GOOD NEWS OF JESUS CHRIST FOR THE PEOPLE OF INDIA

Indian Contextual Christologies

THE GOOD NEWS OF JESUS CHRIST FOR THE PEOPLE OF INDIA

Indian Contextual Christologies

T. K. John S.J. & George Mlakuzhyil S.J.

2021

Cover Design: Mr. Bejoy P. Mukkathu

The multi-coloured RAINBOW is the symbol of "THE GOOD NEWS OF JESUS CHRIST." The RAYS of the revelation of his person, message and mission enlighten "THE PEOPLE OF INDIA." "Indian Contextual Christologies" reflect and interpret Jesus' Good News contextually and theologically.

The *mosaic* of the *Indian Sadguru Jesus* is used with the written permission of Rev. Fr. Mahendra Paul IMS, Superior General, Varanasi.

ISBN: 978-81-949231-5-2

Laser typeset by

ISPCK, Post Box 1585, 1654, Madarsa Road, Kashmere Gate, Delhi-110006 • *Tel:* 23866323

e-mail: ashish@ispck.org.in • ella@ispck.org.in
website: www.ispck.org.in

Dedicated to
Indian Subaltern Groups
(Dalits, Tribals & Women)
and Inter-Faith Dialogue Partners
(Hindus, Muslims & Sikhs)

CONTENTS

Preface

Since many books have already been written about *Jesus Christ* even in the 21ˢᵗ century, *why* to have *another book?* Because of *his unique relevance to the Indian people today.* This volume deals with the *significance* of *"Jesus Christ for the people of India"* in today's context.

In the light of our experiences of teaching in Vidyajyoti College of Theology and in Regional Theology Centres and of giving Retreats and talks and of interacting with various groups of people in India over the decades, we realized that *"the good news of Jesus Christ"* is very *appealing* to theology students, Christian laity, Priests and Religious, and especially to the poor and the oppressed and to many followers of other faiths in our country. Hence we decided to embark on a combined theological project of *writing contextual and dialogical faith-interpretations* of the *person, mission and message of Jesus Christ* that would be *relevant to our people today.* The fruit of our long labour of love is **"THE GOOD NEWS OF JESUS CHRIST FOR THE PEOPLE OF INDIA: Indian Contextual Christologies."**

The **TITLE** underlines how *meaningful Jesus Christ's "Good News"* is *"for the People of India."* The **Subtitle** points to his *relevance* to the **Subaltern Groups** (*Dalits, Tribals, Women*) and **Inter-Faith Dialogue-Partners** (*Hindus, Muslims, Sikhs*) in India today.

We are *indebted* to *many persons* for the *publication* of the present volume. First of all, our whole-hearted thanks to *Jesus Christ* for calling us to be his companions in the Society of Jesus and for inspiring us to venture on writing this book together as friends in the Lord.

We are very grateful to Delhi Jesuit Provincials (Fr. Varkey Perekkatt S.J., Fr. Sebastian Jeerakassery S.J. & Fr. Soosai Mani S.J.) and the Jesuit communities (at Sahayog and St. Xavier's, Delhi) for their fraternal encouragement and prayerful support.

We express our heartfelt gratitude to Fr. Poulose Mangai S.J. (Professor of Theology and Sikhism and Editor of Vidyajyoti Journal of Theological Reflection) for writing the subsection on Sikh-Christian dialogue and to Fr. Victor Edwin S.J. (Lecturer of Islam and Christian-Muslim Relations, Director of VIDIS, Secretary of ISA and CMRSA) for his critical suggestions and valuable assistance in improving the subsection on Muslim-Christian dialogue. We sincerely thank Vidyajyoti librarian (Fr. K. T. Chandy S.J.) and library staff for their timely help in borrowing books.

We are greatly indebted to Mr. Bejoy P. Mukkathu for the artistic Cover Design with the 'Indian Sadguru Jesus' and to Rev. Fr. Mahendra Paul IMS, Superior General, for granting us permission to use the mosaic for the Cover.

Finally, we are very obliged to Rev. Dr. Ashish Amos of ISPCK, Delhi, for publishing this book and making copies of it available to the public at reasonable price.

We hope and pray that the readers will find "THE GOOD NEWS OF JESUS CHRIST FOR THE PEOPLE OF INDIA" meaningful for their life and mission in the Indian context today.

T. K. John S.J.   George Mlakuzhyil S.J.

Sahayog   4 Raj Niwas Marg, Delhi 110054   Jesuit Residence, St. Xavier's

tkjohnsj@gmail.com   *georgemlakuzhy@gmail.com*

November 1, 2020

Feast of All the Saints

INTRODUCTION

0.1. Gospel-based Indian Contextual Christologies

Recently Asian theologians have been highlighting the importance of developing *contextual, Gospel-based theologies* for the pastoral-spiritual renewal of the Church, envisioned by Vatican II and promoted by Pope Francis:

> [O]ne of the fruits of his labour would be the emergence of **gospel-based theologies** - theologies that are not tied down to a rational system or a philosophy as has happened so far in the West...
>
> **Christian theology**" is "**a contextual interpretation of the Scripturally Revealed Word of God** (as epitomized in Christ and constituting the Good news of Salvation) in response to the *socio-cultural challenges* of each place and time...[1]

To develop a *contextual Asian theology*, it is not enough to return to the sources (Scripture and Tradition) but we must return to "***the Source,*" *Jesus Christ of the Gospels,*** and reinterpret God's revelation in him in the *Asian socio-economic context* of "the life-and-death struggles of the Dalits and destitute masses" and *cultural-religious context* of "many religions".[2]

Now if this is true of all contextual Asian theologies, *relevant* **"Indian Contextual Christologies"** cannot be attempted without going back to **"Jesus Christ in the Gospels"**[3] and *reinterpreting* his significance **"for the People of India"** in *today's context.*

The *different Gospel images of Jesus* stimulate us to have *our own faith interpretations* of the *'divinehuman' Jesus Christ, his message and his mission,* which would be meaningful for Indians in the contemporary context.[4] This is what is attempted in this volume: **"THE GOOD NEWS OF JESUS CHRIST FOR THE PEOPLE OF INDIA: Indian Contextual Christologies".**

The **TITLE** suggests that the *person, mission and message* of *Jesus Christ* are *"the Good News for the People of India."* The **Subtitle** indicates that "the Good News of Jesus Christ" is *contextually interpreted* for the *Indian Subaltern Groups* (Dalits, Tribals, Women) and *Inter-Faith Dialogue-Partners* (Hindus, Muslims, Sikhs).

0.2.   Plan of the Present Book

The **FIRST SECTION (I. THE PEOPLE OF INDIA)** deals with the **"Multiple Context of the People of India"**: *historical, political, economic, social, cultural, religious and spiritual* (**Chapter 1**) and **"Indian Subaltern Groups** [*Dalits, Tribals and Women*] **in Socio-Cultural Perspective"** (**Chapter 2**).

In the light of the contextual study of the people of India (in the FIRST SECTION), in the **SECOND SECTION** we formulate **"Indian Contextual Christologies"** in **two Chapters:** *"The Good News of Jesus Christ for Dalits, Tribals and Women: Indian Subaltern Christologies"* (**Chapter 3**) and *"The Good News of Jesus Christ for Hindus, Muslims and Sikhs: Indian Dialogical*

Christologies" (**Chapter 4**). The Gospels *inspire* us to *present Jesus Christ* as "*the Good News*" to *the Indians* (*Christians and others*, especially the *poor* and the *marginalized* and *people of other faiths*).

Finally, keeping in mind the *insights* from the above two SECTIONS, we highlight in the "**CONCLUSION**" the "**SIGNIFICANCE OF JESUS CHRIST FOR THE PEOPLE OF INDIA**" by underlining the *relevance of his person, mission and vision* for *our people today*.

I.

THE PEOPLE OF INDIA

Introduction

Sheltered by the lofty Himalayan ranges in the north and washed regularly by the waters of the Bay of Bengal in the east and the Arabian Ocean in the west is located the subcontinent of India. It is inhabited by the people that trace their roots to at least six anthropological races and nine religions. The Indic civilization is counted among the earliest world civilizations like the Egyptian, the Babylonian, the Sumerian, the Minoan, the Phoenician and the Chinese. The many indigenous people that lived even before the Indus Valley civilization and those that entered India from west-central Asia thereafter further contributed to the diversity and pluralism of the subcontinent.

Academics in search of knowledge, religious seekers for meditative techniques like those for Yoga, traders looking for spices, gold, etc., and artisans for precious wood, and conquerors in search of territorial expansion, -- people of every sector from east and west, had regular contact with the people of this land. Mutual exchange existed from early times with East Asian countries. Indian heritage travelled east as evidences like Angkor Vat in Cambodia and literary forms in Indonesia provide.

Similarly, there were cultural, religious and trade exchanges between India and the West through Arab traders. Cross-cultural exchanges between ancient Phoenician, Roman and Greek cultures existed from early times.

Increasing interest in the people of India globally and locally has been an encouraging development. Academics in many universities from abroad have been focusing on India's experiment with pluralism, democracy and development. India's challenge of poverty and illiteracy has been another area of research and reporting. Considered as a laboratory of religious pluralism, India is being keenly watched by scholars from all over the world.

The phrase "*The people of India*" is an *inclusive* phrase, holding within its fold both the Christians of all denominations as well as the Tribals, the Hindus, the Muslims, the Jains, the Buddhists, the Sikhs, and especially the poor and marginalized such as the Dalits, the Tribals, and the women of all these sections.

From early times onwards the people of India have been raising some of the *deepest questions* pertaining to *life-experience*. Why suffering? What after death? Why inequality among the people?

The *origin, nature and destiny of the human person*, as planned by God, is the frame work of the reflection under way. In the light of current teaching of the Church, people of India were beneficiaries of divine communications and actions. How did the people of India *fare* in terms of the *deepest quest of the human person* and *respond* to the *divine plan for all of humanity?* These have been and are still discussed in many inter-religious and inter-cultural forums.

Right from the beginning of creation the *presence of both grace and sin* had been a main *theme* of the *biblical revelation.* The phenomena like poverty, illiteracy, various forms of violence, exploitation and enslavement of the apparently weaker sections have been among the *dominant concerns* of the *divine restoration plan.* It is therefore quite appropriate to investigate how "the Good News of Jesus Christ" figures in the *life-struggles* of "the People of India" *to fulfill their destiny.*

Reflections on the People of India can be commenced most suitably under the aegis of the following text from the Letter to the Hebrews: "In many and various ways God spoke of old to our fathers [ancestors] by the prophets; but in these last days he has spoken to us by a Son" (Heb 1,1).

An 'ancester' of great antiquity, *Dhrtarashtra,* though blind, was *curious to know* what had been the nature of the forces assembled in the battlefield. Due credit needs to be bestowed on the author of the work here because *jijnasa* (*desire to know,* to probe, to reconsider, to question further the truth at hand, to reassess the existing tradition, practice, values, etc.) is the beginning of all knowledge and wisdom, changes and developments.

Another ancient sage who took to flight after an encounter in the desert was inspired by a strange flame on the mountain bush and was forced to turn back and organize the people for a march to freedom and settlement in peace. His name is

Moses, who came down with a spark from the burning bush and flooded the world with the Judeo-Christian stream.

A modern sage who learned the art of warfare for freedom, truth and justice, in another continent and returned to India to organize the sub-continental forces and won an epic battle not with bloodshed and life-extinguishing weapons but with the unique ethical-moral weapon known as *ahimsa* (non-violence) and *satyagraha* in India. His name is *Gandhi*, honoured as the Father of the Nation.

In brief, ancient wisdom tells us that the first step in the march towards welfare for all could be with the scrutiny of the path with an analytical perception of the field.

The scene of the current phase of the human caravan in India has been quite baffling. Unsettling forces do intervene constantly in the human family's effort to organize life. These are operative globally as well as locally. Assaults on the universally recognized values of dignity, rights and freedoms proper to the human person have been regular. Bulwarks to protect the supreme values enshrined in the historic "Universal Declaration of Human Rights" or the "Preamble of the Constitution of India" are there to give us confidence and hope. Yet even these and the pillars of our national identity are enfeebled by assaults by weapons and forces and structures that are formidable. Operationalization of sterling values is often blocked. The many trends and values that are redeeming and regenerative are there to re-assure all defenders of the human person. A large number of organizations to defend and assist the protection and promotion of justice, rights, freedoms as well as the dignity of the human person are there in the field as resources.

Keeping these in mind, we stand by Arjuna who, although overcome with *vishada* (grief-marked apprehension) at the sight of the forces in Kurukshetra, yet decided to take appropriate remedial steps. Hence the effort in the following pages is to begin with a gaze at the journey of *"the People of India"*

a)   *"The People of India"*

With legitimate racial-cultural pride and joy, we locate '*the People of India*' at the very dawn of world history. With the earliest civilizations, they marched forward. Keeping this perspective in mind, let us listen to the first Prime Minister of free India:

> At the dawn of history India started on her unending quest, and trackless centuries are filled with her striving and the grandeur of her success and her failures. Through good and ill fortune alike she has never lost sight of that quest or forgotten the ideals which gave her strength. We end today a period of ill fortune and India discovers herself again.
>
> At the stroke of the midnight hour, when the world sleeps, India will awake to life and freedom. A moment comes, which comes but rarely in history, when we step out from the old to the new; when an age ends, and when the soul of a nation, long suppressed, finds utterance...[5]

It is India's resetting of her current identity that is of particular concern of the different sections of the people of India. That is what every Indian is looking for. Those who struggled to make India free and set her on the new track had envisioned a new identity for her. What is boldly expressed in the path-making "Preamble to the Constitution of India," the great pledge, is a corporate commitment, a solemn promise:

> WE THE PEOPLE OF INDIA,
> having solemnly resolved to constitute India into a
> Sovereign Socialist Secular Democratic Republic

and to secure to all its citizens:
JUSTICE, social, economic and political;
LIBERTY of thought, expression, belief, faith and worship;
EQUALITY of status and opportunity;
and to promote among them all
FRATERNITY assuring the dignity of the individual
and the unity and integrity of the Nation;
in Our Constituent Assembly
this twenty-sixth day of November, 1949,
do hereby adopt, enact and give to ourselves this Constitution.[6]

At the dawn of our new national identity, leaving behind limited perceptions, narrow loyalties and multiple forms of privations, under the aegis of relentless warriors of freedom we committed ourselves to become a people, the people of India. "We the people of India" have taken on ourselves the onerous responsibilities of leading the country to the envisioned goal.

"We the people of India" is a *unifying and integrating phrase.* The phrase contains J. J. Rousseau's call to revolution to secure freedom for his oppressed country to lead it forward. George Washington's declaration of independence and Jawaharlal Nehru's historic speech on the 'tryst with destiny' and such clarion calls are contained therein. It is a *people's engagement* and *consensual commitment* towards *nation-building.*

"We the people of India" have declared *our national identity* as "a sovereign socialist secular democratic republic." The fourfold epithet of the republic indicates the *lofty ideal* set before the nation by the framers of the Constitution. "The people of India" have *a splendid vision.* The goal set before them is exalted. It needs to be pursued with zeal and tireless efforts. We can recall to our mind that explorers like Christopher Columbus pursued

their vision with unflinching commitment and admirable endurance. It is worth stirring up in our hearts sentiments that will enable the people of India to contribute to the actual realization of the *national goal*: "a sovereign, socialist, secular, democratic republic".

The immediate question that arises in our minds is: *Who are "we the people of India" today?* India of the rich landlords with flourishing agro-industries that always keep their purses fat and bulging? India of industrial magnates that compete with international corporates? This sector of wealth holders wields enormous power politically as well. This is part of the dominant group in India.

There is the India of the *landless agricultural labourers* among the rural population. This sector owns no land but their labour is available to farmers who hire their time and labour at their terms. The labourers have no bargaining power but are at the mercy of the landlords.

In between the rich and the poor, there is the *middle class*. Majority of the rural population has agriculture as their main economic source. Small owners of land raise from it sufficient raw materials for food. Central, as well as the State bureaucracy, is managed by the middle class. This is also known as the *ruling class*.

There is a large section of the *industrial workers*. A small section is organized as "Indian National Trade Union Congress" (INTUC), "All India Trade Union Congress" (AITUC), "Bharatiya Mazdoor Sangh" (BMS), etc. Despite these organized groups, *large sections* of the agricultural, as well as industrial workers (like the migrants), are still *not members of any trade union.* And, therefore, they are *victims of the vicissitudes* of economic and agricultural policies and trends. Market controls their life-struggles.

Not belonging to these sectors is the *large population* of *artisans, petty traders, shop keepers* and *small farmers.* There are also *millions of unemployed Indians* today. 'Street-children', those dwelling in *shanties* without even minimum facilities like running water, electricity, hospitals for medical care, schools, post-offices and other basic services, show another face of modern Indian human community.

The religiosity of the people co-exists with a *life with minimum amenities. Religious symbols* like churches, temples, gurudwaras, mosques abound to give testimony to the claim of *'land of religions'.* However, poverty and stagnation also manifest themselves at various levels. We should recall here that it is this apparent contradiction that provoked economists like Gunnar Myrdal who in his monumental book *The Asian Drama: An Enquiry into the Poverty of the Nations* (1957) raised the sharpness of the *contradiction: great religiosity and abject poverty.* Soothing formulas like *vasudha eva kutumbakam* ('one world family') are uttered at gatherings of activists and scholars to mitigate wounded feelings after terrible communal clashes! Communal clashes, arson and looting, street-fights and stone-pelting, and such indicators of the still existing *symbols of discord,* continue to exist in our country.

Varieties of *celebrations* like marriages, local festivals, national days are also opportunities for further social cohesion. But these are sometimes marred by fundamentalists who interfere and disrupt them and end up in murderous *riots*!

There are *churches* that glory in having golden crosses, *temples* with their deities decked in gold and pots of gold held as deity's possession, *gurudwaras* that manifestly declare themselves rich in gold sheets with which the canopies seem covered. These co-exist with *pavement-sleepers* and *homeless people* who struggle to live on hard-earned money for food, medicine or clothes. Recent information about *millions of houses without toilets* has shocked the *country of economic boom* and the *land of great religiosity.*

b)   An 'Aerial Survey' of the People of India Today

Through a low-altitude aerial survey, one can spot the people in their habitations or places of work or on the move. *Millions of poor* are born, grow and live on the *streets* or under *fly-overs* or in the countless *slums* that flood practically every township in the country. Prolonged life-struggle in the slums results in some being turned into resettlement colonies where minimum amenities are made available to them. *The rich* people live in well-furnished *palatial buildings* with even swimming pools on their terraces. In between these two extreme groups are placed '*the middle class*'. To earn a livelihood, a monstrously graded structure is there: it begins with some taking to *begging* at traffic signals, railway platforms, religious shrines or market places, while on the other end of the socio-economic hierarchy are the *super-rich,* recently termed as the *creamy-layer.*

"We the people of India" can also be located in the nation's *jails, 'red-light areas'* of the cities, *government hospitals, shelter homes* and *orphanages. Refugee-camps* or *temporary huts* with a plastic roof at construction sites are also places where we find 'our people'. Of late there are the *detention camps*, symbols of a new national identity being envisaged and pursued.

Nazi-era gas generation plants had pumping system installed connecting to the chambers. *Poisonous gas* could reach each chamber. Similarly, there are publications and socio-cultural organizations and institutions that regularly generate *hatred-generating literature* that aggravate the *divisive trends* in Indian society. This unhealthy trend needs urgent attention. The sub-continent was once partitioned on the religious criterion. The memory of those days still haunts those who lived through them.

> India is a land of great diversity and composite culture due to a variety of factors such as races, communities, languages, and religions. But India is also *a country of contradictions* (e.g., 'high castes' and 'outcasts', rich landlords and landless labourers, an educated class and illiterate masses, people with palatial homes and homeless slum-dwellers, millionaires and millions of marginalized, super-speciality hospitals for the rich and sub-standard medical care for the poor, a land of religions yet periodic communal conflicts, multiple spiritualities and materialistic consumerism -- extremes seem uncompromising![7]

c) *Gandhiji's Way to Familiarize Himself with the People of India*

Barrister Mohandas Karamchand Gandhi came back from England as a perfect product of Thomas Babington Macaulay's goal of a British education in India: to produce Indians in western garb, to be distant second grader of English sculpting: tie, coat, trousers, shoes, straw hat, and whatnot. Wisdom dawned on him to check the super-imposed newly shaped identity over against the normal Indians. So *he decided to do what Jesus did* (Mt 9,35) to know India and its people: to be in their midst, as a helpful agent, to free them, to raise them up.

With that intention in mind, *Gandhiji* discarded the dress of the 'Inner Temple' barrister and reappeared as *a simple rural Indian*, wearing a simple *dhoti* and a white *chadhar*, and walking with a long *bamboo stick*. He wanted *to know the people of India*. He began the *train journeys across rural India* from north to south, east to west, of peninsular India. He *became a true observer and learner*. Brought up in an urban situation and educated in another culture, Gandhiji began to realize that sufficient *experience of the 'real India'* was *necessary to serve the people of India effectively*. He realized that the majority of the population had to put their seal over his vision and plan to serve them. He came to know the tribals of India, the rich and the poor, brown and fair, Hindus and Muslims, Christians and Buddhists, Jains and Parsees, and above all, rural India. These steps eventually helped him to become a *leader of 'the people of India.'*

The India he saw was ruled by non-Indians. This sad fact propelled him to launch a *struggle to free India from colonial rulers*. For this, he brought together a good mingling of *Indian and western human values*. Henry Thoreau of Civil Disobedience fame and Leo Tolstoy of simple rural life yet of revolutionary vision inspired him to fashion his unique method of campaigning for freeing India from the grip of the colonial power: *ahimsa* and *satyagraha*. He started a *non-violent freedom struggle* for which *satyagraha* (holding on to truth-power) was a *strong moral-spiritual force*.

Gandhiji acknowledged the *impact of Jesus' Sermon on the Mount on his life*: "The spirit of the *Sermon on the Mount* competes almost on equal terms with the *Bhagavad Gita* for the domination of my heart. I yield to no Christian in the strength and devotion with which I sing '*Lead kindly light*' and several other inspired hymns of a similar nature."[8]

Other models for ridding the country of colonial rule or dictatorship were there. It was proposed by the then President of the Indian National Congress, Subhash Chandra Bose, to secure support from two powerful nations, Germany and Japan, to decolonize the country and make India free with their collaboration. World War II was a ripe opportunity to strike, it was argued. But Gandhiji did not want to compromise on his values. Freedom had to be achieved by non-violent means alone. End and means to the end should always resonate. Ethical-moral force, distilled by sound reason, was capable of exerting influence on the mind even of the most hard-hearted tyrant.

d)   Jesus' Way of Knowing His People

Surprised at the simple lifestyle, rare and unique mode of service, close attention to people of all walks of life and earth-bound wisdom, the people of Israel saw in *Jesus of Nazareth*, a man with a rare combination: His lifestyle was that of ordinary folks but his deeds exceedingly surpassed the great ones of the past! By words of his mouth, the water turns to wine. By a mere touch, he heals dreaded lepers and restores them to health. His command over the forces of nature (violent storms) is truly amazing. How he challenges entrenched inhuman traditions defies the imagination. Amazed at his great wisdom and immense power, simple people began to question: "*Where did this man get this wisdom and these mighty works? Is not this the carpenter's son?*" (Mt 13,54-55).

Matthew, one of Jesus' disciples, had already provided a clue to this riddle: "*Jesus went about all the cities and villages,* teaching in their synagogues and preaching the gospel of the kingdom, and healing every disease and every infirmity. When he saw the crowds, he had compassion for them, because they were harassed and helpless, like sheep without a shepherd" (Mt 9,35-36). This *divine wisdom and pedagogy of service of his people* by *Jesus Christ* is well illustrated by the great Indian leader *Gandhiji.*

In the Section on "THE PEOPLE OF INDIA" (in our book), the effort is to look at our country and her people with a sincere desire to know them. This *knowledge of our people* has to be both *experiential* and *substantial* (as shown by *Jesus Christ* and *Gandhiji*). The kind of service to be elicited from every citizen at her/his task of contributing to the national reconstruction has to be preceded by the required and sufficient knowledge of our people. The crucial question is: "*How to do?*"

Chapter 1

MULTIPLE CONTEXT
OF THE PEOPLE OF INDIA

1.0. Introduction

To understand **"the People of India"** today it is necessary to situate them in their **multiple contexts.** We have to feel the turmoil of governance today, note the vexations of people's livelihood, sense the whirlpool of current social dynamics, interact with the many cultures of the day, interrelate with mutually enriching religions, gaze at the depths of our identity, appreciate the priceless values we have inherited and come to terms with the puzzling contradictions of our nation. In other words, we have to examine the **1) historical, 2) political, 3) economic, 4) social, 5) multi-cultural, 6) multi-religious, 7) philosophical-spiritual context** of our people, in the light of which we have to understand **8) our nation of great values** and **9) our country of contradictions.**

1.1. Historical Context

We have to focus upon our present Indian society in its *historical perspective.* Guided by the principle that *'the roots shape the fruits*', the forces and events that contributed to the *dynamics* of the journey of the people of India over centuries are briefly traced here. Tomorrow's India has to be understood as a result of the interplay of the past, the present and the vision of the future.

Historians normally divide the *millennia-long history of India* into **six layers**. This is to facilitate a fair degree of intelligibility to the dynamics at work. A *historical overview* of India's cumulative trajectory can help locate at least the dominant economic, socio-cultural and religious forces that imparted the impulses to its history's march forward. History of any country is more than the narration of events; it is to organize events to get a glimpse into the *ideologies* that generated the events that constitute history.

1.1.1. *Indus Valley Civilization (c. 3000-1500 BCE).*

From whatever evidences are available, some information about this *proto-history phase* is possible. Gujarat-Punjab-Pakistan geographic belt is the designated area. Excavations (for example, in Harappa and Mohenjo-Daro) have disclosed the existence of *a well-developed civilization* that flourished at that time. Pieces of evidence of a *planned city* with provisions for *organized civic life* lend to conclusions about the civilization of that time.

1.1.2. *Indo-Brahmanic era (c. 1500-600 BCE).*

Indo-Aryans entered India, bringing with them a form of *Sanskrit*, used by priests for the fast-developing *sacrificial rituals*. *Religiosity* dominates in the records available. Recognition of an *invisible Power* that is responsible for everything is the starting point of religiosity. Offerings are addressed to *gods* like Agni,

Indira, Soma, Varuna, etc., whose number gradually increases, and sacrifices and rituals multiply in this *Vedic period.* The beginning of the *'grading' of the society* into higher and lower can be located around this time.

During the *Upanishadic period,* the religious mind probes deeper and deeper into the *meaning of existence.* Intimation of the *Supreme Reality* is indicated in the following sample text from the Upanishads: "He is the unseen Seer, the unheard Hearer, the un-thought Thinker, the un-understood Understander. Other than He there is no hearer. Other than He there is no seer. Other than He there is no thinker. Other than He there is no understander. He is your soul, *the Inner Controller, the Immortal"* (Br. Up. 3.7.23).

1.1.3. Indo-Sramanical era (c. 600-300 BCE)

Two significant *beginnings of Jainism and Buddhism* gave India of those times *a new face.* Human sensibility revolts against the infliction of violence upon any living being. The precious value of *ahimsa* is advocated by Jainism and strikes roots to give evidence of an enhanced tone and temper to life. The *four noble truths and eightfold paths* marked by rectitude preached by *Buddha* in a way stand out as *a landmark in the growth of ethical-moral consciousness* of all humanity. (International figures like Nelson Mandela, Edmond Tutu of South Africa, human/civil rights advocates like Martin Luther King Jr. of USA have experimented in their countries and demonstrated to the whole world the power of that ethical-moral force to fight against injustice, oppression and human degradation.)

1.1.4. Indic era (c. 300 BCE-1200 CE)

It is a time of *growth, development and expansion of Hindu, Buddhist and Jain views on life.* Classical Hinduism with its pan-Hindu spread gives a new identity to the subcontinent. Maurya and Gupta empires rose and fell in the North. The rise and fall of the Vijayanagar empire was another event. Chola and Pandya kingdoms flourished in the South.

1.1.5. Indo-Islamic era (1200-1757 CE)

This era is marked by the entry of another major cultural identity. *Semitic* cultural-religious-political force, *Islam*, entered India. Its first phase was seen as *cultural*, as *traders*. But the next phase was as *conquerors and military leaders*. This further changed the course of the history of the people of the subcontinent. The entry of *monotheism* challenged the life and faith in a region where a plethora of godheads had hitherto prevailed, with established rights and privileges.

Establishment of the large *Islamic school* in 1867 in Deoband and the *Anglo-Oriental College* in 1875 in Aligarh influenced the identity of the cultures of the subcontinent. The difference in the belief system gradually intensified leading eventually to the debate on a separate existence. To add to it was the *memory* of the *history of conquests*!!

1.1.6. British India (1758-1947)

It consists primarily of *East India Company rule, British Crown rule* and the *Freedom Struggle* (cf. *Gandhiji's Movements* of "*Non-Cooperation*", "*Civil Disobedience*", "*Quit India*") leading to Independence.

a)   From Traders to Colonizers

An adventurous explorer from the West, Vasco de Gama from Portugal, landed in south India in the 15th Century (in 1498 to be exact). Arab, Portuguese, Dutch, French and English traders landed on both the Coromandel and the Arabian coasts and established *centres for trade*. Gradually these became small *colonies*. After intense rivalry between the agents of the colonial powers, the *East India Company gained complete supremacy* over the subcontinent and eventually, in 1858 the British Crown took over and *made India part of the British Empire.*

b)   India's Freedom Struggle

The *Indian National Congress* (INC) was founded in 1885. In the year 1924 *Gandhiji* was elected the *President* of INC and he took over the *leadership* of *Indian freedom struggle*. An impressive array of national leaders took part in the national struggle for gaining freedom. India eventually became free of foreign domination after a protracted struggle for freedom.

India's freedom struggle has gone down in history as *unique* because it was a *non-violent* people's movement. Other colonies became free after armed and bloody struggles, whereas India became *independent* in 1947 as a result of the *moral-spiritual force* released by *Satyagraha* (holding on to the power of truth) and *non-violent popular struggle* led by Gandhiji. The world has recognized this unique chapter of humanity as *a great civilizational event.*

1.2. Political Context

India was not a homogenous political entity in its early history. There were hundreds of autonomous units called *kingdoms*, each different and distinct, yet in interaction. A *form of democracy* was practiced at the *village level* since much of its administration was by the people through what is known as *panchayat*. The king or emperor had power over the territory or country. The ancient statesman Chanakya's well-known *Arthasastra* expounded *Statecraft* in the fields of administration, politics, economics, etc.

The political situation of India changed when freedom was secured after a prolonged struggle. *Rule by the elected representatives* was established. A *Planning Commission* was created to assist the rulers. The era of self-governance was established which lasted six-seven decades. Rulers elected by the people were at the helm of governance systems and structures. The people of India enjoyed the right and the power to design their destiny. A *sovereign, socialist, secular, democratic India* is *our identity* now. A carefully crafted *Constitution of India* is the *norm* for *governance* and *planning*.

Rulers changed but governance continued. Governance was carried out by a well-established bureaucracy known as the Indian Civil Service during pre-independence times. When power was with the people, the bureaucracy's name was changed into *Indian Administrative Service*. Governance continued through the bureaucracy, although it began to feel the exertion of power by different ideologies and regimes.

The situation began to change almost seven decades after independence. *Another regime*, subscribing to a different ideology, *Hindutva,* which does *not* stand for a *secular* democratic nation but a *Hindu Rashtra,* came to the helm of affairs. It has come to power in the Centre and some States. It brands

Christianity and *Islam* as *foreign religions*. But historian Romila Thapar (formerly of Jawaharlal Nehru University) has stated that the *Aryans* entered the North-West of India through the Hindu Kush pass and settled down in the Punjab.[9] Historical data like this *question* the stand of the historians of rightwing ideology regarding the *origin of religions*. Objective/impartial historians affirm that, except the primal religions, both *Hinduism* and *Christianity & Islam came to India from outside*. [Global movements of people were part of early world history.]

After *Narendra Modi* was elected as the *Prime Minister* in 2014, he made his first visit to the United Nations assembly to represent the India of the new regime under Bharatiya Janata Party. The Prime Minister of India held out the *Bhagavad Gita* to gift to the assembly of nations. This symbolic gesture declared a *hidden agenda*. The text represented not "We the People of India" of the Preamble of the Indian Constitution but the majority religion of the country, Hinduism. The hidden ambiguity was evident. For the giver of the text represented the dreamers and planners of a 'Hindu Rashtra' (the ideology of the RSS). The newly elected Prime Minister has been a committed *pracharak* (propagator) of this so-called 'cultural organization' (RSS).

The *previous Congress regime* had governed the people with the assistance of a *Planning Commission* and *Five Year Plans*, which were dropped by the *present BJP regime* and it started its own *Niti Ayog!* Now many are asking the question: "For whose justice (*niti*) and development (*vikas*: 'sub ka vikas' or *Hindutva ka vikas*) is the Prime Minister working?"

The *Hindutva* agenda of gradually *moving away* from the 'secular' identity of the Indian Nation is overtly being pursued.

Most significant in this connection is the *National Register of Citizens.* What is at stake here is the *Indian identity* of the citizens!

The Indian Parliament, through *Citizenship Act* (CA) of 1955, provided *citizenship* to those who fled from persecution in Pakistan, Bangladesh (erstwhile East Pakistan) or Afghanistan after 7 years of residency in India or 12 years' residency for those from other countries. Of late, different parts of the country have been experiencing turmoil because of the *Citizenship (Amendment) Act* (CAA) of 2019, passed by the Parliament in three days without much discussion with the opposition! The Bill offers citizenship to Hindus, Sikhs, Jains and Christians but *excludes Muslims,* fleeing the above countries due to persecution! Concern has been expressed at this *exclusion of Muslims* not only in different groups in India but also in international organizations like the Office of the United Nations High Commission on Human Rights which called it *'fundamentally discriminatory'.*

The *National Register of Citizens* (NRC) surveyed *the population in Assam* and made the results public in August 2019. The report showed that *1.9 million residents* were *not on the list* and were in *danger of losing their citizenship.* It happens that *many* of the *missing* in the list are *Bengali Muslims*! These *identity-verifying steps* are seen by some as basic steps to ascertain the constitutive nature of the population. Because of the common border with Bangladesh, the possibility of a regular influx of the Muslim population to Assam and the fluid nature of the population became a concern for the ruling regime in Delhi.

Some feel these are steps to gradually *move away* from the *Gandhi-Nehru vision of India* to a *Hindu Rashtra.* Now the only saving factor is the existence of a *vigilant and free Press* in the midst of much of the *social media* being dictated by the *Hindutva forces*!

1.3. Economic Context

The *scale of economic status* in India begins with the *landless labourers* at the bottom-most level, followed by the small landholders known as *marginal farmers*. Above them all, atop the socio-economic hierarchy, are the *landlords*, or today's *corporates, industrialists* and the *big business class*. The present picture shows a *society of unequal distribution of wealth and power*.

While India's super-rich [1%] possess more than half of the country's wealth, more than one-third of the Indian population lives below the poverty line![10] This *unjust economic inequality* stares at all the true citizens of India and demands just redistribution of the country's wealth.

Jesus' wise teaching about paying taxes (Lk 20,20-26) instructs that all have to acknowledge legitimate authority but, since everything ultimately belongs to God, even the rulers must recognize God's ownership of everything and therefore wealth must be distributed equitably among the population including the poor and the marginalized and must not impose unjust laws and exploitative taxes on the subjects, particularly the poor. Hence the necessities of life of the poor must be exempted from taxation. If not, the poor have the *right to protest against the unjust government* which imposes an unbearable burden of taxes on them, for instance, the present GST (Goods and Services Tax) on essential goods needed for the survival of the poor and the deprived in India. Just as Mahatma Gandhi started a non-violent agitation against the British rule and its colonial taxation with his *Salt March*, the poor citizens of India today have to fight peacefully and perseveringly for their economic freedom against the selfish and exploitative 'government of the rich, by the rich and for the rich.' Often the Government ("the suit-boot *Sarkar*") spends the taxpayers' money as though the tax collected is its private property! The tax belongs to the people and must be spent for their welfare and not for the politicians' luxurious living! "Give back to the people what belongs to them!"[11]

1.4.   Social Context

Indian society (especially *Hindu community*) has a *hierarchical structure* based on the *caste system* (which has its negative influence also on Christian and Muslim communities in India). Prof. (Emeritus) Satish Deshpande (Delhi University, Department of Sociology) gives the following description of *caste*:

> A caste is a *closed, ascriptive group* whose *membership* is decided *by birth* and is *hereditary* (i.e., one inherits the caste of one's parents); *mandatory* (i.e. it is not a matter of choice); and *unalterable* (i.e. caste identity cannot be changed.[12]

> Caste implies *rules of conduct* on their members, the most prominent being those on *marriage* (endogamy, or marriage within the caste group, is a common requirement); *social interaction* (including especially the sharing of food and water); and *occupation* (castes were traditionally restricted to a particular occupation, though these restrictions are much weaker now than they used to be).[13]

Hindu community is *hierarchically structured* based on the network of *castes: Brahmins, Kshatriyas, Vaishyas,* and *Shudras.* The *Brahmins* are on the *top* of the *pyramidal* caste social order. Their functions were the performance of rituals and instructions on *dharma.* Below the Brahmins are the *Kshatriyas* whose duty was to protect the society from any threat from outside. *Vaishyas,* who were the third caste, were assigned the responsibilities of agriculture and trade in society. *Shudras,* who belonged to the fourth caste, were the labourers and service providers. Thus the *Hindu hierarchical social structure* was organized *caste-wise.*

There are *different explanations* regarding the *origin of the caste system* in *Hinduism*:

a) One is the *organization* of human society *according to* the *profession.* A *honeycomb* can provide us as an example. The wisdom operative in the organization and functioning of the culture in the honey-comb can be instructive at this juncture of human re-organization in India. Something of the natural traits operative in the honey-comb can act as a mirror or wisdom book in *re-organizing services* in the human species too. There are *various functions* for a group to live like searching and bringing the pollen from flowers, categorizing and processing the raw material so that honey is produced, feeding the young ones just out of the egg, safeguarding the comb especially the queen bee from marauders like ants.

Similarly, the *human society* too has *various needs.* But the humans do not go by instinct but by intelligence and freedom. Although human freedom, the distinctive endowment of the humans, often militates against this fixed-rung performance practice, attempts have been fairly successfully made in the early phase of history to *apportion to each group-specific functions.*

When we look back at the history of Indian societies, we notice that a way of *organizing the society according to functions* began to take shape. This is what a Vedic scholar says:

> The period of the *Brahmanas* is a very important one in the history of Indian society. For in it the system of the *four castes* (i.e., the *varnas*) assumed definite shape, furnishing the frame within which the highly complex network of the castes (i.e., the *jatis* of today) has been developed...[14]

Thus economically productive functions like *agriculture, trade* and related activities were assigned to a group called *Vaishyas*. *Security* of the village or the wider unit of the society was entrusted to another group called the *Kshatriyas*. Familiarity with *knowledge sources*, like *scriptures,* and regular performance of rituals and sacrifices fell in the scope of another group, the *Brahmins. Sudras* were assigned *to be at the service* of the *Brahmins, Kshatriyas* and *Vaishyas*. Gradually conviction was created that this manner of organizing the society was of *divine origin.*[15]

Strict *compliance* was enforced with *sanctions*. In *Manusmriti,* the law book that controls the individual and community behaviour, relationships and observances of the members of the Hindu community, all these functions were prescribed and enforced. Anyone breaking caste-enjoined law or prescription had to face the consequences enjoined by *Manusmriti.*

b) Another explanation for the *origin of caste* in India is based on the *episode of invasions* and the consequent *conqueror-conquered relationship*. During the early days of migration and settlements of peoples, it was quite natural that clashes between different groups that tried to settle down could have taken place. These could lead to fights and the conquered group became captive in the hands of the victorious. Infliction upon the victims of various kinds of tasks became normal. In this situation, the loser group became *victims* of many restrictive laws and tasks.

The loser was *condemned to do all the menial tasks*. This is held by some as the *origin of the caste system* in India.[16]

This *social structuring* was *institutionalized* over time. The *four castes* are *hierarchically structured* with the assumption of more or less of right, competence, merit, power and worth in the descending order (*Brahmins, Kshatriyas, Vaishyas, Shudras*).

1.5. Multi-Cultural Context

1.5.1. A People with an Ancient Heritage

India is located on the globe north of the equator (between 8.4 and 37.6 degrees' north latitude, and between 68.7 and 97.25 degrees' east longitude). The land stretches 3214 km north-south and 2933 km east-west. That explains the geographic diversity and weather variations. The geographic range led to a diversity of traditions and values. *Diversity* is a *distinctive mark* of the Indian people who belong to the one country but belong to several races, believe in the one God of the different religious traditions. *Geographical, racial, social, cultural and religious diversity* has contributed to the emergence of a *composite culture*.

Indus Valley Civilization (also known as *Harappan Civilization*) (c. 3300 - c. 1300 BCE) was the earliest city-based Indian civilization. Harappan culture began to decline even before 1500 BCE and entry of migrants from Iran known as *Indo-Aryans* was a new phase of India's history. The combined forces, along with the vast indigenous population, were engaged in the great task of making the history of the Indian people.

The *Ajanta rock-cut Buddhist caves*, that date from second century BCE to about 480 CE, contain *paintings* and rock-cut *sculptures* which are considered as among the finest surviving artistic and sculptural achievements of the ancient people of India.

1.5.2. Composite Culture of India

The people of India are marked by racial, linguistic, cultural and religious pluralism. In the words of Damodar Dharmanand Kosambi: "A dispassionate observer who looks at India with detachment and penetration would be struck by two mutually contradictory features: *diversity* and *unity* at the same time."[17]

The same author further observes that there is no national language, but *many languages* are part of *one nation*. There is no one Indian race but the *many races* constitute the *one people*. Geographic features are diverse and even conflicting: the snow-clad mountain peaks of the north and the hot desert land in the west and the many lagoons in the south point to the *geographic diversity*. Food habits, dress, manner of relating with friends, etc. vary from region to region. *Shared cultural values and practices* do facilitate mingling of people across the subcontinent.

The *foundation* for this *diversity of the Indian people* is primarily *racial*. For, at least *six anthropological races* have been intermingling with each other from early times in the India of today. Anthropological Survey of India holds that these are the Negrito, the Mediterranean, the Australoid, the Brachycephalic, the Mongoloid and the Nordic races. *Racial diversity* is present at the root of the Indian people.

1.5.3. Multiple Tribal (Indigenous) Cultures

There live in India a large number of *indigenous peoples*, known as *Tribals*, who with their specific features add to the composite culture of India.

We have in the *North-East* many *tribal communities*, belonging to the *Mongoloid race*. From *Assam through central India and Rajasthan* the indigenous/tribal communities constitute *another major block* with their specific cultures and religions. We have in the *peninsular India* several groups of tribal people still retaining their links with their ancestral heritage.

The *tribal religion* is a journey of the mind from the effect to the cause. According to some groups among them, the *green vegetation* is animated by a *life force* (like *elan vital* of H. Bergson). For example, one central Indian *Oraon tribe* gives special homage to the *Karam tree*.

1.5.4. Multiplicity of Languages

Next mark of our *diversity* is *linguistic*. For it is a fact that we constitute one nation but India has about 22 (official) major languages, written in 13 different scripts, with over 720 dialects.

1.5.5. Architecture, Music, Dance, Literature and Medicine

There is plenty of evidence for the *diversity of skills in **Indian sculpture and architecture**. Taj Mahal* in Agra is still reckoned among the wonders of the world. Most perfect in form and design, Taj Mahal stands as an eternal monument to human love, skill in sculpting and form in designing. Another architectural wonder is *Kutab Minar* in Delhi.

The *Indian temples*, of which the Meenakshi temple in Madurai, Konark temple in Puri, Brhadeswara temple in Tanjore, and Khajurao temples in Madhya Pradesh, Vishwanath temple in Varanasi in Uttar Pradesh, the marble temples in Bilwara, Gujarat, are among the countless temples, standing monuments testifying to the high architectural and sculpting skills. The credit goes to the Indian architects who developed the theory and science of architecture (*vastukala*).

Similarly, India's achievement in **music** is another major landmark. *Carnatic* music and *Hindustani* music are schools that developed *Indian music* as *fine art*, apart from *folk music*.

Another area of high excellence achieved in India is **dance** as an art form. *Bharatanatyam, Kuchipudi, Mohinyattam, Kathakali* and folk dance are highly perfected dance forms attracting artists from abroad even today. An important fact to be remembered is that these sophisticated forms were developed to high perfection because these were mostly associated with *temples*.

If Aristotle had developed the canons of poetry in the West, definitely rivalling his works or even surpassing them are the precious works in the field of **literature** in India. India's *Kavyasastra* prescribes and evaluates works in literature. At all India level, we have great works in Sanskrit like *Ramayana* and *Mahabharata*. Poets like Kalidasa and his *Abhijnana Sakuntalam* stand on a par with Shakespeare and his famous dramatic works like *Romeo and Juliet*.

One wanting to taste the beauty and aesthetic experience should enter the treasure-troves of the *regional works of literature and art* in Bengali, Tamil, Telugu, Oriya, Malayalam, Marathi, Kannada, Assamese, Gujarati, Kashmiri, Hindi, etc.

Ayurveda is a uniquely **Indian system of medicine** which treats illnesses using a combination of *herbs* and *foods*. Indian *ayurvedic* physicians have studied the specific medicinal properties of thousands of herbs in India and examined the medicinal impact of various types of foods.

1.5.6. Influence of Indian Culture Abroad

When the Aryans from central Asia arrived in India and came in contact with the Indus Valley Civilization, a new phase of Indian history and civilization began. There was *cultural interaction with the near East* right from early on in history, which promoted the expansion of different branches of knowledge in the Near East. Signposts of *Buddhist-Hindu contact with the near East* are in abundance in *Indonesia, Thailand, Cambodia* and other countries.

Hsuan Tsang, a Chinese Buddhist monk and pilgrim, visited India between 627- 664 CE to obtain Buddhist scriptures. *Angkor Wat* in Cambodia, an extensive temple complex of 262 hectors, is testimony to ancient India's eastward cultural spread and impact. Kabul and Hindukush in the western Himalayas acted as the gateway to central and western Asia. *Taxila* near Rawalpindi in Pakistan flourished around 1000 BCE. *Surat* on the Gujarat coast had been acting as the gateway to the Arab countries and beyond which promoted *East-West trade and cultural interaction.* The life-enhancing items like *tea, coffee, coconut oil,* etc. were among *items of export* from India. *Nalanda Mahavihara* (a large Buddhist monastery in the ancient kingdom of Magadh in north India) was *one of the intellectual circles in India* around that time.

Many *Indian names* figure among the names in some *neighbouring countries.* In countries like *Thailand, Cambodia, Indonesia, Myanmar,* etc. there are vestiges of Indian cultural elements, which can be regarded as *signs of cultural interaction.* In *Bangkok* in Thailand, a major road is named as *Rajaveethi Marg. Amkor Vat* in Cambodia, a magnificent *ancient temple,* now in a dilapidated state, is another landmark of *cultural diffusion*. A version of *Ramayana*, the great Indian epic, is famous in *Indonesia*.

It has to be admitted that one *outcome* of the *western entry into the world of Indian cultures and religions* had been the birth of what is known as '*orientalism*'. Fascinated by the wealth of Indian religions and cultures as well as the literature, especially Sanskrit, some scholars began to study the language, translate some selected classics into European languages. The event had a great impact on the history of *east-west cultural exchanges*.

1.6. Multi-Religious Context

1.6.1. Religious Quest of India

Religion is regarded as the '*meaning dimension' of culture* since it articulates to itself its self-understanding not only concerning other identities but still more with the powers beyond nature, called super-natural or divine. This self-understanding is expressed through words, symbols, rituals and belief systems. People of India do have a great *fascination for the divine*. *Religiosity* is recognized as *a special trait of India* in general. It is manifested by the people in diverse forms. From time immemorial this trait did mark our ancestors. The tradition has continued down the centuries.

a)   Natural phenomena and genesis of religiosity
Nature's marvels were the *starting point of religiosity*. For instance, lightning and rain fall from heaven. Light, that illumines all beings falls from above. The sources of that light (the sun, the moon and the stars) are all up in the skies. Grains for the daily living depend upon the rains that come down from above. Fruits

in their varieties grow on trees because of the rain from above and light from the sun. The *primal man and woman* frequently looked up to heaven in the course of their life struggles.

b)   *Growth in Hindu religiosity*

The earliest extant written religious literature we have is the *Rig Veda* of *Hinduism*. Most of it was composed between 1700-1100 BCE. A common feature of the early religiosity in India, as we have from the texts of the Rig Veda, was praising the heavenly powers for their many bounties. We see in the hymns of the Rig Veda, pleas for progeny and other favours from the powers above. A common prayer was protection from enemies. Some pleaded for relief from change and decay. Others prayed for rescue from the sway of the *asuras*. Right from the early phase of India's recorded history, the *phenomenon of existence* has been traced to the 'powers above'.

Soon these 'powers above' started getting distinct identities. *Names* began to be attached to them, such as Agni, Indra, Varuna, Prajapati, and so forth. Favours like protection of the petitioner and his cows were sought from them. Cows were important because they provided milk, and milk-products were normally offered to these powers in and through the sacrifices. In the course of time, these deities were either *clubbed together* (e.g. *Ashwins*) or seen as *twins* (Indra-Varuna or Mithra-Varuna).

A later important development is the emergence of *two major deities Vishnu* (whose *avatara* is Krishna) and *Siva* (the great cosmic dancer) in *two Hindu religious sects*, namely, in *Vaishnavism* and *Saivism* respectively.

A most distinctive feature of the *Upanishads* was the *ceaseless quest* for the *meaning of life*, for *light* to illumine the life-quest, for *freedom* from the darkness of ignorance that blocks knowledge, for *solutions* to the eternal questions regarding *suffering and death*. This led to the next phase of *Upanishadic thought*, the deepest realm of the religious quest, as revealed in the *Upanishadic prayer*: "From the unreal/untruth (*asat*) lead me to the real/truth (*sat*); from darkness (*tamas*) lead me to light (*jyoti*); from death (*mrtyu*) lead me to immortality (*amrt*)" (Br. Up. 1.3.28).

The Upanishads provided scope for *philosophical elaboration*. The *six systems of philosophy* were followed by *three more* in the form of *Advaita* of Sankara, *Vishitadvaita* of Ramanuja and *Dvaita* of Madhva.

1.6.2. Religious Pluralism in India

Diversity in religions is another feature of the people of India. *Ten religions, five* of *native origin* and *five* of *exotic origin* and later native by domicile contribute to the religious diversity in India. *Tribal religions, Hinduism, Jainism, Buddhism* and *Sikhism* are of *native* origin. *Judaism, Christianity, Islam, Zoroastrianism* and *Bahaism* are of *exotic* origin but most of them came to India very early in history and made India their home. Consequently, we have five religions of *native origin* and five *by domicile*, contributing to the unique title as '*the land of religions*'. *All ten* are legally, culturally and psychologically held as *Indian religions*.[18]

a) Many *Tribal or indigenous religions* predate Hinduism. *Tribal belief* systems contain many symbols of their sense of *searching for the agency* responsible for the phenomenal world, *a great power* controlling their lives and everything else in the universe. They are named *Dharmes, Singbonga*, and so on.

b) Hinduism has various phases (Vedic, Brahmanic, Upanishadic, Philosophical) and two main sects (Vaishnava and Siva traditions). The *Hindu religiosity* of the people has influenced their life to such an extent that even the land and all its products are seen from a religious perspective. For example, the *land* is addressed as *bhumi devi (goddess).* It has led to an *evolutionary perception* of all reality. The *ten Avataras* (incarnations) in popular religiosity are expressions of this perception. In the list some trees (*vat*), birds (*mayur,* peacock) and animals (*hanuman*) are *sacred.* Further up in the stages of evolution are *Varaha* (boar), *Narasimha, Vamana, Parasu Rama, Balarama, Rama, Krishna and Kalki.* These are the *personified stages* of the *evolutionary concept of life* in a comprehensive manner. *The climax* of the evolutionary unifying process is described in the Upanishads: "As a spider might come out with his thread, as small sparks come forth from the fire, even so from this Soul come forth all vital energies, all worlds, all gods, all beings" (Br. Up. 2.1.20).

c) Buddhism started as a protest movement against Hindu casteism and ritualism and became a world religion. Siddhartha (563-483 BCE), the founder, was confronted by the most vexing problems human beings face: pain, suffering and death. Gautama Buddha's explanation and solution appeal to many minds even today, to peoples the world over.

d) Jainism, somewhat similar to Buddhism, was founded by Mahavir (599-527 BCE), called *Jina* (spiritual conqueror), a contemporary of Buddha. Jainism insists that pain should not be inflicted upon any living being, even the tiniest. *Compassion* towards every living being is central to Jain teaching.

e) Sikhism, perhaps the last to be born in India, shares much with Hinduism and Islam. Guru Nanak (1469-1539 CE), the founder of the Sikh *Panth*, holding the *One God* (*ik omkar*) as *the supreme Being* adds to the richness of religious diversity in this land. He gifted to India a developed notion of God as one. He knew from experience the divided nature of Hindu society because of caste. He stressed, therefore, the sense of community in the new *Panth*. Three *special features of Sikhism* are *one Godhead, one community, no priestly class.* The community took responsibility for the management of religious matters. These were fresh attempts by Guru Nanak, the founder.

f) Judaism is the ethnic religion of the Jewish people. It is a *monotheistic* religion with the *Torah* as its foundational text. Jews were present in India from very ancient times (e.g. Cochin Jews in Kerala).

g) Christianity professes faith in the person and teachings of Jesus Christ, who claimed himself to be the Son of God and the promised Messiah of the Jewish Scriptures. St. Thomas (in South India) and St. Bartolomeo (in the Konkan coast) are, by tradition, two of the disciples of Jesus, who introduced Christianity to India in the first century CE.

h) Islam, belonging to the Semitic family, came to India through the Arab traders and later through colonizers. The creation of a new language called *Urdu* is among the many contributions of the believers in Islam. The Lodhis and the Khiljis and the imperial Mogul regime bequeathed their Islamic heritage to India.

i) Zoroastrianism was founded by the ancient Persian prophet Zoroaster. It is the religion of the Parsee community, which migrated to Gujarat to escape persecution by the Muslims in

Persia/Iran. Today the *Parsees,* having identified with the native population closely yet retaining their specific identity, contribute to the diversity and unity of the country.

j) Bahaism, belonging to the Islamic tradition in a new form, has become a modern contributor to the Indic heritage.

© The coming to India of Judaism, Christianity, Islam, Zoroastrianism and Bahaism was an important phase of the *meeting of religions in India*, a phenomenon further contributing to the *diversity-unity* of the country. The concept of God is expressed through their rituals, doctrines and celebrations. Thus, there are in India *ten religions* that serve the people of India in various ways. These do contribute to India's meriting that unique compliment, *'the land of religions'.*

Just as mountaineers venturing to reach Everest peak have been trekking through diverse routes, the Supreme Godhead had been the point of divergence and convergence in these religions. All these vindicate the tribute of Pope Paul VI who touched upon the *'relentless search' for the Supreme* which had been *a most distinctive mark of Indian religions.*[19]

It is worth noting that racial, linguistic, cultural and religious diversity contributed to the functional interaction across the people of the nation. *Unity and diversity* from early times were *integral* to the mind of Indians. Factors like these have contributed to the making of the *great Indian heritage.*

1.7. Philosophical-Spiritual Context

The *lofty thoughts* bequeathed by thinkers and philosophers travel beyond territorial borders of kingdoms and are owned and cherished by people of all States. Such thoughts further help in knitting together the diverse races of the land. Thus *thinkers* like Buddha and later Nagarjuna, *philosophers* like Sankara, Ramanuja and Madhva, *emperors* like Asoka and Akbar, *national leaders* like Mahatma Gandhi, Vinoba Bhave of '*bhoodan*' movement, *poets* like Valmiki, Tulsidas of *Ramayana*, Manikavachakar and Vallathol, have contributed to the *philosophical-spiritual make-up of the Indian nation.*

1.7.1. Philosophical Systems and Theological Schools

People of India are known for their *ceaseless quest for knowledge* about the self and the Self, for reasons for suffering, for remedies for ailments, for the mystery of life after death, and the state of the *jiva* in that state. The manifold answers these questions have brought in have attracted not only the different groups of people in India but also people from outside. This enabled the people of India to come into contact with peoples of other nations.

The inquiring mind of India's ancient people produced *six philosophical systems* and *three theological schools*. The *six systems of philosophy* are *Purva* and *Uttara Mimamsa, Nyaya* and *Vaiseshika, Samkhya* and *Yoga*. They reveal the *systematic thinking skill* as well as the *ability to debate*. One can be quite sure that the origin of the *Indian syllogism* is illustrative of the culture of argumentation that must have flourished in different schools. The depth of the journey of the mind is manifested through these philosophical edifices.

The *three schools of theology* are *Advaita* (non-dualism) propounded by Sankara, the *Vishitadvaita* (qualified non-dualism) by Ramanuja, and *Dvaita* (dualism) by Madhva. These are special to India because it is not pure abstract thinking but thinking and probing about God and the human being. Therefore, it is a *combination of philosophy and theology*.

1.7.2. Spiritualities and Margas (Paths/Ways) to God

Spiritual quest had been a special interest among the peoples of India. The word "spirituality" conveys a particular interpretation of empirical life. Investigating the origin, nature and destiny of the *individual human being*, sometimes named as *jivatma*, received top priority. Thinking and planning for its fundamental needs became a dominant concern. Several *spiritualities* and corresponding *margas* (paths/ways to God) were developed and made available to society as a result.

The *marga* that prescribes *rituals and sacrifices* to attain liberation is known as *karma marga*. The path dominated by meditation (*dhyana*) to seek and secure identification or union with the Supreme is known as *jnana marga*. The path held out as the way of *loving surrender* to *Bhagavan* is known as *bhakti marga*.

The early phase commences with elaborate rituals, and deriving meaning for them by various interpretations. This paved the way for the *spirituality* of *ritual action* known as *karma marga*.

Dissatisfied with rituals and their regular performance, the dissenters developed the role of *meditation* in attaining liberation of the *atman*. This grew extensively and came to be known as *jnana marga*. Sankara developed the *Advaita* philosophy/spirituality, which was qualified by Ramanuja and is known as *Vishitadvaita*.

The aspirations of the *common folks* needed ways for their actualization. The *bhakti* school of spirituality provided that *marga*. It is known as *bhakti marga*, the *way of devotional love* to the *Bhagavan*. *Shrimad Bagavatam*, the *Bhagavad-Gita*, etc. provided the devotional literature, which was/is much appealing to the ordinary people.

A beautiful '*bouquet*' is thus shaped by these *three illustrious schools of spirituality* that assist the pilgrims in their *quest for God*.

The *Kashmir school of Shaivism* has given to the world three spiritual ways or means (*upayas*) to God Consciousness or *Shiva Consciousness* ("*Shivo Hum*", I am Shiva). They are *sambhavopaya* (supreme means or path of pure Consciousness), *saktopaya* (intermediate means or path of the Mind), and *anavopaya* (inferior means or path of the Body), plus an additional one called *anupaya* (no-means), which is the state of *samadhi* or enlightenment.[20]

Besides early Bengal Vaishnavism, the contributions of Rabindranath Tagore, Sri Ramakrishna and Vivekananda have helped the dissemination of India's spiritual findings at a global level. The *devotional poems* by Tulsidas and Surdas have contributed to the spiritual journey of their disciples. In the South we have great *spiritual poetry*, offering *bhakti* steps by Manikavachakar. In Rajasthan, the *popular spirituality* of Mira Bai has offered an approachable way to God for people of all kinds. *Tantric spirituality* is another approach to God.

The *two religious epics* of India, *Ramayana* and *Mahabharata*, can be regarded as containing within them, the essentials of

India's ethical/moral and philosophical values. They rank with *Paradise Lost* by John Milton and *Divine Comedy* by Dante. The great *religious poetry* of *Bhagavad-Gita* (Song of the Lord), which is part of Mahabharata, has been considered by scholars both in India and abroad, as the most translated book after the Bible and the Qur'an. It is *a treasure house of devotion to the Lord (Krishna).* Its poetry is simple and resonating with the elegant *bhakti spirituality* in India.

In current times the *spiritual masters* like Shivananda, Aurobindo Ghosh and J. Krishnamurthy have put Indian approaches to spirituality on par with other great schools in the Christian and Islamic traditions.

The *comprehensive nature of Indian spirituality* has been influencing Indian art, architecture, sculpture and music, all of which are embodiments of a *spiritual vision.*

The *Yoga school of spirituality* closely collaborates with this striving for *spiritual union*, although there is no explicit mention of God as the goal of *yoga sadhana.*

There are also *other schools of spirituality* found in India like the *Buddhist, Jain and Sikh schools* and *Sufism in Islam.* There is a *variety of Christian spiritualities* like the *Dominican, Franciscan, Ignatian* schools of spirituality.

The picture is impressive and quite fascinating. The fascination will be turning into *challenges* with the picture of the great rivals in the religious-spiritual world. *Creation* and *Incarnation* are two 'unique' offers for the pilgrims in the *Judeo-Christian world.* Here too *Hinduism* offers to the world another interesting contribution. It is the world of *Puranas* leading to special schools of *avatara.*

1.8.   A Nation of Great Values

Cultures and religions sprang up and made their contributions to the process of *humanization* of peninsular India. Just as many small *streams* make their contributions to the flow of the mighty *Ganges* that merges with the Bay of Bengal, so the many cultural and civilizational *values* continue to contribute to the great *harmony of the people* of the subcontinent.

It is to the credit of our ancestors that priceless and perennial values have been bequeathed to us and the world at large. The following are some of the **great values** cherished by ***the people of India***.

1.8.1. Yoga. It is a school of spirituality where restlessness and disquiet of mind are systematically detected and treated, and *tranquility* is gained through self-discipline and meditation. It is emerging as a global quest since centres devoted to it are on the increase.

1.8.2. Shanti. Every human being is searching for *peace* of soul. Individuals devote time regularly to discipline the inner storms and stresses and to practice various forms of meditation to attain peace. Techniques like *Vipasana* are increasingly practiced by people of all walks of life. It is an offshoot of Indian quest by Siddhartha and Buddhism.

1.8.3. Sagara Mathana. It narrates the *Puranic* myth of 'churning of the ocean' by *devas* (gods) and *asuras* (demons) as a result of which the mythical drink *amrt* (the nectar of immortality) surfaces. It signifies the tireless and ceaseless hard work needed to achieve great things in life. (One recalls the life-long research of Madame Marie Curie and Peer Curie that gifted Polonium to the scientific world.)

1.8.4. Dharma Yudh. The term *dharma* is a rich word implying duty, responsibility, justice, righteousness, (Hindu) religion, etc. "The concept of 'Dharma' is one of the greatest contributions of India to human thought. The word 'dharma' comes from the Sanskrit root '*dhr*'. It means to hold together, to unite, to integrate. Hence, 'Dharma' is that which holds together…"[21] In classical Hindu tradition *dharma* designated 'duty' or 'the fulfilment of religious and ethical obligations'.[22] The great religious epic, *Mahabharata*, which recounts a *just war* in compliance with the demands of *righteousness*, points to the pro-good stand expected of everyone, but at great cost.

1.8.5. Nishkama Karma. The phrase in Sanskrit may be rendered as '*self-less action*' *of service* because service in itself is worthy of every man and woman. It is the high point of the sense of *duty*. (It can be compared to the 'ethical imperative' of the German philosopher Emmanuel Kant.)

1.8.6. Bhutdaya. The compound word in Sanskrit may be translated as '*kindness to every form of life*', as a result of which no pain is to be inflicted on any living being. *Compassion for all living beings*, as taught and practiced by Mahavir, the founder of Jainism, is of perennial value. When modern weapons that can inflict massive destruction, bloodshed and loss of life, are made or bought at a great price, counter values like *bhutdaya* (regard for life in all beings) enhance the quality of a culture.

1.8.7. Ahimsa. It is traditionally translated as '*non-violence*' or '*non-injury*' to any living being (in thought, word or action) since any form of violence is unethical. *Ahimsa paramo dharma* means *non-violence is the highest form of righteousness*. (At the international level, the political neutrality of *non-alignment*, at a time when the armed world with nuclear war-heads lined up like the Kauravas and Pandavas in the Kurukshetra war, was derived from *ahimsa*.)

1.8.8. Satyameva jayate (*"Truth alone triumphs"*) is owned and cherished by the entire nation as its *motto* because of its unifying, educating and soul-elevating powers.

***1.8.*©** Drawn from India's *rich heritage* of many cultures, religions and spiritualities, the above-mentioned *noble values* (churned by trials and errors, failures and successes) *appeal*: 'O Indian, be worthy of these precious treasures of a great past that produced men and women of eminence.' They challenge every Indian to pause, reflect and act in our times marked by divisive and sectarian advocacies.

1.9.   A Country of Contradictions

Even though India is a nation of great values, on close examination of current realities, we find that it is also *a country of contradictions*.

1.9.1. The *first* contradiction in India today is the presence of a vast population of *landless and homeless poor* and many *rich landlords* living in luxury. The contrast between the landless agricultural labourers and the rich families (in possession of vast stretches of land) is quite sharp. It is saddening to note that the great majority of the *landless* belong to the Scheduled Caste (*Dalit*) community.

Land is required not only for *cultivation* (to have food) but also to have a *home* (for protecting oneself from inclement weather and for raising a family). Hence land must be a fundamental right of every citizen. '*Land for the tiller*' was the war-cry of sections of the agitating labour-class in Kerala decades ago and the consequent land reforms in that State have led to a near-total realization of the slogan. That has led to a fairly satisfactory settlement. But that is an exception in the country.

Whereas many *rich families* live in *palatial homes, millions of poor Indians* today are still *homeless,* who have to sleep under bridges or on sidewalks in cold winter and burning summer. *Millions* are forced to live in very small huts (*jhuggi-jhopadis*) without basic facilities. The so-called '*slum population*' of the country testifies to the lope-sidedness of perception and governance in India.

1.9.2. The *second* contradiction is the distressing picture of *illiterate people* in a country of ancient *wisdom and knowledge.* Right from early in its history (e.g., Indus Valley civilization), the pursuit of knowledge had been a commendable trait of our people. But this treasure of knowledge was unfortunately kept locked up within the hold of a small group of people (the Brahmins). Acquiring knowledge was denied to "the untouchable" (Scheduled Castes or Dalits) of India. Today many of them are educated, but many more remain without that right to knowledge, and the majority of the SCs (Dalits) belong to that deprived group.

India has the *largest* population of *illiterate adults* in the world (*287 million,* which is *37%* of the global total)! The damage *illiteracy* does to the human mind is unimaginable. But *26%* of the Indian population is *still illiterate.* The percentage of illiteracy among *women* (*35%*) is almost double that of men (18%). This has serious consequences for society, given the universally recognized role of women to shape up well-formed citizens in any society.

1.9.3. The *third* contradiction is the *inequality between men and women* despite the obvious truth that every 'man' is born of a 'woman'. For example, frequently female fetuses are aborted; girl children are not educated; wives eat only after their husbands are fed! Such injustices against females are perpetuated despite solemn declarations on the equality of men and women as in the following UNDP statement:

> The vision is of a world in which men and women work together as equal partners to secure better lives for themselves and their families. In this world women and men share equally in the enjoyment of basic capabilities, economic assets, and freedom from fear and violence. They share the care of children, the elderly and the sick, the responsibility for paid employment and the joys of leisure.[23]

1.9.4. The *fourth* contradiction pertains to the peculiar way *Indian society is structured*. Even though a 'socialist, secular, democratic republic' is the assurance to the people of India through the Preamble of the Constitution, India is mainly a country of *hierarchically organized society based on the caste system*.[24]

1.9.5. The *fifth* contradiction is that, even though India is reputed for the rich heritage of what is known as *spiritualities*, there is a modern *contrary tendency* to *materialism and hedonism*. In *Hinduism,* there are *three* distinct *spiritual paths* of action, knowledge and loving devotion (*karma marga, jnana marga* and *bhakti marga*). A life of *renunciation* is considered helpful in attaining the ultimate destiny of the 'soul'.

In contrast, we have a contrary view of adhering to *materialistic* life. The *Charvaka* school in India ignores the reality of the *atman* (soul) after cessation of life. This school holds that it is best to take the best advantage of the short life-span by enjoying this empirical world to the fullest sensual satisfaction that it can offer. The current proclivity, both in the West as well as in the East, is to satiate one's sensual inclinations to the maximum. In one way or other, *hedonism* has been growing as a major *counter-cultural force.*

1.9.6. The *sixth* contradiction is that, even though India is a *land of religions*, frequently 'communal riots' occur due to *conflicts of religions.* The ten religions that live in India have made their distinctive contributions to the Indian heritage, acclaimed by admirers the world over. *Symbols* of these religions like *Sarna*, temples, mosques, churches, Gurudwaras, dot the land from north to south. *Diversity of religious symbols* do proclaim the richness of the evolving heritage. Each religion does attract a large number of *pilgrims* to its recognized *shrines.* Processions, celebrations, rituals, specific to each of these sacred symbols further highlight *religious diversity. Sacred books* specific to each of these religions also contribute to the vast wealth of knowledge systems in the land.

Despite these religio-cultural riches, there are frequent 'religious conflicts', which are due to various reasons. Many sociologists consider religion as a source of violence. The frequent *communal conflicts*, especially during religious processions or disputes over sacred symbols or sites like the temple or mosque or church, are blots on the sanity of the adherents of religions. Some *Hindutva* trends propagate *fear of contamination* through contact with other religions and urge Hindus to withdraw towards *self-conceived purism.* Such a negative trend is found also among some *fanatic* groups in other religions. *Fundamentalism* is the name of that negative trend *masquerading* as 'self-preservation' or 'identity affirmation'. They weaken the global trend towards universal convergence. At a time when races, religions, cultures and civilizations are moving towards global perception and transaction, any *retrograde move* can delay the process of the *current interaction initiatives* at various levels.

Frequent *communal conflicts* challenge the followers of religions to vindicate their claim that religions generate and disseminate *peace*. The risen *Jesus* greeted his bewildered and frustrated disciples by bequeathing them *peace* (*shalom*). *Shanti* is a rare blessing with which elders, venerable men and women, impart tranquility of heart to seekers of blessing. *Promotion of peace* is a benign contribution by well-wishers across the land.

1.9.© We may *sum up the contradictions* in our country as follows:

> India is a country of contradictions, the land of life and death, prosperity and penury, religiosity and inhumanity, a country that considers life as sacred yet lets millions of humans live in inhuman conditions as bonded labourers, child-labourers, slum-dwellers, quarry-workers, etc. It is a secular, socialist democracy but millions of its citizens (e.g. Dalits, Tribals, and women) are discriminated against based on caste, colour, creed and sex. Modern India has taken giant steps in science and technology, agriculture and industry, yet even after 60 [73] years of independence one-third of its population lives below the poverty line. Every corner of our country is dotted with temples and mosques, daily visited by thousands of religious devotees for prayer to and worship of God. But the demonic demolition of the *Babri masjid* and the barbaric destruction of hundreds of human lives in the frenzy of the religious riots that erupted in different parts of the country point to the fire of hatred that burns in the hearts of many, kindled by fundamentalist and fanatical forces and exploited by unscrupulous and power-hungry politicians in collusion with inhuman and ungodly religious

leaders, who are ready to sacrifice human lives to placate the bloodthirsty and death-dealing demon of power.[25]

1.© Conclusion

When a stone was flung on the still surface of a tiny lake with clean water by an innocent lad, some ripples were generated. A frog lurking by the bank, waiting for a tiny prey, jumped in to seize the 'prey'. That caused more ripples and all crossed and crisscrossed. Tickled by the frog-jump and the phenomena of waves, more stones were hurled and the ripples increased, moving in all directions. This went on for a few minutes and the lake surface was all ripples moving in all directions.

The scene is comparable to the spectacle of the subcontinent. From ancient days, races, cultures and religions were born, spread, interacted mutually and continued the process till today. People from outside came and people from India travelled far and wide. Values and ideologies followed the voyagers in and out. The process goes on. The ripples of people on the move, ideas generated and disseminated, of conflicts and contradictions, of claims and counter-claims, all contributed to these still travelling ripples.

Chapter 2

INDIAN SUBALTERN GROUPS IN SOCIO-CULTURAL PERSPECTIVE

2.0. Introduction

Personal experience alone is not enough to *know people in depth. The relevant scientific method* is an essential requirement to avoid superficiality. If to 'know' just one human person is a complex and arduous task for anyone, even for a psychologist, how much more difficult it is to know the people of a large nation! The growing *human sciences* of our times testify to the *complexities and demands of knowing the people of a nation* like India.

Modern thinkers like Karl Marx at the global level and *Indian innovative humanists* like the late B. R. Ambedkar, D. D. Kosambi, Jotirao and Savitribai Phule and others propose a *socio-cultural perspective* derived from liberative humanism. It looks at the *existing social structure as unjust and discriminatory, detrimental to genuine human development and welfare* of the *dominated sections of society* (like the *poor*, the *unemployed*, etc.) and especially of the *deprived subaltern groups (Dalits, Tribals, Women)* in India.

2.0.1. Basic Human Needs

The most *basic needs of all human beings* are *food, clothes, shelter, health, security, education, equality, freedom, social acceptance, participation,* development of human *creative potentials,* right atmosphere to attend to the *religious yearning.* These *basic needs* may be *categorized* under the following *headings:*

a)   *Subsistence*

The first fundamental requirement for a person's normal life is *subsistence.* These are *food, clothing, shelter, health,* a *living environment* that assists one to maintain one's *identity* as a *human person.* Wherever these are lacking, one experiences a deep kind of want. *Poverty* is the most visible indicator of the below-subsistence-level existence of millions of Indians, despite the enormous development the country has made in the last seven decades.

Any city in India will provide indicators of the *lop-sidedness of governance* in India: people being born, living and dying, on *city streets* or in *slums! Insufficiency* of the minimum required *nourishment* begins when one is in the womb or is just born. It continues in and through childhood, youth, adulthood and old age. Visible marks like being *ill-clad* and *seriously sick,* yet *without medical care,* leading to *early death,* are further realities of *the poor in India.*

b)   *Security*

All human beings need the *protection* of their *identity, education* and *recreation.* Being already choked by poverty, the fulfilment of these needs escapes *the poorer* section of the people regularly. They are exposed to many forms of *insecurity.*

c)   Social Acceptance

Third in the order of needs is *acceptance* in the society *as an equal* and *availability* of elements that take care of *self-esteem, partnership* and *collaboration*. Authoritarianism, oppression, exploitation and marginalization are signs of rejection of the people. *Caste-system* contributes to the *rejection* of some sections of society especially the *Dalits*.

d)   Participation

Fourthly, there is a need for *participation* in common programmes in which society is engaged and expects collaboration from the members (men and women). This would imply cultivating a *sense of solidarity* with the group and exercising one's *rights and duties* as a member of society. Associations, clubs, etc., do contribute to the satisfaction of this need. The *most serious obstacle* to this is the man-made *barrier* of the *caste system*.

e)   Favourable Atmosphere for Developing One's Talents

Fifthly, there is a need for expressing and developing one's natural talents, endowments, inventiveness and other potentials. *Creative exercises* like writing, painting, sculpturing, singing, dancing, acting, etc., are required for the realization of one's inborn creativity and integral human development.

However, the *suffocating atmosphere*, generated by factors like social fragmentation and religious obscurantism that create rigid socio-religious barriers, prevents the full blossoming of one's *identity* as *a human person* and as *a citizen of India*.

f)   Freedom

Sixthly, there is the most important need of the human person to exercise one's *freedom* and *autonomy* in the community and society. This contributes to one's growth and development as a person. Freedom is the most distinctive trait of the human person. However, many of the social mores, traditions and behaviour patterns (e.g., those dictated by the *caste-system*) are rigid and inhibitive. Gulliver landed in Lilliput and when he woke up he found that the pygmy-like inhabitants of the place tied him down with a network of strong threads because of which he found it impossible to extricate himself and stand up on his feet. This is the terrible experience of many *Dalits* today.

g)   Transcendental Needs

Finally, every human being is entitled to fulfil one's *transcendental needs*. This is the realm of religion. India is blessed with many religions in their diversity. Society is expected to provide space, time and opportunity for the exercise of one's inborn rights and the pursuit of one's *religious needs*. No power on earth, the State or society or institution can prevent one from exercising the natural right to freely *"profess, practice and propagate"* one's *religious faith*. *Religious liberty* means that one is also free *to choose* the religion (which freedom is now being denied to many especially the *Tribals* and the *Dalits!*)

© In *conclusion*, every human person has *social, cultural, economic, professional, political, religious and spiritual-transcendental needs and rights.* The body-soul-spirit composition of the human person has limitless aspirations that open up to the transcendental horizon.

2.0.2. *Fundamental Human Rights*

All humans are born to bloom, endowed with *inalienable rights* and are rightful heirs to a *share of the resources* of Mother Earth. These rights are divine in origin, *fundamental* in nature and *universal* in recognition. It is incumbent on every citizen anywhere in the world to honour them unreservedly, promote them wholeheartedly and guard them zealously.

Depriving any citizen of any of the *fundamental rights* by any authority (religious or State) in any manner must be held as an act of *illegal usurpation*, most irreligious and as an affront to both the Creator and the human conscience. *Natural law* and *civil law*, as well as the *Universal Declaration of Human Rights*, demand unreserved compliance with the fundamental rights of peoples. The *Preamble of the Constitution of India* assures "to secure to all its citizens" *justice, liberty, equality and fraternity*. But even seven decades after independence, these *basic human rights* have been largely denied to the *majority* of the population.

The *Puranic myth of the churning of the ocean* by *devas* and *asuras* describes how *poison* and *nectar* came up from the subliminal layers of the ocean. The former was dangerous to the living beings but the latter was beneficial to them. The *devas snatched the nectar* and vanished from the scene. In actual life, the *labour for the churning* comes largely from the *poor* and *subaltern groups (Dalits, Tribals and Women)* but the *benefits* in the vast reservoirs of the nation are diverted to the *creamy layer* of society (the *super-rich* and the so-called *upper castes*, the *landlords* and the *corporates*, the *vested interests*).

2.0.3. *Deprived Subaltern Groups in India*

While on the one hand, the upper classes are experiencing phenomenal growth and wellbeing, the *subaltern groups (Dalits, Tribals* and *Women)* are choked, deprived and disfigured as humans. Their *foremost grievance* all through history has been: "We belong to the *deprived sections* of the country!". This central grievance requires active listening and honest response. A country that promises and professes *equality for all its citizens* has the responsibility to heed the grievances of the deprived ones.

To respond to the crying needs of the *Dalits, Tribals* and *Women*, a first necessary step is *to know* them. A proper *social diagnosis* is necessary to assess the actual situation and to grasp the gravity of the affected condition. *Correct information* on the economic, political, social, cultural and religious situation is a major step. Then there is the need to *locate the blocks* that intervene and prevent human development to the full. Adequate knowledge of the actual situation prompts committed individuals to find the *skill* required to search and find out the *reasons* for the blocks and *means* how to deal with them.

Our national identity is shaped by the *Preamble of our Constitution* which describes our *Republic* as *Sovereign, Socialist, Secular and Democratic*. It guarantees *Justice, Liberty, Equality and Fraternity* to every Indian citizen. These are the *four pillars of our national identity* and they are to be the *lights* for our steps. They are our *dreams* to be realized, our *standard* under which we assemble and our *store-house* of energy and resources for our untiring efforts to *actualize* our dreams.

Standing opposed to the above four pillars of our nation are the *four words* that are *symbols* of a *culture of exploitation*: *Caste,*

Domination, Homogenization and *Patriarchy.* These defy the plan of the Creator and Designer of the world we live in, blur our vision of a just and egalitarian society, and deflect us from our path towards mature citizenship needed for the emergence of a welfare State. Consequently, the groans of the affected people are not heard, and their centuries-old sufferings are neglected!

2.0.4. *Present Challenges of the Subaltern Groups*

Although post-independence *all power* is vested in the hands of the *citizen*, there are *many challenges* the nation has to face in order to attain *appreciable welfare* for all, especially for the *poor*, the *marginalized,* the *deprived* and the *downtrodden.*

A very important challenge is *to free the suppressed groups from the exploitation of the dominant groups* in India. D. D. Kosambi has placed before the readers the great *divide of the people of India*:

> The subtle mystic philosophies, tortuous religions, ornate literature, monuments teaming with intricate sculpture and delicate music of India all derive from the same historical process that produced the famished apathy of the villager, senseless opportunism and termite greed of the cultured strata, sullen un-co-ordinate discontent among the workers, the general demoralization, misery, squalor and degrading superstition. The one is a result of the other; the one is the expression of the other. The most primitive implements produced a meagre surplus which was expropriated by a correspondingly archaic social mechanism. This maintained a few in that cultured leisure which they took as a mark of their innate superiority to the vast majority living in degradation. It is necessary to grasp this to appreciate the fact that history is not a sequence of haphazard events but is made by human beings in the satisfaction of their needs.[26]

Kosambi sees *history* as a *process of conflict* where the large *dominated group* is ever at the mercy of the *dominant group. Two powerful forces or ideologies* are responsible for this distressing *culture of domination.* Indian traditional social structure is based on the *Hindu caste system and patriarchy.* Modern *capitalistic structure* too is built on an *unjust system of domination and marginalization.* One re-enforces and strengthens the other since they feed on each other and get strengthened. Consequently, the *dominated cultures and structures* remain in *perpetual enslavement.*

2.1. Dalits ('*Panchamas*') in Indian Caste Society

The *panchamas* were regarded as "*untouchable*". We now touch upon an intractable '*phantom*'[27] in human affairs, especially having its roots in religion with ramifications in all walks of life, even in burial grounds. It is known as "*untouchability*" built on the *illusion* of *purity and pollution.* It is a *biased social criterion* based on the *unverified assumption* that *certain human beings* are '*impure*' and hence '*polluting*'. Any disintegrated or rotten material, because it has become decomposed, can be contaminating or defiling by being filthy. But the *belief* that *a human being* can be '*polluting*' is *a misconception born of ignorance and prejudice*! *Pollution* was introduced *to fence off the Dalits* from the others. The puzzle remains unsolved: how could a human person, endowed with freedom, rights and dignity, be treated as 'polluting'!

In the Chandogya Upanishad we have an account of the nature of this treatment: "But those who are of stinking conduct here – here the prospect is, indeed, that they will enter a stinking womb, either of a dog or the womb of a swine or the womb of an outcast (*chandala*)" (Ch. Up. 5.10.7). Hence a terrible *stigma* was attached to the *panchama* who was branded as '*polluting*'! *Manusmriti* has enjoined upon the society the nature of the *habitation of the panchamas*:

> The dwelling of Chandala and Chavpakas (*sapaka*) (should be) outside the village; they should be deprived of dishes (*apapatra*), their property (consists) of dogs and asses. Their clothes (should be) garments of the dead and their ornaments (should be) of iron, and their food (should be) in broken dishes, and they should constantly wander about.[28]

Caste confines the citizen to one's own limited space in the grossly *fragmented Indian social structure.* Caste also fragments society *hierarchically*, in a graded scaling that ascribes disproportionate possession of humanity and value. Thus the higher one is in the social hierarchy, greater is the worth accorded. Inversely, the lower one is placed on the social ladder, the less worth is ascribed.

2.1.1. Dalits (Scheduled Castes) and the Caste System

Instead of the term *panchama,* the State documents use the term '*Scheduled Castes*' (SCs).[29] Today they are known as '*Dalits*', which is a neologism, a term used by the SCs themselves. It is a *protest word* for it communicates the judgmental message that 'we are such because it is the society that has reduced us to this state'. The late Dr. James Massey, himself a '*Dalit*', and an internationally recognized scholar, says that the word is derived from the Sanskrit root *dal* which means 'burst, split, broken, or split asunder, downtrodden ....'[30]

Dalits faced *many disabilities.* They had to *live outside the caste village* and *work for the* so-called *upper castes* as *landless agricultural labourers* or *do menial jobs.* To impose strict adhesion, *sanction* was attached. By enforcement of *purity-*

pollution dynamics, the *institution of caste* became *rigorous*. The Dalits could *not enter temples* set apart for the so-called upper castes. *Dalits' economic resources* were *meagre. Education* was strictly *out of purview* for them. *Literacy* consequently was *minimum. Social discrimination* of the *panchamas* was enforced in every sphere of life. They were *denied commensality (eating together with other castes)*; *marriages* were *only within the same group*. It was *a form of apartheid* (one-time prevalent in South Africa).

Here are *two episodes* to help us to understand the *plight of the 'polluting', 'untouchable' Dalits* in the *caste-ridden Indian society*.

After unloading the sugar cane bundles at the processing mills a bullock cart was treading back to the village in Maharashtra. The cart man noticed a lad and a lass with their books in the bag heading home. Parental feelings prompted him to stop the cart near them and offer them a lift. Joyously the kids managed to board the cart thrilled at the gracious offer. A short conversation followed: their names, name of the school, name of the village they live in, class in which they were studying, name of the teacher, and such. Interval. More of chitchat. Finally, the cart man asked about their caste. As soon the word 'Mahar' was heard, the shock stirred up in him impulses over which he had no control. He stopped the bulls, jumped out of the cart, stood by the other side of the road, breathless and fuming, and in blaming tone he raged at the kids: "Why didn't you tell the truth earlier?" *Untouchability!* The cart man felt contaminated by the presence in his bullock-cart of two innocent kids who belonged to the so-called *panchama* (fifth) caste or *outcaste!* The embarrassed and confused kids felt like two criminals! The shock was ineradicable! It got deeply imprinted in their innocent hearts for all their life! Perhaps the shock worked out its effect and shaped the *future Ambedkar*, the Lawgiver and the great social reformer.

On his return from England after his studies, Barrister Bhim Rao Ambedkar was appointed Dewan by the Maharaja of Baroda. He noticed that the *glass used by him for drinking water won't be touched by his attendants*: their master was from *Maher caste*!

Painful episodes like these haunted Ambedkar's imagination and reason. *"I was born a Hindu but I will not die a Hindu"* was his final resolve. His writings and speeches thereafter are there as a testimony to their validation.

James Massey and Samson Prabhakar make the following comment on the *hideous caste system* and the *inhuman untouchability* based on the delusion of *pollution*:

> The *hideous social institution* known as *caste* and its product *untouchability* had blackened the human landscape on the subcontinent. The many unique human achievements in philosophy, literature, spirituality, music, art and architecture, all stood eclipsed by this most deforming and dehumanizing social institution. To think that the human mind that had penetrated the very nature of the Godhead did also invent the hideous *delusion* that a human being can be 'polluting' another, that its nature is made of 'polluting' elements, and that this delusory social construct can contaminate another, is beyond the grasp of imagination, still less of rational thinking. Some insidious force invented in the past this delusion and foisted it on the society that accepted and internalized it, which in its turn went on transmitting from generation to generation. The humanity in India lay concealed under this dark 'carpet' woven by some

schemers in the past. The time has come to expose and explode this *millennia-long delusion.*[31]

Dalits lost their *rights* to *justice, liberty, equality* and their *legitimate roles in society* because of the *unjust caste system.* They were *kicked out* of the normal society by the connivance of the so-called upper castes, and their expulsion was sealed by branding them as '*untouchables*'. On what ground did the inflated status of the so-called upper castes push the Dalits down to hell-like status and declare that these human beings are to be kept outside of society? The lie was spread among the so-called upper castes that the *panchamas pollute* others! The *sealing wax* was supplied by *religion.* The process was complete when their economic activity was restricted to doing *only menial works.* So the Dalits *lost their rightful place as equals in the society* and were *denied their rights to land and education, shared rituals and worship of common deities.* In truth, they were *deprived of all rights*: social, economic, political, cultural and religious. India's so called wisdom shone away from this *dark dungeon* of the world of *panchamas.*

To free the *panchamas* of the stigma of *untouchability,* protest movements were initiated from time to time. *Siddhartha* (Gautama Buddha), the founder of Buddhism, remains top in the list of *social protesters.* Quite a few medieval *sages* like *Kabir* and *Tukaram* made strenuous efforts to free society of the evil of caste and 'untouchability'. Occasionally protests came from the so-called upper castes, but frequently from the so-called 'outcastes'. But the impact was only partial. The hierarchical ordering of the society proved so far too powerful and rigid to admit of any re-structuring.

India's still existing *bonded labourers, landless agricultural workers, migrant seasonal labourers*, all belong to *Dalits*. The great majority of *slum dwellers* in modern urban centres are drawn from this sector. From these clusters stream forth every morning a large number of *women* to reach the apartments in the colonies and mansions of the rich layer of the Indian population. There they are *employed in all menial tasks*: cleaning, sweeping, mopping of bedrooms, verandahs, and tidying up of tables, windows, etc. The *menfolk* come out of their huts on foot or cycles to be *guards* and *watchmen*, to be *sweepers* in schools and colleges or office rooms.

The *Dalits* are condemned to *socio-economic dependence* on the higher-ups in the caste hierarchy. The *economic dependence* of these men, painful as well as humiliating, compounds their dependence on others. This is not merely based on material wealth. Economic dependence turns out gradually to *social dependence* on the scale of *human worth*: the feeling that one is of *low-grade humanity*! Indeed, this form of *socio-economic slavery* is more painful and degrading than any other because one is permanently seen, treated and measured as *low*.

The *Dalits* have *no power* and *no share* in the exercise of *governance*: hence comes *political dependence or servitude*. Although they have the voting rights, they belong to the 'ruled class', not to the 'ruling class'. For it is through participation in power that one's freedom is exercised. And *freedom*, the constitutive element of the human person, is *denied, ignored, dominated, suppressed*, yes, *trampled underfoot*! If the footwear could speak, what would it pour out? Steaming out of their soul is the hurt and humiliation of being used and down-graded as a *thing* rather than as a person. Others decide for them, use them for their needs and discard them at will. Shoe-polishing, toilet and sewage cleaning, scavenging, sweeping of public roads, disposing of cadaver, all such *menial tasks* have been forced upon the *'low-grade' citizens* of India. Most of the *political leaders* in India follow the 'raja' culture and the *government officials* the colonial 'sahib' culture, both of which have made deep inroads into the human psyche in India.

The *outcastes* were *denied* their *right* to pursue *learning*: hence *cultural stagnation and dependence* were created. A kind of *permanent mental amnesia or inertia* was injected into the minds of the *panchamas*!

2.1.2. Dalit Conversion to Escape Hindu Caste Discrimination

Since Buddhism was against caste discrimination, many Dalits became *Buddhists*.[32] Since Mohammad and Guru Nanak were against the caste system, a large number of Dalits were converted to *Islam* and *Sikhism*. Likewise, many Dalits embraced *Christianity* because of their thirst for liberation from the oppressive caste structure and their longing for human dignity and self-respect.

This appears the right place to raise the question: is *caste practice* permitted in religions that profess egalitarian values and hold on to monotheism? For instance, apart from many of the tribal religions, Christianity, Islam and Sikhism, the three monotheistic religions living and practicing in India, do claim and are known to teach and profess egalitarianism.

In the *Christian* tradition, the initiation rite declares that the baptized are members of the body of Christ, irrespective of caste, colour, race and gender and that all are one in Christ. All belong to the one community and consequently enjoy equality with all other members. This fundamental oneness is ignored and tarnished if a divisive claim is introduced. However, practice belies claims, teachings and assumptions, because *caste is still practiced in Indian Christianity!*

> *Casteism within the Church* is a scandal to the Christian faith in India. Christian communities in several parts of India show more feelings of caste exclusiveness and hold more tenaciously to undesirable caste customs. In many places, different congregations have their separate places of worship and cemeteries. Today, there are many fights and quarrels between different caste groups due to the appointments or transfers of priests from one parish to another. Even in the selection and appointment of bishops, caste plays a major role. So it seems that Dalits in general and Christian Dalits, in particular, continue to live under the burden of oppressive forces within the Church and outside. There has been a spate of newspaper reports regarding 'Christian casteism' in many parts of India. *Christians of Dalit background* in the Christian community in India *suffer three-fold discrimination*: one *at the hinds of the Hindu community*, second, *from Government of India*, when it denies them constitutional rights which it grants to the Dalits in general, and three, *from Christians of upper-caste background.*[33]

Does it mean that rituals and sacraments like *Baptism* and *Eucharist* produce hardly any behavioural change in the recipients? Eucharist, the symbol of unity and community-building, has not succeeded in warding off anti-community practices in the Church!

2.1.3. *Dalit Mass Movements of Liberation in the 19th and 20th Centuries*

Mahatma Jyotirao Phule, a social activist, reformer and writer (1827-1890), fought for the eradication of caste system and untouchability of Dalits and the emancipation of women through their education in Maharashtra. Similarly, *Dr. Babasaheb Ambedkar* (1891-1956), the Father of the Indian Constitution, campaigned against the social discrimination of the Dalits and inspired the Dalit Buddhist movement. He *denounced* the unjust caste system (*Varnashrama dharma*) and *advocated* socio-economic-political democracy for the Dalits and insisted on *reservation* (protective/positive discrimination) for the Dalits. His *motto* for the *Dalit liberation* was: *"Educate! Unite! Agitate!"* In Tamilnadu *Periyar E. V. Ramasamy* (1879-1973), a social activist and politician, founder of the Self-Respect Movement and *Dravidar Kazhagam*, led the Dravidian Movement to oppose the Brahmin domination of Dalits and to eradicate Dalit untouchability and to fight for their right to enter temples. He insisted on justice, equality and self-respect for the Dalits.

Powerful *reformers and social critics* like *Ramaswamy Naickar* in the South, *Jotirao and Savitribai Phule* and *B. R. Ambedkar* in Maharashtra, turned their torchlights on the plight of the Dalits. Floodlights of *Kabir* in the North and *Sri Narayana Guru* in Travancore exposed the *inequalities and hideousness of the evil system* that continued un-resisted for millennia.

Kerala's poet *Kumaranasan* exposed the iniquitous nature of such relationship in his touching poem about an untouchable beggar-woman, *'Chandalabhikshuki'*. That piece of poetic literature indeed created a social revolution in his time and for subsequent decades in Kerala.

V. S. Naipaul's novels (*India A Wounded Civilization* and *Area of Darkness*) depict the disturbing picture of *enslaved Indians*. *Manual scavenging* is a stark *example of the exploitation of the Dalits* by the caste people even today. An *elderly Dalit woman*, for whom this detestable profession was the only livelihood, narrates *her horrendous experience*: "Had fever. Felt my hand would burst. Felt my eyesight would go. Couldn't eat... the stench, the filth, it would come before me. Twenty years ago, we stopped head-loading here. But still I handle shit every day."[34]

2.1.4. Present Situation of the Dalits

The *Dalits* are *deprived* of their authentic *human identity and self-worth* especially because of the blind acceptance and transmission of the myth of *'pollution'* from generation to generation. And so, most Dalits are still *denied* their dignity, freedom and equality as human beings, not to speak of recognition and rightful place in society. Due to a subtle and malicious kind of deprivation and oppression, they remain socially, economically, culturally and psychologically *down-graded and exploited*. Worse, development avenues are denied to them. They are still *segregated* in most spheres of social life. Though nominally co-equal, they are still *kept out of many temples and housing societies*. Their residences are expected to be in a separate location, known in some places as *cheri*. In some regions they are *denied land ownership*, use of *common wells* and *village water taps. Restrictions* still exist regarding the use of *roads, buses,* etc. especially in rural areas.

Even though *'untouchability'* has been *legally banned* (by an act of Parliament) and is a punishable offence, it *continues to be practiced* especially *in Indian villages*! It is *a blot on humanity* that the *Dalits* are subject to gross *inhuman treatment*. Since they are regarded as *polluting*, they are condemned to *menial occupations* like *manual scavenging* (even though it is legally forbidden). Dalits are assigned to do *all unwanted jobs* like disposing of dead animals, cleaning bath rooms in private homes, sweeping apartments and roads, etc.

It is more than seventy years since India became independent. Even though education is slowly mitigating the rigours of caste practice, still Dalits are under subjugation and non-Dalits are under delusion (that they are on a higher grade of humanity). The Dalits are still expected to be at the beck and call of the so-called upper castes, especially in the village set up. If the Dalits disobey, they are beaten up, their dwellings are set on fire, and some women are brutally raped and even murdered! Many of the so-called upper castes resent the *new trend* of *Dalits' awakening* and *asserting their rights*. In many places *crimes and atrocities* committed on the awakened Dalits by the so-called upper castes are *on the increase*.

2.1.5. Dalits' Growing Awareness of Their Multiple Deprivation

The Dalits are *fast growing* in *awareness* of their centuries old *multiple deprivations*:

a) At the *human* level: deprivation of dignity, equality, freedom and other fundamental rights. Caste system was created by vested interests, which led to the enforced *devaluation and de-humanization* of the Dalits.

b) At the *social* level: Dalits were *denied* entry into *hotels and restaurants* where the other castes ate. Dalits were *forbidden to marry outside caste*. The social ostracization affected their persona most acutely. A kind of submission to the situation began to be internalized. Social interaction with the other caste groups was cut off. Dalits' *houses* had to be *outside* the perimeter of the village.

Degrading restrictions: Dalits are *not allowed* in some parts of India to wear *shoes*. In areas where the dominant castes live, Dalits may not use *bicycles* or *motorcycles*. In some villages a Dalit may *not sit on a chair*, and if a Dalit occupies a seat in a transport vehicle, he has to vacate it as soon as an upper caste person boards the same bus.

> In most of the villages they have to suffer residential segregation and in towns, it is difficult for its members to even rent a house in a decent residential locality. On account of their poverty and unhygienic living conditions, they suffer from malnutrition, physical disabilities and diseases such as tuberculosis, leprosy, malaria, venereal disease, etc. in large numbers…They continue to be the most disadvantaged group among the Indian people.[35]

c) At the *economic* level: deprivation of business and employment avenues. Further, *Dalit women* are subjected to *gender discrimination*.

d) At the *educational* level: Education was the monopoly of the Brahmin caste. *Dalits* were *denied/forbidden entry into educational institutions*. Study of the *sastras* (sacred scriptures) was *not permitted* to Dalits. Nowadays the backward castes are given scholarships by the government and many Dalit children do go to school, but many of them also drop out!

e) At the *religious* level: *entry of Dalits* into many *Hindu temples* is not permitted for fear of *pollution*. If they defy this bar and enter temples or other sacred places like holy river-beds, they are beaten up and put to flight! If by chance they enter and pay homage to the deity, their offerings are not accepted by the priests, if they come to know the offering is from a *panchama*. And if the priest still accepts them, he will be ostracized by the other priests.

2.1.6. Deprivation of Dalits' Rights as Mutilation

The five *jnanendriyas* (senses) and the five *karmendriyas* (limbs) constitute the *human body*. Similarly, *human dignity* and *rights* (*justice, liberty, equality and fraternity*) are constitutive of the *human person*, created in the image and likeness of God (Gen 1:26). These are also guaranteed to every Indian citizen by the Constitution (cf. *Preamble*). What the *two wings* are to the birds, these core values are to the human person. Clip one wing, and the bird is permanently grounded! *Depriving Dalits* of any of these constitutive components is tantamount to *mutilation of a perverse kind,* which seriously damages them and prevents their wholesome development as humans.

2.1.7. Domination by the Upper Castes and Its Impact on the Dalits

Domination generates a superiority complex in the dominating community and a *submissive psyche* in the subjugated community. This warps the *self-image* of both the dominator and the dominated, which in turn disturbs social interaction.

We know only too well about the *damage of domination* of a nation or a culture. We recall at this juncture that almost three-fourths of humanity - their lands, cultures and economies - were *dominated and subjugated* by the colonial powers in recent centuries. That domination was achieved by use of threats and force. It was an *unethical and immoral aggression* by the stronger on the weaker. Violence on humanity by armed humanity was de-grading. The *quality of culture and civilization was adversely affected* by that mega injustice. The people of India were subjected to anti-civilizational deviant behavior by the colonizers and consequently a submissive mentality crept into the psyche of the ordinary *Indian.* Similarly, the *Dalits* became *submissive* to the *dominating upper castes* for centuries!

2.1.8. Domestication of Dalits as Dehumanization

Domestication is a consequence of domination. *Animals* are domesticated through a process of interfering with their proper instincts. Elephants, donkeys, ponies, dogs, cats, cows, buffaloes and horses are first taken control of by the humans. By the use of force, they are conditioned to forget their natural instincts and become useful instruments for the satisfaction of human needs. From the *grade of living and feeling beings,* they are lowered to the *grade of tools.* It is nothing but a subtle form of violence.

In somewhat the same way, the Dalits did *internalize their instrumentalization* by the higher castes and accepted it as their *fate!* Eventually, it became part of their very *psyche.* This prevented their wholesome development as humans and *negatively affected their social relationships.* In short, *Dalits' domestication* is their *dehumanization* (*reducing* them to the *level of animals* and refusing to accept them as human beings).

2.1.© Humiliation, rejection, oppression and multiple forms of violence have been the experiences of Dalits. Suppressed and silenced by the so-called upper castes for centuries, the community of Dalits now is *growing in consciousness.* Education has facilitated this growing awareness. They are conscious of their situation and are steadily waking up and vigorously asserting themselves. They are determined to be rid of this unfair stigma. The Dalit awakened roar has been resounding across the subcontinent and beyond. *Social quakes* are repeatedly felt. Wave after *wave of protest* keeps emerging. Dalit voices are becoming louder and shriller.

2.2.   Tribals in Ancient, Colonial and Modern India

2.2.0. Introduction

A *tribe* is a particular social group in a traditional society that is formed by families linked by social, economic, religious and racial bonds. The group or community has a common culture and its specific language. Terms like '*Adivasis*' and '*indigenous people*' take one to the primordial days of India's history.[36]

The Indian Constitution has recognized *tribal communities* in India by placing them under '*Schedule 5*'; hence they are known as '*Scheduled Tribes*' (STs). They comprise about *8.6%* of India's population (according to the 2011 census). There are *645 STs* spread all over India. Although almost every State has some tribal population, States like Madhya Pradesh, Maharashtra, Gujarat, Rajasthan, Jharkhand, Bihar, Bengal, Odisha and the North-Eastern States have a large number of Tribals.[37] The largest tribal group is the *Bhils*, residing in the western part of India. This is followed by the *Gonds*, with their habitat in central India.

The *Adivasis* are located and identified as *Anusuchit Jan Jati* (Scheduled Tribes) at least in *nine States* and they live in small groups in other States. *Adivasis* living in the designated areas are conferred special constitutional provisions for their protection and development according to their own genius.[38] But some States do not recognize these rights and privileges. For instance, the large tribal populations that migrated from central India to Assam are not granted the privileges that are due to the *Adivasis* because they are considered as '*outsiders*'.

Adivasi culture is *communitarian* and their *religiosity* is *mostly nature-centred*. A special feature of the tribes is their *integrated view of life.* Dr. Agapit Tirkey gives an account of the *integral life of the tribes* in and around *Jharkhand:*

> The culture of this plateau has attained distinctiveness by fostering a balance between nature and culture, egalitarianism in social structure, accommodative history, equal sharing of economy, secularism in religious pursuits, democratic political thinking and people-oriented art and literature.[39]

Many tribes in the North-East (e.g., the Nagas) also have a similar *holistic view of life.*

> The *Naga-tribal world-view* is aptly described as the *holistic vision of life.* This idea of the holistic view of life transcends the idea of dualism or duality of the western world. For the Nagas there is no distinction between sacred and secular, physical and spiritual, earthly and heavenly. All these together constitute *wholeness of life.* This holistic vision or primal vision can be called '*Undifferentiated Unity*'.[40]

2.2.1. Tribals in Ancient India

The Creator of the cosmos (Yahweh, God), meeting and talking to a man and woman living in the forest-like garden called Paradise, is the primal scene in the Book of Genesis (1-2). Simplicity, satisfaction, harmony and contentment are writ on the scene. Everyone was at ease in the first phase of creation.

The above was also more or less the atmosphere in which the *Adivasis* (*tribes*) had been living for millennia. *Simple living, oneness with nature* and a deep, *participatory community culture* were the general tone and temper of their life, occupation and history.

The *tribes* lived very close to the *rhythm of Nature. Nature* was everything: the bedrock of life, work, teacher, scripture, religion and even God. They invested heavily in toil on the soil or in the sylvan forests which in due turn rewarded them with nourishing leaves and fruits, healing and medicinal roots, and with protective leaves for their roofs. Sentiments of *gratitude* to the benevolence of nature were expressed through certain festivals marked by *singing and dancing.* Rituals abounded corresponding to the different phases of life and season either to placate the gods or to plead for their cause. Reserved and honoured in one corner of the village was the *sacred grove* (*Sarna*) for hosting the Power(s) responsible for all creation, for the veneration of God. No religious symbols like temples or mosques were constructed. The culture and world view of the tribes were reflected in their festival songs and rhythmic movements. They beautifully vibrated with the dynamics of a green land, luscious forests and ever-flowing rivers. There was a *resonance* between the blood flowing through their veins and the life-stream coursing through the body of *Mother Nature.* Often their very names were paraphrases of plants, trees, birds or animals, indicating a profound link between man and nature.

Almost parallel to the process of Dalit exploitation was the *exclusion of the Tribals (Adivasis) by the Aryans* (the late-comers to India) who proved to be more *powerful* than the original inhabitants. There is irony and poignancy in this tragedy. The *Adivasis* had a *heritage* of a *unique* kind. They had a very high sense of *community* and *group living.* They treasured *human togetherness* to the belligerency of the invaders and the subtle diplomacy of the landlords. So, many of them decided *to preserve their identity and heritage* by *withdrawing to the forests.* They lived on the produce of the jungle or by cultivating pieces of forest land.

2.2.2. *Impact of British Colonialism on Tribal Society and Culture*

Tribes generally lived as self-contained units until the arrival of the British. This meant that tribes lived outside of Indian society and not as a part of it. Interaction certainly occurred between the two, but it was not until the arrival of the British that the tribes came under the same political and administrative structure as the larger Indian population. They were subjected to the same laws, rules and regulations. Through land, labour, credit, and commodity markets, tribes were brought under a single economic order. In this new politico-administrative system, however, *tribes faced the steady erosion of control, and access to, natural resources such as land, forest, and water*. Both the colonial administration and the non-tribal Indian population - particularly traders, merchants, and money lenders - were responsible for this phenomenon.[41]

With the tribal territories falling into the ever-expanding British colonial power, *another domination* was added to the already existing one. Consequently, a *twofold domination was foisted upon them*:

> Tribes thus had to experience *twofold colonialism*: one in the hands of the *British* and the other in the hands of the *non-tribal Indians*. Tribes who had control over natural resources and enjoyed their autonomy of governance were *pushed to the margin* of the new political and economic system through fraud, deceit, debt, usury, and other related processes. This *marginalization* was intricately linked to the *process of integration* that resulted in widespread discontent, culminating in a series of *revolts and rebellions*, throughout the eighteenth and nineteenth centuries. The *riots* were directed *against both the British and non-tribal Indians* who had moved into the tribal areas.[42]

The *revolting tribes* were *defeated*. Might prevailed over right. That was the culture of the dominant community of the times. The tribes preferred to keep their identity as a community and their culture safe from disintegration and disappearance and so *withdrew* to safer places like uplands or semi-forest areas *to maintain their identity*. There is poignancy and irony in this tragic period in history. The earliest inhabitants that had a heritage of their own and treasured their human togetherness did not want to be harassed by the dominant groups' belligerency and opted to move out without warfare with the invading Arians and British. And so the *tribes* preferred to *withdraw* into sylvan lands and semi-forest uplands *to preserve their heritage*.

The *tribal and non-tribal encounters* had unpredictable *consequences for tribal culture and identity*. Prof. Wati Longchar laments:

> The *coming of the British* affected all areas of life in tribal society. The British, with the introduction of a new political process, economic system, communication network of roads, post and telegraphs, telephones, wireless and radio, books, journals, newspapers, cinemas, contributed to intensifying this *erosion of tribal identity*.[43]

Longchar lists the following elements in *socio-cultural changes* as a result of the encounter:

a) *Shrinking of the village-based community* which functioned almost as an autonomous identity, now finding itself as part of a mega State and *losing* of the *decision-making machinery*. There was *erosion* of many *customary laws* based on land and its products.

b) *Introduction of the money-based economy* led to the *alienation of the tribes from toil on the land*. Without working on the soil and living on its products, the tribes had to resort to non-traditional avenues of work for their livelihood.

c) Gradual disintegration of village polity. The newly emerged wider interaction with other tribal as well as non-tribal groups *threatened both community and individual identity.* A new outlook and identity began to emerge.

d) Closeness to the earth gradually vanished as a result of *factory-made utensils.* Wooden and bamboo cups, plates and other utensils were replaced by aluminium. Another culture, another world of different values and techniques, gradually impinged powerfully upon the traditional ones.[44]

2.2.3. Modern Development, a Threat to Tribal Identity

A very serious issue that the tribes of India face today is the *threat to their identity* as a *consequence of modern development. Land and forest* have been central to the Tribal existence for millennia. Let us listen to Wati Longchar, a Tribal scholar from the North-East:

> Land, forest, river, mountains and the entire cosmic universe are inseparably related to tribal identity. Contrary to the colonizers' description of the land as 'wilderness' or 'empty space', the land is our temple (cathedral), our university, our hospital, our market, the vast hall where we congregate and celebrate, our parent, our life. It is in the land that we worship, heal the sick, educate our children and feed our people. The loss of land and the destruction of the tribal peoples' environment is an affront to our identities, the loss of our spiritualties and our self-determining existence. If the land is lost, the family, clan and village and the tribe's identity too will be lost. A person who is not deeply rooted in the land cannot become a good citizen. He/she is a stranger without an identity and a home.[45]

This loud declaration should reach the ears of the global human community, especially of the powerful majority that has been entrenched in the destruction of the environment in the process of maximising profits out of the land and its produce like forest, rivers, hills and mountains. The number of hills and mountains that have been disappearing by scooping mud out of them for converting into paddy fields/vegetable farms or over which apartments and shopping malls are being raised stand as monuments to the folly of utilitarianism. Utilitarian view commercialises everything ("what can it fetch in the market?") Even human beings are assessed primarily in economic terms and not perhaps according to their inherent value.

Sure enough, significant *areas of tribal homeland face a major threat*. Many tribal villages are located just a few feet above vast *deposits* of coal, iron, copper, bauxite, aluminium and such other commercially valuable raw materials. Similarly, thousands of villages are found perched on river beds and adjacent to rich cultivable lands. These are now threatened by *mega dam projects* to feed the power needs of industries and housing complexes. Canal networks also gobble up their land for carrying water to distant fields. The tribes that inhabit these lands are in danger of losing their ancient culture and heritage. On the one hand, the need for water and power is accepted by all. On the other hand, there is great *loss of very ancient tribal cultures* that pre-date the Indus Valley Civilization. *Dispersal of the tribes* in the process of *re-location* leads to the *disintegration of their culture*. It is with due attention to these value systems that interference with nature should be considered.

Deep intrusion into the Tribals' life and occupation has imperilled their very identity. They demand these days that their way of life and culture be affirmed, respected and accepted in the nation. The serious challenges threatening them have led to their *massive dispersal and have damaged their cultural heritage* itself.

2.2.4. Present Deprivations of the Tribals

a) First of all, the *Tribals* suffer from *loss of control over and use of natural resources* like *forests* (the place of their habitation for centuries), due to *mining of minerals* and *industrialization* that have been making rapid strides, making inroads into their land, leading to their *massive dispersal and displacement*. Dubious efforts are underway to circumvent the few special privileges that were hitherto enjoyed by the Tribals for generations to safeguard their special *identity as indigenous people* of the land. They are exploited by *greedy landlords, corrupt forest officials* and *mighty industrial and mining magnates*. To facilitate the latter groups, *new forest laws* have been passed by the State, which have led to vast *deforestation* and terrible *ecological disasters*!

b) Another connected issue of the Tribals is how to face *rehabilitation in non-tribal areas*, which *disrupts their natural rhythm of life*. The *shelters* built for rehabilitation are often *unfit* for the tribal way of living. Tribals, used to living in identical groups, frequently find themselves relocated amidst *mixed ethnic groups*. This proves to be very *disastrous* to their *cultural identity*. There is the grave danger of *erosion of their own culture* due to the *admixing with other cultures*. It happens that a dominant culture directly or indirectly imposes its imprint upon them, however surreptitiously. In other words, given the predominance of multi-cultural tendencies, *micro-cultures* (like those of the Tribals) are faced with the *threat of gradual disappearance*.

c) Furthermore, *each tribe* has *its* particular *language/dialect*. When it becomes part of the wider national identity, *State language* becomes the *medium of communication*. The *tribal language is left out* of *schools and colleges*, where the national or State language is used. Over time, this can *adversely affect the survival* of *every tribal language*.

d) Insufficient education of the tribal children is another major issue. Used to tribal laws, customs and traditions, there has been inadequate incentive from within the tribal communities and from the non-tribal population, including State officials, for educating all the tribal children.

2.2.5. Religion of the Indian Tribes

The visible and invisible cosmos can be intelligible only when *an all-knowing and all-powerful Supreme Being* is acknowledged. It is incumbent on all created realities and especially on human beings to express their indebtedness in myriad forms. Rituals and celebrations, as well as compliance with the natural and moral laws, are among the indicators of an acknowledgement of the *Supreme Being (God)*. Such expressions are universally seen and recognized. *Every tribe* has *its own God*. Thus the Santals worship *Cando Bonga*. The Gonds have *Baradeo*. The Bhils' deity is *Mahadeo*. The Oraons' God is called *Dharmes*. The Mundas call God *Singbonga*.

The *tribal rituals and celebrations* are always and everywhere *life-centred. Protection of life* (from natural disasters or diseases or threat from other tribes), the birth of a child, rites of passage of the members of the society become occasions for the rituals. Sprouting of seeds, the flowering of trees, harvesting, etc. are celebrated. The *powers of nature* and the *Supreme Power* (God) are the focus of such rituals and celebrations.

The appropriation of tribal deities by the Hindus also has been sometimes reported. For example, *Lord Jagannath of Puri* was *originally a local tribal deity* who has been *Hinduized!* Even the emergence of *Lord Krishna* is attributed to such local or territorial development. In places like Kalighat, Kamakhya, etc. where *animal sacrifice* is held as *a Hindu religious ritual,* the appropriation phenomenon is held to be further verified. In the case of *Matkai temple* in Bollinger district of Odisha, controversy has been going on between the Khons tribe and Hindu priests. The Hindus believe *Matkai* represents *Shiva and Durga* phenomenon. But *animal sacrifice* was/is *common among tribes,* whereas from Vedic times it was *not a practice in Hinduism,* where milk and milk products were the materials for sacrifice.

2.3.   Women in Patriarchal India

2.3.0. Introduction

Women have experienced *inequality, injustice* and *lack of liberty* in our country from time immemorial. *Her natural right as an equal to man* was gradually subjected to *manipulation* by the evolving *patriarchy.* As a result, *her freedom* was *curtailed; her position in the family* got *eroded* and eventually *in the society* too, and particularly *in professions,* in the *places of worship* and *in power-centres* where decisions are made. The debate today about *her right to family property* is a vestige of that erosion and denial of justice. *Dowry* system evolved that rendered *woman as an economic commodity* at the time of marriage negotiations! She was regarded as a gain to the receiving family but a burden to the family that marries her off. Hence *her care, education, rights and freedom* received *low priority.* In the affairs of the society and in matters of religious rituals, the *woman slipped* gradually to the *lowest rung*. Custom, tradition, ideology and religion stood by or approved of this *decline*.

The *women* of India have been subjected to many disabilities and modes of deprivation, from which *recovery, albeit slow,* is taking place. Popular expressions like 'fairer sex', 'better half', etc. have their place around coffee tables, but the reality is far from such utterances. Many solemn *documentary assertions do not correspond to the life-practices* either in the State or in the Church. The *disparity* is *alarming*, although assurances through Constitutional documents are categorical. Life, both in the secular and sacred realms, does not match with the ponderous statements.[46]

One is puzzled by a *contradiction*: *Indian society* pays the *highest honour* to celestial beings like *goddesses* but *minimum recognition is given to women* in society! Are not *women devalued* and *held in low esteem* in the *patriarchal* society? That is a crucial question that is sufficient matter for investigation.

2.3.1. Glorification of Goddesses in Hindu Religion

The *Rig Veda*, the earliest religious document available to us, provides us with clues to know about our human situation. Both gods and goddesses do figure in what is held as Scripture. The *goddesses* like *Ushas, Urvashi, Yami* do figure among the male gods. Homage is paid and offerings are made to them. They are *honoured highly* along with other celestial figures. For instance, Goddess *Ushas* is as much venerated as Lord *Indira, Varuna, Mithra* and other gods.

In the *sectarian religions* the *female* figures regularly. Thus in *Saivism the divine* is conceived as *bi-sexual*. In the Supreme Being the female is present proportionate to the male constituent.

Lord Siva is depicted as *Ardhanarisvara*, a symbol of the *male-female merger in the divine.* The two genders are considered separately also as in *Siva* and *Parvati.* In *Vaishnavism, god Vishnu* is closely associated with *goddess Lakshmi.* These do highlight the *supreme regard* with which the *female* is considered *in the godhead* in *Saivism* and *Vaishnavism.*

Shrines are dedicated to *goddesses* like *Saraswati, Lakshmi, Parvati, Sitala Devi, Candima* etc. Many *temples* like *Meenakhsi* temple in Madurai, *Chamundaswari* hill shrine dedicated to the goddess, are also in honour of the female deity. Some *cities* are *named* after *local female deities.* For instance, the planned city of *Chandigarh* is named after *goddess Candi,* a local goddess. The southernmost township of India *Kanyakumari (Cape Komrin)* is another example. A large number of local female deities get such honour across India.

Goddess Saraswati is given special recognition as the symbol and embodiment of wisdom, eloquence, poetry, culture, art and even music. Today education of a child commences with due homage to *Saraswati, the goddess of wisdom.*

Durga Devi has captured the heart and sensibilities of the people of Bengal, Assam and adjacent places. *Devi Mahatmya* extols the beauty, loyalty and at the same time the power of the *goddess Durga.* Her victory over the powerful Asur Mahisha inspires the devotees to hold her in high honour and emboldens them to take a stand when faced with evil. All Bengal echoes with the *glorification of Goddess Durga.*

2.3.2. Actual Place of Women in Indian Society

Women are praised sky-high in some of the highly ornate *Indian literature. Sita,* the spouse of Lord Ram in Ramayana, is the *ideal wife. Panchali* of *Mahabharata* is extolled by literary critics and religious leaders as the *ideal woman. Romantic novels, sonnets* and such works in literature devote much space to the *glorification of women.*

But when one comes to the human community *in actual life, women* are subject to *multiple deprivations* in most places like the family, social gatherings, places of employment, professions, legislatures and judiciary. Regarding the *discriminated condition of women in India,* Cardinal Oswald Gracias states:

> The violence and discrimination that women face across the country are documented by various National and International Agencies. Recently there had been an upsurge of shocking statistics that shows the sad plight of women in the country. Discrimination, which starts in the womb through female feticide follows her throughout her life in various forms such as sexual harassment, physical and emotional abuse often culminating in abandonment, rape, bride burning, dowry death and honour killing.[47]

De-grading of the woman begins already *before birth.* Although punishable by law, female feticide is prevalent in many Indian families. Woman, who is the receptacle, preserver, nurse and nourisher of human life on earth, is subject to the callous phenomenon of modern mercantile and consumerist civilization, that of *female feticide!*[48]

There is *joy* in the family if the new-born is a *male child,* but if it is a *female child,* there is *gloom!* From birth, the girl child's behaviour is extremely controlled. *Girl's education* is *neglected. Marriage negotiation* is painful in the case of the *young woman,* whereas the young man is precious because he will bring home a bride with dowry and gold ornaments apart from other gifts like vessels, crockeries, refrigerator, television set, motorcycle, car, etc. The still prevailing *dowry system* makes the *woman an economic commodity*: gain for the new family she comes into and loss for the parental family. Why this anomaly is the perturbing question today. *Dowry-related conflicts* do make the life of the bride anxious. *In-laws* turn against the new bride if sufficient dowry does not accompany her to the new home. This often ends up in the *brutal burning of the bride to death*!

Domestic and sexual violence against women has been a phenomenon that disturbs family life. Wives are beaten up by their husbands. Girls are abused sexually and even raped not only by neighbours but also by relatives.

> The issue of *violence against women* is as broad as it is long, as violence against women is expressed in many ways. However, a *feminist analysis* would trace the increasing violence against women to many causes including those outside the direct *male-female 'oppression'* defined in *patriarchy and gender relations*. It would point to the increasing distance between the poor and the rich, the steady growth and expansion of *consumerism, violence in media, alcohol abuse, objectification of women* and *commercialization*. However, if women are in leadership, they can influence the development and direction of society towards less and less of violence and onwards to a more just and equitable goal.[49]

Representation of women in *civic administration* (e.g., in *Panchayat Raj* institutions, in All India Central and State services), *Judiciary* (e.g., in the district courts, high courts and the Supreme Court), *Parliament* (both in the Upper and Lower Houses) and *State Assemblies* is much less than that of men, which is an index of the *non-egalitarian status of women in India*. For instance, analysis from the available data shows that in the 2013 and 2017 elections for various State Assemblies the percentage of women representation was around 14% in States like Bihar and Rajasthan. At all India level, women were 9% in the State Assemblies and 5% in the State Councils. The proposal to have at least 30% of women representation in the Parliament and State Assemblies is not accepted even today! Marginal presence of women in the judiciary is quite a shocking picture for the public. When one moves from the public to *private sectors*, the picture is even more astounding because *women are much less than men* in industry, trade, banking, insurance, etc.

Till recently *woman* had no *share in the ancestral property*. After the recent Mary Roy intervention in the high court in Kerala, the woman is also a legitimate sharer in the family property. This has enhanced the image, rights and role of woman in the family and the society at least in the State of Kerala.

Yet theoretical or legal stand on the rights of women in the traditional Indian society is one thing but its actualization in family, institutions, etc. is another. When *Panchayat elections* were recently held in some States, it was reported that many *Dalit women* were elected. But when these elected '*mukhyas*' began to preside over the meetings, it was objected to and brawls took place in several places. First of all, *a woman,* secondly *a Dalit woman,* was too much for the *patriarchy-dominated mind-set of the so-called upper castes*!

2.© How to Liberate the Indian Subaltern Groups (Dalits, Tribals and Women)?

The time has come to raise vital questions about the *depressing picture of the deprived and the disadvantaged people in India.* Three such sections of Indian society together called '*Indian subaltern groups*' (*Dalits, Tribals and Women*) were briefly considered above. *Disturbed and puzzled by their predicament,* concerned citizens are prompted to *raise questions. What blocks the integral human development of the poor and especially the marginalized and exploited sections in India? What are the forces responsible for this painful phenomenon of deprivation of the Dalits, Tribals and Women? When will they have justice, equality, liberty and fraternity in our country? Who will liberate them from the centuries-old slavery to the oppressive forces?*

In the *Vedic myth*, God *Indira* found that the regular *flow of water*, essential for the cultivation of grains for livelihood for people downstream, was *blocked!* Indira discovered that the malicious demon *Vritra* blocked the flow by using his body, laid between rocky-passes. God Indira engaged the demonic monster with his valour and thunderbolt, and subdued and destroyed him. Water began to flow once again (*Rig Veda*, 1.32).

To the French sociologist Auguste Comte (1798-1857) is attributed the well-known and frequently quoted summation of human behaviour: '*homo homini lupus*' ("One man is a wolf to another!"). Everyone knows the rapacious behaviour of a wolf: pouncing upon a living prey prompted by its carnivorous instinct. Likewise, *the so-called upper castes, the rich and the mighty,* and *the patriarchal men* have been *preying* upon the *Dalits, Tribals* and *women!*

The next significant questions are also disturbing: *How is it that for centuries the deprived situation continued unabated? How is it that the deprived remained submissive without raising questions or making efforts to shake off the suppressing forces or to break their fetters?*

Plato's example of the '*caveman*' may provide some clues to explain this *behavior of the deprived*. Plato refers to the *change* that happened to a group of men punished by the State and kept in a subterranean dungeon with just sufficient air to breathe and minimum light that broke in once a day when the sun passed over the place. It happened that when they sighted the sun for a short while, the memory of their former normal habitation revived and tears began to flow down their faces. But once they got habituated to their dark abode, the memory of their homes began gradually to fade. Eventually, the *short passage of the sun* just over their prison *failed to stir up emotions* altogether.

When Jeanne Jacques Rousseau raised the *banner of revolt* against multiple forms of oppression and floated the historic phrase "*social revolution*," it began to stir up the sentiments of *protest* among the people. But till then the people of France had for centuries got used to the chains. *Enslavement* once *internalized* is not easily broken down.

The phenomenon of *deprivation of the subaltern groups* in Indian society continued *for millennia* without being courageously and effectively questioned. Only with the *education of the deprived groups* did *information about their social situation* begin to filter through the multiple channels of cultural diffusion and communication and *stir up their protesting spirit* against *marginalization, exploitation and oppression. Dr. Ambedkar's advice* to the Dalits decades ago is valid today for the liberation of all the subaltern groups in India: "*Educate, organize and agitate.*" As proven by *Mahatma Gandhi* during the Freedom Struggle, educated (conscientized), organized (united), democratic (value-based), *non-violent protest* (which is a democratic right) is an efficient and effective way of *achieving true liberation of the Dalits, Tribals and women* in our country.

II.

THE GOOD NEWS OF JESUS CHRIST FOR INDIANS
Indian Contextual Christologies

In the light of our study of "THE PEOPLE OF INDIA" in their varied contexts (cf. SECTION I), in this **SECTION II** we interpret **"THE GOOD NEWS OF JESUS CHRIST FOR INDIANS"** in view of developing **"Indian Contextual Christologies."**

Here we *attempt* at *contextualised faith interpretation* of the *person and mission of Jesus Christ* (revealed in the four Gospels) to help the various *subaltern and religious groups* in India to understand Jesus Christ in *their distinct contexts*. Hopefully, it would be significant for *Indian subaltern groups (Dalits, Tribals and Women)* for their *integral liberation* and meaningful for *Indian religious groups (Hindus, Muslims, Sikhs* and *Christians)* for entering into deep *interfaith dialogue*.[50]

Chapter 3

THE GOOD NEWS OF JESUS CHRIST FOR DALITS, TRIBALS AND WOMEN
Indian Subaltern Christologies

3.0. Introduction

Mahatma ('great-souled' literally) is a frequently heard nomenclature in India. A particular line of development in the human social level is the eminent place accorded to outstanding human persons. Worthy of admiration and emulation are these men and women, past and present, in the society. They are held as models for their commitment to some noble cause. Persons like *Mahatma Gandhi* are found uncompromising in their stand for *truth and freedom*. Also, there are those like *Ambedkar* who have made a remarkable contribution by the advocacy of the rights of the *downtrodden (Dalits)*. Similarly, *Fr. Constance Lievens SJ* fought in the courts for the legal *rights of the Chhotanagpur Tribals* over their *land* and *freed them* from the landlords and money lenders. Some like *Mother Teresa* are exceptional examples of *love for the last and the least in society* and *selfless service to the abandoned*.

In the twenty-first century, *Indian Christian theology* provides privileged places to the *subaltern groups.* "Indian theology purposely privileges society's underprivileged or 'subalterns' in its faith-reflection. Paralleling Yahweh's *anawim,* the groups accorded special attention are *Dalits* (former untouchables), *Adivasis* (tribals), and women."[51] In this chapter we would like to attempt *Indian Contextual Christologies* from the *perspective* of the *subaltern groups: Dalits, Tribals* and *Women* in our country.

3.1. The Good News of Jesus Christ for Dalits (Dalit Christology)

3.1.0. Introduction

Dalits are *oppressed* (socially, culturally, economically, politically and religiously) in the context of the *Hindu caste system* in India, as we have seen above.[52] *Caste ideology* is based on the *wrong assumption* that *Dalits* are *sub-human. Dalitness* has *four* interconnected *constituents: a) pollution* (impurity), *b) poverty* (economic), *c) pathos* (suffering), and *d) powerlessness* (political).

Dalits are branded as *polluting by birth* and *ritually impure, socially outcast* and *untouchable* during their entire life and even after death! They are the *most oppressed and exploited group* by the so-called upper castes in Indian society. Dalits are *economically poor* (mostly landless labourers), *politically powerless* (voiceless), and *religiously condemned as sinners* (due to the presumed bad deeds [*karma*] done in their previous births)! They are *deprived of human dignity, denied of equality and dispossessed of liberty,* and are reduced *to live like slaves of the upper castes* and *forced* to be at their beck and call *to do all menial works* for nominal wages. If they protest against any injustice done to them, they are *brutally beaten up*, their *huts* are *burnt down*, their *wives and daughters* are *raped* by the upper caste goons!

Many *Dalits* have been *converted to Buddhism, Sikhism, Islam and Christianity as a protest* against their oppression and dehumanization by the Hindu caste people.[53] But the *Dalit converts* continue to be marginalized and discriminated even today! *Dalit Christians* are oppressed and persecuted and their women are abused and raped by the caste people. They are *discriminated against* by the central government by denying them 'reservation' for the Scheduled Castes (SCs). Besides, they are *looked down upon* by the *Church hierarchy and caste Christians* in many parts of India.

Doing "*Dalit Christology*" means to articulate the mystery of the *person, mission and praxis of Jesus Christ* in the context of the *Dalits' experience of exclusion and oppression* and *their struggles for liberation.* This can be done in the light of the *personal and communitarian faith* in the *crucified Jesus and risen Christ* to bring about *integral Dalit liberation.*[54]

3.1.1. Relevance of the Gospels' Jesus Christ to the Dalits

A relevant *Dalit Christology* interprets the *person and mission of Jesus Christ* revealed in the Gospels from a *Dalit perspective*, that is, based on *their life-experiences* of *marginalization, oppression* and *dehumanization.* Such a Dalit interpretation of Jesus Christ of the Gospels will inspire them to be actively engaged in a *prophetic protest* against their exclusion and exploitation and in a *Christlike praxis for their integral liberation.*

a)   *Relevance of Mark's Jesus Christ to the Dalits*

(i)   *Identity of Markan Jesus and that of the Dalits*[55]

Mark begins his Gospel by identifying "*Jesus*" as "*Son of God*" (Mk 1,1). His *filial divine identity* is confirmed by the heavenly Father at *Jesus' baptism*: "You are *my Son, the beloved*; with you I am well-pleased" (1,11) and during *his transfiguration*: "He is *my Son, the beloved*" (9,7). Even though Jesus silences the demons who declare him as "the Son of God" during the exorcisms (cf.1,24.34; 3,11,5,7), he is finally confessed by the Gentile centurion immediately after his death on the cross: "Truly *this one* was *God's Son*" (15,39), indicating his *humandivine identity*.

The *humanity* of Jesus, the Son of God, is highlighted throughout his public ministry and passion in the Markan Gospel. His many *miracles* manifest not only his *divine authority* but also his *human concern* for the sick and the suffering, the deprived and the downtrodden.

The *vicious caste system* has been casting aspersions on and downgrading "*Dalit identity* through the derogatory titles like *chandala, paraya, palla, chakkiliya, mala, madiga, bhangi, chamar, atisudra, anasika,* untouchable...".[56] The caste obsessed people refuse to accept the Dalits as children of the soil and treat them as slaves and as the refuse of society and trespass their human rights and dignity with impunity!

In this context of the denigration of the Dalit identity, the self-designation of Jesus as "the Son of Man" and his identification with the suffering people of his time ("*the suffering Son of Man*"), as we have seen above, are very meaningful for the Dalits.

When the power-seeking ideologues were indiscriminately labelling the socially marginalized as the 'morally sinful', he [Jesus] advocated the *preferential love for the so-called sinners*. That is why he, as *the Son of Man in deep solidarity with the defaced people*, could daringly *rupture the anti-human cultural traditions and anti-life religious conventions* to promote the overall welfare of the suffering humanity. For this clear stand, this Son of Man had to pay the price rather dearly by way of being tormented, tortured, tried and terminated in the most ignominious manner. Yet he could courageously take it as the opportunity to effectively *serve the suffering humanity* as part of his *Sonship with the humans* [10,45] and *Sonship with God*.[57]

There are many *similarities* between the *Markan Jesus* and the *Indian Dalits*: both have *experienced* injustice and inhumanity, exclusion and rejection, oppression and persecution, humiliation and condemnation, and even cruel murder at the hands of so-called religious and political powers. But the *crucified Jesus' resurrection* fills the Dalits with the *hope* that the *God of life is with them* and *will raise them up*, provided they, like Jesus, the suffering Son of Man, are *ready and willing to suffer and die for the liberation* of their exploited sisters and oppressed brothers, the downtrodden daughters and despised sons of God.

The Markan Jesus, *the divinehuman Son of God*, gives the Dalits a *new identity* as the *humandivine children (sons and daughters) of God* and as *his brothers and sisters*, provided they are willing to *do the will of God* (Mk 3,34-35), the Father, even if they have to suffer and die for others, as Jesus the *Son of God* did (cf. his *prayer* in Gethsemane: "*Abba*, Father, … not my will but *your will*": Mk 14,36).

(ii)   *Markan Jesus, the Liberator of Dalits*

Dalits have *to be freed* from the inhuman *caste system*, which is built on the biased category of "purity and pollution." It makes the so-called "upper castes" and the "outcastes" believe that the former are "pure" and the latter are "polluting" by nature! Hence the Dalits are branded as contaminating "untouchables" by the caste people! Over the centuries the Dalits themselves have internalized this false belief and accepted their dehumanized state as their inevitable fate!

The Evangelist Mark, who plays the role of an announcer (*sutradhara*) in the ancient Indian theatre, announces the arrival on the scene of "Jesus, Son of God" (Mk 1,1), "who brings something entirely new and unique. The fire he brings is going to make the face of the world new because what he inaugurates is something celestial to change the terrestrial."[58] "The time is fulfilled, and the *kingdom of God* has come near; *repent* and *believe in the Good News*" (Mk 1,15). So that the *reign/rule of God* may become a reality in the society, all must have a change of mind and heart and accept in total trust *God's reign* as *the good news* of justice, dignity, liberty and equality especially for the downtrodden.

Jesus has a significant role to play in the liberation of Dalits from the dungeon of the oppressive caste system. Like Mathariswan, "the bringer of the celestial fire upon earth" (according to an ancient Indian myth),[59] the Markan Jesus brings the *heavenly fire* of the *reign of God* (Mk 1,15), which will *enlighten* the minds of the repressed Dalits and *burn up* the discriminating and oppressive caste system.

The *Markan Jesus' liberating message* of the *imminent reign of God* among all the people has the power to *challenge the inhuman caste people* and *empower the Dalits* to claim their legitimate right to be treated with *human dignity and equality* as the *sons and daughters of God*.

The *Markan Jesus' miracles* manifest his genuine *concern for* the welfare of the body, mind and spirit of all and especially of the poor, the sick, the marginalized and the dispossessed (like the *Dalits*). Thus he *feeds* the hungry crowds; he *heals* the physically sick, the blind, the deaf, the dumb, the paralyzed, the lepers, and *raises the dead*; he *cures* the mentally sick and *casts out demons* from the possessed.

The *Markan Jesus* had a *preferential option for the marginalised and discriminated* in his society (like the *Dalits* in Indian society); he *befriended* the sinners and tax-collectors, the prostitutes and those exploited by the dominant groups; he *freed* them from their illnesses and bondages and *empowered* them to regain their human dignity. His preaching and teaching of the kingdom of God (especially through his *parables*) gave the poor and the oppressed *hope of a new era of freedom and fellowship, dignity and equality*. All this enraged the unscrupulous socio-political-religious authorities of his time and put him on a collision path with them, ultimately resulting in his execution by crucifixion. But by *raising Jesus to new life*, God revealed to the Dalits convincingly that it is life (not death) that is the last word in the *liberative plan of God*.

> Apparently, there might be a pattern of victory of the power-wielding oppressors to the effect of decimating the assertive victims like Jesus and the Dalits. But the divine affirmation of the dignity of every human being will never be cowed down by death-promoting forces, for the God worshipped by Jesus and the Dalits is an enlivening God of life and not of death.[60]

a)   Relevance of Matthew's Jesus Christ to the Dalits

Because of centuries of subjugation and discrimination of the Dalits as *untouchables* and *outcastes* by the so-called upper castes, the *Dalits* have *lost* their *sense of human dignity*. The theory goes that their present low status as outcastes is the result of their bad *karma* in the previous birth (due to the Hindu caste fatalistic theory of *karma and rebirth*) from which no one can save them!

Like many of the Dalits, Jesus is a *Servant, God's Servant*: "Behold, *my servant* whom I have *chosen, my beloved* with whom my soul is pleased. I will *put my Spirit* upon him, and he will proclaim justice to the Gentiles… and in his name will the Gentiles hope" (Mt 12,18.21; cf. Is 42,1-4). The Dalits can confidently hope in *Jesus, the beloved Servant of God*, and can identify themselves with him since they too are specially *chosen* and *Spirit-anointed* by God to bring justice to all. "This liberative mission implies reaching out with hope to those who are sinned against. Such are those who have become the victims of social structure; and in the Indian context it means the structure of caste."[61]

Jesus is not only the Servant of God but also *the suffering Son of Man*, who is an inspiring figure to all and especially to the *suffering Dalits* in India because he laid down his life *voluntarily* for the liberation/salvation of others particularly the outcasts and the oppressed, and so he was *glorified by God*. The *passion-death-resurrection of Jesus* gives the *suffering Dalits hope* that they too would be *vindicated by God*.

Jesus, *the beloved Son of God*, has taught us that God is "*our Father*" (Mt 6,9) who *loves* and *cares for all his children* who put their trust in him (cf. 6,25-33). Jesus, the *enfleshed Son of God*, lived a life of solidarity with and compassion for the dispossessed and marginalized like the Dalits and died in disgrace on a cross but he was raised to new life by God the Father. Jesus, the *divinehuman Saviour*, enables the *Dalits* to become the *humandivine children of God* with *dignity, equality and liberty* and invites them to join hands with him to establish God's reign of justice and love, freedom and fellowship, in the caste-ridden Indian society.

It is also significant that *Jesus begins his public ministry in Galilee ("Galilee of the Gentiles"*: Mt 4,15). It is to them that Jesus proclaimed, "Repent, for the kingdom of God is at hand" (4,17). Just as the *Galileans* (in constant contact with Gentile culture) were *despised* by the Jewish elites in Jerusalem, so the Dalits are looked down upon by the so-called upper castes. Jesus' *teachings on God's kingdom of justice and freedom* is especially valid for *the downtrodden Dalits* living in segregated sections outside the caste village.

Besides, *Jesus chooses his first disciples* from the *Galilean fishermen* (4,18-22), indicating his preferential option for the ordinary working-class rather than the elite from the city of Jerusalem. He even chose a *despised tax collector* (Matthew) as *one of the Twelve* disciples (9,9).

Jesus *heals* by *touching* an 'untouchable' *leper* segregated from society (Mt 8,1-4), *cures* the *Gentile Centurion's paralysed servant* (8,5-13), and *casts out the demon* from the *daughter of a Canaanite woman* (15,21-28), manifesting thereby that he is the *Messiah* and the *Saviour of all people* including the *Gentiles*. He dared to *heal the lame and the blind in the Temple*, even though it displeased the chief priests and the scribes (21,14-15). This reveals Jesus' special concern for the *marginalized sections of society* in his time, who are like the *excluded Dalits* in India today.

> Jesus made a sharp distinction between the perpetrators of unjust inequalities and their victims. The *perpetrators* were the Pharisees and the scribes (Mt 23,2), the Herodians (Mt 22,16),

chief priests (Mt 21,45-46), lawyers (Mt 22,35), the rich (Mt 19,13-24), the Sadducees (Mt 16,11), and kings like Herod (Mt 14,1). The *victims* were the tax-collectors and prostitutes (Mt 21,31), the women (Mt 26,7), and people affected by leprosy (Mt 8,2). *Jesus made his preferential option for the victims* because they were made unequal through unjust means. They were sinned against. The caste culture and practice is similarly a system of graded social inequality.[62]

Jesus gave *a new criterion* of *doing* the heavenly *Father's will* to build *a new community of brotherly and sisterly relationships* (beyond the immediate family ties: Mt 12,46-48): "For whoever does the will of my Father in heaven is my brother, and sister, and mother" (12,50). This will inspire the *Christian Dalits* to relate to *Jesus Christ* in an intimate way and to *others* (*beyond their own family*) as their brothers and sisters in Christ.

At the end of Matthew's Gospel, the risen Lord commissions the disciples to go and "*disciple all nations*" (*mathêteusate panta ta ethnê*: 28,19), all the peoples of all races and cultures, without excluding anyone. This must give *hope* to the *excluded and discriminated Dalits* who are called to become *Jesus' disciples, brothers and sisters,* and form *communities of justice and equality, freedom and fellowship.*

"Jesus," who "will save his people from their sins," is "*Emmanuel*" ("*God-with-us*": Mt 1,21.23), that is, in *solidarity* with the suffering people like the *Dalits*. Before his ascension the risen Lord assures all his disciples of *his saving presence* with them till the end of the world: "And behold! *I am with you always* till the end of the age" (Mt 28,20). This gives *hope of liberation* to the *oppressed Dalits*.

c)   Relevance of Luke's Jesus Christ to the Dalits[63]

Right from birth, *Jesus identified himself with the poor, the marginalised, the discriminated, the despised and the outcasts*, who are *like the Dalits* in India. For instance, after his birth, *baby Jesus* was "wrapped in *swaddling* [used] *clothes* and laid in a *manger*" (Lk 2,7.11) (which symbolize his *poverty*) *outside* the guest-house (which shows his *solidarity with the Dalits* who are forced to live *outside* the caste village).

Even though Luke's Jesus is the *Saviour of all*, Jesus is the *anointed Prophet* who brings the *good news to the poor, freedom to the prisoners, sight to the blind* and *liberty to the oppressed* (cf. Lk 4,18-19).

> Jesus after making his mission statement in Nazareth worked constantly for the implementation of the same without any break, by preaching the good news, by his actions of healing the sick, raising the dead, and by offering his fellowship and solidarity to the poor and sinners. This included the physically weak, economically poor, socially outcast, and politically powerless people as well (10,25-37; 15,1-7; 17,11-19; 18,9-14).[64]

During the "*Sermon on the Plain*" Jesus declares as "*blessed*", the (economically and socially) *poor*, the (physically) *hungry* and the (helplessly) *weeping* because their suffering situations are going to be radically changed in "*the kingdom of God*" already present here on earth (6,20-21).

It is for the "*daily bread*" (Lk 11,4) that the *Dalits* do hard work every day. "Almost all the Dalits in India spend the whole day in work which even includes the dirtiest of jobs, to earn their *daily bread*. But only about fifty percent can get the minimum of one full meal a day, while the other fifty percent (out of 250 million at present), do not get even that."[65]

During his *public ministry*, Jesus had special concern for the *outcast* (untouchable) *lepers* whom he *heals* (by *touching*) and whom he *rehabilitates* in society (cf. 5,12-16; 17,11-19). Unlike the Jews of his time, Jesus *visits a Samaritan village* (9,56) and praises the caring "*Good Samaritan*" through his moving parable (10,25-37).

Like the *protesting Dalits* who are *persecuted* and even *murdered* by the so-called upper castes, Jesus was *opposed, arrested and condemned to death unjustly* by the religious and political leaders because he had a preferential option for the poor and he questioned the unjust socio-cultural-religious-political system of the time. Just as God the Father *raised the crucified Jesus from the dead*, if Dalits are ready to suffer and sacrifice their lives for the liberation of their Dalit brothers and sisters, God will raise them to *a new life* of dignity, equality and liberty. The *way of the cross* is the *path of Dalit liberation*.

To conclude, even though *Luke's Jesus* is the *Saviour of all*, he is especially the *Saviour of the poor and the oppressed* (4,16-22; 6,20-21; 7,22), *sinners and tax collectors* (15,11-32; 18,9-14; 19,1-10; 23,39-43), *the outcasts* (7,36-50). In short, the *Lukan Jesus Christ* is the *Dalit Saviour/Liberator* par excellence.

d)   Relevance of John's Jesus Christ to the Dalits
John's Gospel presents *Jesus* as the *divinehuman mediator of life* especially to those who are *dispossessed of life* in various ways. His miraculous "*signs*" and "*works*" not only manifest his being *the Messiah* and *the Son of God* respectively but also point to him as *the giver of life* to those who are *denied life*. Thus, he provides plenty of quality wine to those who have no wine to celebrate life during a marriage party (2,1-11); he gives life to the royal

official's dying son (4,46-54); he cures a helpless cripple (5,1-9); he gives an abundance of food to the hungry crowd (6,1-15); he saves the disciples from drowning in the stormy sea (6,15-21); he protects the woman caught in adultery from being stoned to death (8,1-11); he gives sight to the blind beggar (9,1-7); he raises the dead Lazarus to life (11,1-44).

Since Jesus is the *giver of life* especially to those who are *deprived of life*, the oppressed Dalits will discover the *Johannine Jesus relevant*, just as the persecuted Johannine community found the life-giving Christ of the Gospel meaningful for their personal and communitarian life. "The *Dalit reading* of the Gospel of John will abundantly bring out the *liberative potentials* of the Gospel to march towards *a life of dignity* to all especially to those it has been denied for centuries."[66]

3.1.2. Jesus' Option for and Identification with the Dalits

John describes the *incarnation* of the Son of God as the divine Word's 'enfleshing' as a *weak and mortal human being*: "The Word became *flesh*" (*sarx*: Jn 1,14). This was the eternal Son of God's *voluntary immersion in the vulnerability* of the oppressed human situation like that of the Dalits.

a)   Jesus' Birth in a Stable and Dalits' Birth outside the Village
Jesus was *a Jew by birth* (since he was born of the Jewish virgin Mary) (Mt 1,18-24).[67] But he *opted to be born in a stable* in Bethlehem (cf. Lk 2,1-7) rather than in a king's palace in Jerusalem (cf. Mt 2,1-7). This is *like the birth of a poor child* in a dilapidated *Dalit hut* outside an upper-caste village or in a *shanty* in a slum on the outskirts of a city like Delhi or Mumbai. In short, *Jesus* was *a Dalit by option*.

The *good news* of the *birth of the Messiah* was *announced* by an angel of the Lord, not to the rich and the powerful in the capital city of Jerusalem but *the poor* (*anawim*) and *lowly shepherds* keeping watch at night over their sheep in Bethlehem: "*To you is born* this day in the city of David *a Saviour*, who is *Christ the Lord*" (Lk 2,8-11), and they are given a simple but sure *sign* how to recognize the *new-born Messiah*: "you will find *a babe wrapped in swaddling clothes and lying in a manger*" (2,12). It shows the *solidarity of the Saviour* with *the poor and the marginalized* like the *Dalits*.[68] *The good news* for the shepherds and the despised (like the *Dalits* of today) is that *Jesus, the Messiah,* is *their Saviour*. This gives *hope* to the marginalized and deprived *Dalits* in India.

b)   Jesus' Flight into Egypt and the Dalits' Migration to Slums
To save the *infant Jesus* from the murderous plan of king Herod, *Joseph and Mary* had to *flee* with the *new-born Messiah to Egypt* and become *refugees* in *a foreign land* (Mt 2,13-15).

> Apparently, the land outside the precincts of the 'holy' gave refuge to the 'holy family'. It was as if the Dalit residential areas, the *thatti* and the *cheri*, outside the village – consigned to be unholy and polluted – extended a refuge to God… Behold, God comes to the unholy grounds of the unholy populace seeking refuge! And there indeed He finds a shelter.[69]

Many poor and oppressed *Dalits* today are forced to leave their villages to *find refuge* in faraway *city-slums* where they have to earn their livelihood by doing menial jobs. *Jesus' identification with the marginalized and the vulnerable from his childhood* gives the *Dalits* the *assurance* that *God in Jesus is with them;* Jesus, *Emmanuel* ("God-with-us": Mt 1,23), accompanies them *in their life-struggles.*

c)   Baptism of Jesus, the Beloved Son of God, in Solidarity with Dalits, the Children of God

When Jesus was baptized in *solidarity* with ordinary *people* (cf. Lk 3,21), the Holy Spirit in the form of a female dove (*peristera*) descended upon him and God the Father's voice was heard: "You are *my Son, the beloved*, with you I am well-pleased" (Lk 3,22; Mk 1,11; Mt 3,17). Even though this theophany at the time of Jesus' baptism manifested primarily his being *the beloved Son of God*, it also points to *all the believers in the Word of God* to be the "*children of God*" (*tekna theou*) "who were *born from God*" (*ek theou egennêthêsan*) (Jn 1,12-13), and therefore *beloved sons and daughter of God*, created in "the image and likeness of God" (Gen 1,26). They are "*born anew/from above*" (*anôthen*) (Jn 3,3), from the Spirit of God (3,5). This filial relationship with God gives *all Dalits* the *dignity of the children of God*, who belong to the *family of God*. This should enable the Dalits to *challenge* the *Varnashrama caste system* that degrades them as outcastes and denigrates them as untouchables.

d)   Temptations of Jesus and the Dalits

Like all ordinary human beings, Jesus had to *face three temptations (tests)* by the devil (cf. Lk 4,1-13; Mt 4,1-11), which shows that Jesus ("the Son of God") was *truly human* (since he was tempted to have riches, glory, power and pride). But unlike most human beings, he was *successful in all the tests* because he was determined *to do the will of God* (his Father) (cf. Lk 4,4.8.12; Mt 4,4.7.10). *Dalits* who are prone to fall into these temptations will be able to overcome them if they are constantly *aware* (like Jesus, the beloved Son of God) of *being children of God* who are called to fight against the enslaving evil of the *demonic caste system* today.

e)   Rejection of Jesus and the Dalits

Like the excluded and marginalized Dalits (who are forced to live outside the caste village), Jesus also *experienced rejection* by his people at Nazareth (Lk 4,22.28-29). He said: "the Son of Man has nowhere to lay his head" (Mt 8,20). Jesus *identifies himself* with the *poor* and the *Dalits* who have to live on the fringe of society.

3.1.3. Jesus' Preaching and Teaching in Favour of the Poor and the Oppressed (Dalits)

a)   Jesus' Proclamation of God's Reign, Good News for the Dalits

Jesus proclaimed the *imminence of God's reign* to the Galileans and invited them to *believe in the good news* (Mk 1,14-15). "This message brings hope to the Dalits who see the possibility of making complete reversal of the prevailing worldviews, values and belief-system upholding the discriminative caste system."[70]

b)   Jesus' Mission Manifesto of Liberation of the Poor and the Oppressed (Dalits)

In Luke's Gospel Jesus started his *liberative mission for the poor and the oppressed* by stating that the Lord has anointed him with His Spirit to *bring the good news to the poor and the destitute,* to *proclaim release to the captives and sight to the blind,* to *free the oppressed,* to *announce the Jubilee year* of the Lord (Lk 4,18-19). In short, Jesus' *mission manifesto* and declaration of the *Jubilee Year* are particularly "for the *poor (deen), captives (bandi), blind (andhey)* and *oppressed (dalit)*."[71]

c)   The Blessedness of the Poor (Dalits) in God's Kingdom

Jesus' *first beatitude* in Luke's Gospel is: "Blessed are *you the poor* for *yours* is *the Kingdom of God*" (Lk 6,20). The *kingdom of God belongs* to *the poor and the oppressed* (the *Dalits*). The *parable of the labourers* in the vineyard highlights Jesus' *concern* for the *unemployed and underemployed* and his sense of generous *social justice* for the *last ones* (cf. Mt 20,1-16). In the *last judgment* of the nations, Jesus will *identify himself* with the last and the least, the marginalized and the deprived (*Dalits*) (cf. Mt 25,31-46).

d)   The Parable of the Good Samaritan and the Dalit Fishermen
        in Kerala

In the "parable of the Good Samaritan" (Lk 10,29-37), unlike the Jewish priest and the Levite who passed by the wounded Jew lying on the roadside, *a despised Samaritan* was *compassionate* to the dying Jew by *caring* for him lovingly and proved himself to be *a true "neighbour."* Hence Jesus' instruction is: *"Go and do likewise"* (Lk 10,37).

The *Dalit (Christian) fishermen* who *risked their lives to save* the flood-affected people (irrespective of caste, class, colour or creed) during the catastrophic *floods in Kerala* in 2018 are *modern-day Good Samaritans* who inspire all of us to *"go and do likewise"*. They are *role models* for all to become *catalysts* for the *transformation* of Indian caste society into a *caring community*.

e)   Jesus' Advice to be Large-hearted

Jesus' advice to his narrow-minded disciples is to have *a large-hearted and inclusive attitude* (Mk 9,38-40) towards those who do good to others (irrespective of whether they belong to the group of disciples): "For he who is not against us is for us"

(Mk 9,40). This is an invitation to the Dalits to collaborate with those who are "casting out the demons" of discrimination and dehumanization in our country.

f)   New Relationship through Doing the Will of God, the Father
When Jesus' mother and brothers come to meet him, he tells the people that what matters most to him is *not family ties* based on blood relationship but *true discipleship* which enables one to have a *new* (brotherly, sisterly and motherly) *relationship* based on *doing God the Father's will* (Mt 12,46-50; cf. Lk 8,19-21). Just as in a good human family the father's will is willingly and lovingly accomplished by all the family members (mother, sons and daughters), so all who do the will of the Father become true members of *Jesus' new family of disciples*. If Jesus' disciples are his new brothers and sisters, they are also expected to have *brotherly/ sisterly relationships* with one another. "Relating in new ways to other people should be a challenge in the Indian context where we have been encouraged to relate within the caste boundaries and family orbit alone, which has for centuries provided the fertile grounds to breed caste-based discrimination."[72]

g)   The Parable of the Vineyard and the Wicked Tenants
The greedy wicked tenants in the parable ill-treat and/or kill the servants (prophets) and the son/heir of the owner of the vineyard. This is similar to what the covetous caste groups have done to the Dalits.

> The parable is analogous to what has happened to the *Dalit communities*. They have been *dispossessed* forcefully of what was lawfully theirs: their land, heritage and culture. They have been robbed of their dignity, freedom and equality. They have been *debarred* from collecting what they lawfully owned from their lands and fields. Their *saints* have been *rejected*, even *killed*.

However, the *coming of Jesus* is the *mark of hope* that God would not allow the *illicit domination of the casteist groups* over the *Dalit communities* to continue forever; rather they, despite their rejected status, would become the *cornerstones* by becoming indispensable to create history (Mk 12,10-11).[73]

h)   Jesus, the Light of the World, the Hope of the Dalits

Jesus told the people: "I am the *light of the world*; whoever follows me will never walk in darkness but will have *the light of life*" (Jn 8,12; 9,5). He is the *light of revelation* for the whole of humanity living in the darkness of ignorance, evil and sin, and those who follow him will have "the light of life", leading to the fullness of life. "*Jesus as the light* which could not be overcome by the darkness [Jn 1,4-5] becomes the *hope for the Dalits*. Their thirst for dignity, justice and equality cannot be conquered by the anti-life forces of dehumanization, discrimination and inequality. The hope that the *light of life* that will ultimately shine strengthens the Dalits in their ongoing struggles for freedom and dignity."[74] For this to become a reality, however, the *Dalit disciples of Jesus* have to become "*the light of the world*" (Mt 5,14) by *collaborating* with him in the *work of liberation* (Jn 9,4-5). *Their lives must be kindled* by the *Paschal candle*, the symbol of the crucified-risen Jesus.

i)   Jesus, the Good Shepherd and the Life-Giver

Since *Jesus' mission* consists of giving *life in abundance* (Jn 10,10) especially to those (like the Dalits) who are denied life, he compares himself to a shepherd who knows the sheep and their needs, cares for them and leads them to pasture (10,3-4.9). He identifies himself as *the good shepherd* who *lays down his life* for the sake of the sheep (10,11), as the *loving leader* who is ready and willing to sacrifice his own life for the protection and welfare of his people (cf. 15,13).

Just as Jesus, "*the resurrection and the life*" (Jn 11,25), *raised the dead Lazarus to life* (11,43-44), he will "resurrect the Dalits from the destructive forces of oppression, exploitation and dehumanization."[75] Just as *Jesus' power of giving life* to Lazarus was interpreted by the *Jewish leaders* (the chief priests and the Pharisees) as *a threat* to their vested interests (11,47-53), the *rise of Dalit power* is taken as *a threat to the caste leaders* and therefore they are bent on suppressing it even by eliminating the Dalit leaders. Like Jesus, they too must be ready to struggle, suffer and even *lose their life* (12,25-26.33-34) to assure a new life of dignity and liberty to all the oppressed Dalits.

j)   *The Disciples'/Dalits' Future Persecution and Life-Giving Suffering*

Jesus foretold that the disciples would be persecuted and even murdered and he warned them: "whoever kills you will think that they are offering worship to God" (Jn 16,2). This is equally true of the maltreated Dalits in India today: "Discriminations and atrocities are carried out against the Dalits in the name of God and religion."[76]

Jesus also told the disciples that they must be *ready to suffer like a woman in travail*: "When a woman gives birth, she has pain because her hour has come, but when she brings forth the child, she no longer remembers the anguish, for the *joy* of *a child being born* into the world" (Jn 16,21). Similarly, "the sufferings and struggles they [Dalits] encounter in *bringing forth a new life of dignity and justice* are indeed *liberative*. Their sweat and blood *give birth to a new life* for *generations to come*."[77] If the Dalits are Christians, *Jesus' victory over death* (through his *resurrection*) will give them *hope* in their struggles for *Dalit liberation* (cf. Jn 16,33).

3.1.4. Jesus' Liberative Praxis

a)   *Call of the Fishermen (Lowly Dalits) and the Choosing of the Twelve*

Jesus calls *ordinary fishermen* (Simon and Andrew, James and John, belonging to the lower social strata) to be *his disciples* (Mk 1,16-20; Mt 4,18-22; Lk, 5,10-11), which indicates that he has a *preferential option* for the *lowly* (like the *Dalits*), rather than those from the socially privileged strata (like the Brahmins). Even a *despised tax collector* (Levi/Matthew) is included among his close disciples/collaborators (Mk 2,14; Mt 9,9; Lk 5,27-28).

From among the many disciples, Jesus *chooses twelve* "apostles" to be his special emissaries. He *commissions* them as his *co-workers* and *shares his authority* not only in proclaiming the reign of God but also in establishing it through healing illnesses and driving out demons (Mk 3,14-15; Mt 10,1; Lk 6,13).

> *The twelve apostles* who were endowed with authority were not from the privileged or dominant sections of the Jewish society. What brings them closer to the *Dalits* is *their disadvantaged social background.* They were illiterate, daily wage earners, … Jesus was prepared to work with such ordinary folk to serve and save the abandoned people. He sought to restore them with God-given dignity. The *Dalits* who have been robbed of their self-respect are no better than these disciples, yet the fact that Jesus intends to accompany them *as his co-workers* is the good news.[78]

b)   Jesus' Table Fellowship with the Sinners and Outcasts (Dalits)

Jesus' table-fellowship with the *"tax-collectors and sinners"* and social outcasts was criticized by the ruling class (especially by the scribes and the Pharisees) (cf. Mk 2,15-16; Mt 9,10-13; Lk 5,29-30) but his rebuttal was: "I came not to call the righteous, but sinners" (Mk 2,17). Jesus' *sharing food with the poor and the marginalized* was a sign not only of his *compassion* for them but also of his desire to enter into *communion* with them. His dining with them manifests that his mission is to establish *God's kingdom-community* without any discrimination based on caste or kind of work (unlike the caste-community which forbids Dalits from eating with the caste people!). *Jesus' table fellowship with the sinners and the outcasts* indicates their *inclusion in the Kingdom of God* and the *community of salvation* (Lk 19,9). It is an *affirmation of the dignity of the Dalits* as *the children of God the Father* and as *Jesus' brothers and sisters.*[79] This will *create within the Dalits* a *consciousness* of *their worth and dignity.*

c)   Jesus' Healing Touch of the Lepers and Loving Touch of the Untouchables (Dalits)

The *social situation* of the *lepers* at Jesus' time was similar to that of the *Dalits* who are forced to live in *Harijan Bastis* which are outside the village or in *separate colonies* on the outskirts of the towns and cities. Like the lepers "who stood at a distance" (Lk 17,12), the Dalits are also supposed to *keep a distance* while talking to the so-called upper caste people especially in the villages.

The *social condition of a Dalit leper* in India is *doubly terrible* because he is considered as an *untouchable* first because of his *birth as a Dalit* and secondly because of his *leprosy* which is believed to be due to his *karma* (his bad deeds done during his previous birth/life).

Rejecting the Jewish practice of untouchability based on the false belief of 'purity and pollution', Jesus *lovingly touches the untouchables* like the *lepers* (Mk 1,40-42; Mt 8,2-3), the *dead body of the ruler's daughter* (Mt 9,25) and allows himself to be touched by a *bleeding woman* (Mt 9,20-21). Jesus also *asks a drink* from the vessel of a *'polluting' Samaritan woman* (looked down upon by the Jews as 'menstruating from birth till death'!) and reveals himself to her as the *Samaritan Messiah* (Jn 4,7-26). *Jesus' stopover* in the *Samaritan village* (4,40) shows *his solidarity* with the *despised Samaritans/Dalits*.

Although untouchability is legally banned in India, *Dalits* are still treated as *untouchables* by the caste people in many parts of our country even today. *Jesus' healing of the untouchables* by touching them and *his staying in the Samaritan village* are *prophetic protests against the heartless dehumanization* of human beings "created in the image and likeness of God" (cf. Gen 1,26-27). This inspires the *Dalits*, who are despised as "*untouchables*" by the caste people, to protest in word and deed against the inhuman *caste system* until it is eradicated from our motherland.

d)   Jesus' Miracles in Favour of the Last and the Least (Dalits)
The *miracles* of Jesus *reveal the Reign of God* and manifest *his love and compassion for those who suffer* in body, mind and spirit. So he *feeds* the hungry crowds; he *heals* the physically ill, the blind, the deaf, the dumb, the paralyzed, the lepers, and raises the dead; he *cures* the mentally sick and *casts out demons* from the possessed. Most of the miracles are performed in favour of

the last and the least, the suffering and the marginalized, the outcasts and the untouchables (*the Dalits of Jesus' time*). For instance, Jesus showed *preferential love* for the *most helpless cripple* for 38 years (Jn 5,2-9) and empowered him to stand on his own feet and walk by telling him: "Rise, take up your pallet and walk" (5,8). Thus Jesus conferred on him not only *healing* but also *a new life of liberty and dignity.*

> For centuries Dalit sisters and brothers have been languishing under the yoke of untold oppression and dehumanization in all the arenas…. In India today they are [the] most oppressed people, denied human dignity at all levels. Therefore, for Christians, the *preferential option for the Dalits* is both a historical and moral imperative. When the Dalit mission receives preferential attention in the Churches, we become the *true disciples of Jesus* who always *opted for the most in need.*[80]

All those who are the sons and daughters of God must, like Jesus the Son of God, work for the liberation of the oppressed Dalits and be ready to face opposition and persecution (Jn 5,16-18; cf. also 9,22-34) by the dominant classes and castes.

e)   *Jesus' Reinterpretation of the Sabbath and His Healings on the Sabbath*

When the Pharisees criticize Jesus' hungry disciples plucking and eating some heads of grain on a Sabbath, he defends them by pointing back to the *original purpose of the Sabbath law* (in fact, every law), viz. the *welfare of human beings*: "The Sabbath was made for man, not man for the Sabbath" (Mk 2,27). Hence Jesus *interprets the law* in favour of the hungry, the suffering and the marginalized and so he *heals the sick and the handicapped even on Sabbath days,* for instance the *man with a withered hand* (Mk 3,1-5),[81] the *cripple* (Jn 5,5-9) and the *man born blind* (Jn 9,1-14).[82] *Jesus' violation of the Sabbath laws* to heal the handicapped shows the way for *the Dalits to violate the discriminatory caste laws* of *Manusmriti.*

f)   Jesus' Abolition of Purity & Pollution and Warning against the Pharisaic Leaven

Jesus *rejects* the wrong idea of *clean and unclean foods* (Mk 7,14-19; Mt 15,10-11.17-18) and strongly opposes any discrimination of persons based on their birth or food habits. He *abolishes* the traditional laws of *purity and pollution* (on which is based the inhuman *caste system* and the labelling of *Dalits* as *unclean*).

Jesus warns his disciples to "beware of the *leaven of the Pharisees*" (Lk 12,1; Mt 16,6.11; Mk 8,15), namely, to guard against their *hypocritical teaching* (Lk 12,1; Mt 16,12). It is similar to the intolerant caste theory of *karma and rebirth* and *Manusmriti's* discriminatory prescriptions for the performance of the *dharma* (duty) of the outcasts (Dalits) to do menial works like removing night soil, burying dead animals, etc. The Dalits must disobey such unfair caste laws and discard such demeaning works.

g)   Jesus' Walking on the Stormy Sea and Calming It

Like the terrified disciples who cried out at the sight of a *ghostlike figure walking on the stormy sea* (Mk 6,49-50; Mt 14,25-26), the Dalits do get scared and scream when the caste criminals attack them. "This experience [of the disciples] lies close to the Dalit heart that screams with terror at the sight of the casteist attacks, arson, rapes and killings. It is like being caught in a stormy sea far away from the civilized world, where no one ever hears their cry."[83]

If the *Dalit Christians* have the *firm faith in Jesus*, who is *in their boat*, who *calms the storms*, and who asks them the challenging question *"Why are you afraid?"* (Mk 4,40), they will have the *courage to face the threatening waves of the caste system* without any fear of getting drowned in the sea of caste discrimination, opposition and persecution.

h)   Jesus' Curing of the Demoniacs

Like the *cured Gerasene demoniac* (Mk 5,18-20), if the *Dalit Christians* were to *bear witness to the liberative divine intervention* of the Lord Jesus in their lives, they would become *co-liberators* with him to free all Dalits from the *clutches of the caste system* in India.

When Jesus *healed dumb demoniacs* and *enabled them to speak,* he was accused by the Pharisees of casting out demons by Beelzebul, the prince of demons (Mt 9,32-34; 12,22-24; Lk 11,14-15). Similarly, those who are engaged in the *liberation of Dalits,* by empowering them to *protest* against the enslaving demonic forces operative in a caste-based society, are *demonised* by the Brahmins and Hindutva groups. "Those who become the voice of the voiceless invariably face such false allegations, as Jesus did… We, like Jesus and in the name of Jesus, need to cast out the demons that keep them mute."[84]

i)   Jesus' Humble Entry into Jerusalem and Prophetic Cleansing of the Temple

Jesus' *riding on a donkey* and entering Jerusalem symbolize his *"humble" entry* into the capital city (Mk 11,4; Mt 21,5-7; Lk 19,30.35; Jn 12,14-15), which identifies him with the *Dalits* who use *donkeys* for short rides or for carrying loads.

By *casting out the traders from the Temple's Court of the Gentiles*, Jesus protests, like a prophet, angrily and violently against the desecration of the place of worship by the vested interests: "Is it not written, 'My house shall be *a house of prayer for all the nations*'? But you have made it a den of robbers" (Mk 11,17; cf. Jn 2,14-17). Thus he *restores the Gentiles' right to worship in the Temple.* This is very significant for the *Dalits* who had to undergo a long *struggle for their temple entry rights.*

Even now *Dalit Christians* have to *face caste discrimination* in some *Churches* and *segregation* even in *cemeteries* (e.g., in Tamilnadu)! "The *Dalit Christians* in many places have *constructed separate churches* or have sat in *separate places at worship inside the church* or have been *buried in a segregated area of cemeteries.*" [85] If Christ were to visit the caste-Christians' Churches today, he would certainly cast out the upper caste parish priests and re-establish inclusive worship of God, the Father, by all his children! The Dalit Christians must continue to protest courageously against all discriminatory and unchristian practices.

j)   Eucharistic Meal

Sharing of the same loaf of bread and *the same cup of wine* (sacramental symbols of the *body* and *blood* of Jesus) (Mk 14,22-23; Mt 26,26-28; Lk 22,19-20) indicates *communion* not only with *Christ* but also with all the members of the *Christian community* (without any discrimination or exclusion), which is very significant especially for the *Dalit Christians.*

> Sharing a piece of a broken bread indicates the fact that those who were going to share that *one bread*, representing *Jesus' own body*, were to become *part of that body.* In the same way, those who were going to drink from the *one cup*, representing *Jesus'*

blood, were going to become *blood relations* from that moment onwards.[86]

k) *Jesus' Servant-Leadership, a New Paradigm for Dalit Leaders*

By *washing the disciples' feet,* Jesus taught them a new paradigm of *"servant-leadership"* (Jn 13,2-17), which is valid not only for Church leaders but also for Dalit leaders.

> Jesus, the Teacher and the Lord, stoops down in service to wash the feet of his disciples (vv. 4-5). This is unconventional and unheard of among the Jewish Rabbis who seek honour and service from their disciples. *Jesus is a different type of teacher and master.* By taking upon himself the *washing of the feet,* which is usually done *by slaves,* Jesus shows again that he has come *to serve and not to be served.* Washing the disciples' feet is *symbolic of his emptying himself* which will be *completed in his death on the cross.*[87]

l) *Jesus' New Commandment of Love and Dalit Vision of an Egalitarian Community*

The *new commandment of love* that Jesus gives his disciples is: "Love one another as I have loved you" (Jn 15,12.17; cf. also 13,34). Christlike *agapê* (selfless, self-giving, self-sacrificing *love*) is the *essential characteristic* of Christ's community of disciples (cf. 13,35), where there would be *no discrimination* based on caste, colour, sex or social position but rather *equality and love, fraternal fellowship and friendship.* This *vision of Jesus* resonates with the *vision of the Dalits:*

> The *Dalit vision of humanity* is one of *egalitarianism and fellowship* in a world that is stratified as an unequal and unjust caste-based society. Jesus' vision of a fraternal and egalitarian society is a clarion call to break down not merely the caste-ridden structures in the Churches but the whole caste-based Indian society and to build ourselves into a *society of equality, love and fellowship.* Only

this type of community will announce that we are indeed the *true disciples of Jesus.*[88]

3.1.5. *Jesus' Passion & Death on the Cross and Dalits' Sufferings*

Jesus' preferential option for the poor and the marginalized in the Jewish society and religion and *his critiquing of the Jewish authorities* (high priests, scribes and Pharisees) angered them. Their opposition to him increased day by day and they plotted to do away with him. He had already foretold the *Son of Man's suffering, rejection and death* (cf. Mk 8,31; 9,31; 10,32-34). Jesus was *not* even given a *fair trial* either by the Jewish or by the Roman authorities.

Even though Jesus had committed no crime, he was *arrested* by the soldiers/police and questioned by Annas and *slapped* by an official. Jesus, however, dared *to question* the one who struck him (cf. Jn 18,23). Again, Jesus was *bold to challenge* the arrogant and threatening *Roman governor* who claimed to have the power to release him or to crucify him: "You would have no power over me unless it had been given to you from above" (Jn 19,11). "Jesus' courageous stand is an inspiration to the Dalits to continue to stand firm and determined in their convictions even if the opposing forces seem to overpower and to conquer."[89]

Innocent Jesus was *unjustly condemned to death* and was *crucified between two criminals* (Lk 23,32-33).[90] He was *mocked* by the *passers-by* and the *rulers* (chief priests and scribes), who challenged him to come down from the cross (Mk 15,29-32; Mt 27,39-43; Lk 23,35). "The *Dalits* stand *dispossessed, disgraced and discarded* for no fault of theirs. *Christ* finds himself *today ridiculed in the Dalits.*"[91]

The *crucified Jesus identifies himself* with the *persecuted Dalits*. Before his death on the cross, he *cried out*: "My God, my God, why have you *forsaken me?*" (Mt 27,46). This is *the anguish of abandonment and final plea for vindication of Jesus*, the Suffering Servant.

Since the Gospels *identify Jesus* with Isaiah's innocent *Servant of God* who *suffered* for the salvation of others, *Dalit Christians* are called to *follow Jesus*, the *Suffering Servant* who summons them *to suffer in solidarity with all fellow Dalits* (of all faiths) in their struggle for emancipation from caste discrimination and oppression. Through the *Christian Dalits' voluntary martyrdom* for the sake of others, the crucified Jesus touches the hearts and eyes, ears and mouths of the Dalit leaders so that they may see the plight of their oppressed brothers and sisters and hear their cries for liberation and organize them to *agitate against every form of discrimination, domination and oppression. Dalit leaders* must be ready to *follow* the *self-sacrificing example of Jesus* if they want the *total liberation and integral welfare (fullness of life)* for their suffering sisters and oppressed brothers.

India must *quake* at the *Dalits' death-cry* that should break open the rocky hearts of the killer-castes before every *believing Indian* will publicly acknowledge the *Dalits* as *children of God* (cf. Jn 1,12-13), just as the *Centurion* confessed "Truly this [*Jesus*] was *God's Son*" (Mt 27,51-54).

3.1.6. Jesus' Resurrection and Ascension, Dalits' Hope

The "young man," "dressed in a white robe," sitting in the empty tomb of Jesus, told the women the *good news* of the crucified Jesus' resurrection (Mk 16,5-6) and asked them to give his disciples the *message of hope*: "he [Jesus] is going before you to *Galilee; there you will meet him*, as he told you" (16,7).

> *Jesus would meet them* not in Jerusalem but *Galilee* [Mk 16,7], analogous to our *thatti* or *cheri* – this indicating that the source of life was not in the place where the temple was situated but away from the borders where the 'unclean' people lived (v. 7). The *hope of the world* is with the *wounded people*.[92]

The *resurrection of the crucified Christ* gives the *persecuted Dalits hope of final victory* over their oppression and death. This is very *relevant*, especially for the *Dalit Christian women*.[93] It should inspire *Dalit Christians* to form *Basic Christian Communities*, which, in turn, must become the *salt* and the *leaven* of the whole Dalit community. Formation of leavened *Basic Human Communities of Dalits* will energize the various *Dalit movements* to continue their *struggle against caste oppression* and *achieve total liberation*.

The *ascension of the risen Jesus* into heaven means that *his presence* is no longer limited to one place but that he is *always and everywhere present to all* (cf. Mt 28,20) who continue his *mission of integral liberation*. The *ascended Jesus' presence* with the struggling Dalits against the unjust caste system instils in them *courage and confidence*. "The Dalits must imbibe the qualities of conviction and trust to build up their levels of confidence to struggle and resist the forces of caste. Jesus was taken up into heaven from where his presence with everyone in all places who carry [sic!] out his mandate is maintained."[94] Then the *Reign of God* of social *justice*, human *dignity*, true *liberty*, casteless *equality* and universal *fraternity* will become *a reality* for all (particularly for the *Dalits*) in our motherland.

3.1.7. Dalit Titles for Jesus Christ

a)   Jesus Christ, a Dalit by Option

Jesus is a *Dalit by option* because he *voluntarily underwent Dalit experiences* of poverty, mockery, contempt, rejection, persecution, suffering and death.[95] *Like a Dalit* who is *born* and *dies outside the caste village*, Jesus was *born in a stable* in Bethlehem and he *died on Calvary outside the city* of Jerusalem.

b)   Jesus Christ, the Liberator of the Dalits

Jesus Christ of the Gospels (especially the Synoptic Gospels) not only *speaks against every form of injustice and discrimination* but also *acts in favour of the unjustly treated and inhumanly marginalized*. So many *Dalits* have believed in *Jesus* and accepted him as *their liberator*.

Through *Jesus' liberative mission to the poor and the oppressed* and *his special love for the socially outcast* (like the lepers, the tax collectors and the sinners), he has revealed himself to be *"the Liberator of the Dalits"*.

The *(Christian) Dalits* feel the inner urge to proclaim this *good news of liberation* to all their discriminated brothers and sisters. *Christ on the cross* gives them the *strength to suffer for others* because they know that they too, like the crucified Jesus, will be *raised to new life*. Since the *crucified Jesus* is also *the risen Lord*, he *gives hope* to all those who are engaged in the struggle for the *integral liberation of the exploited*. The *risen Lord* is the *pledge* that God is on the side of the *suffering Dalits* and that the *Christ-inspired liberative praxis* will *lead to final victory*.[96] He *inspires* them *to courageously continue the mission of integral liberation* of all.

c)   Jesus Christ, the Life-Giver to the Dalits

Jesus Christ, the incarnate Son of God, the crucified-risen Lord, is revealed in John's Gospel as the *Life-Giver* (Jn 10,10; cf. also 20,31). The *Dalits*, who have been *denied 'life'* for centuries, are happy to welcome *Jesus Christ* as the *giver of (true) life* so that *all the loving children of God* may live with dignity and equality, freedom and fellowship, peace and joy, here on earth and hereafter. *Jesus Christ* invites his Dalit brothers and sisters for the *celebration of life*. His life-death-resurrection is a *clarion call* for *liberation and fullness of life*, freedom, dignity and equality for all.

3.2.   The Good News of Jesus Christ For Tribals (Tribal Christology)

3.2.0. Introduction: How to do Tribal Christology?

Francis Minj SJ, a tribal theologian, asks the question and answers it as follows:

> What would be the method of doing Christology in an Adivasi context? Adivasis express themselves in symbolic and metaphorical terms, not in conceptual or abstract ways. Doing an Adivasi Christology, in this sense, would require metaphors chosen from Adivasi cultural resources.[97]

To do a meaningful *Tribal Christology*, we have to take into account the *multiple contexts* in which the Tribals live,[98] their *holistic world view* (e.g., their connectedness to God, community and creation/land/nature), their *negative experiences* (e.g., poverty, exploitation by *dikus*/outsiders, displacement due to dams, deforestation, mining, etc.), their understanding of *liberation* and *salvation*, their *hopes and aspirations* (human dignity, tribal identity, etc.), their *symbolic ways of expression* through stories, songs, dances, *myths and metaphors*.

1)   Tribal World View

The Tribals have a *holistic faith vision* of *God, community and world/nature*. They believe in the *Supreme Being* (called by various names by different tribes, e.g., *Dharmes* by Oraons, *Singbonga* by Mundas and Hos, *Ponomesor* by Kharias, *Cando Baba* by Santals, etc.), who is the *Creator, Protector* and *Provider*. He is the ultimate source of all "good" (creation, land, life, birth, health, happiness, prosperity, family, clan, tribe, etc.). Children, crops and cattle are God's great gifts. There exist *an accepted hierarchical order and harmonious unity between God and all creatures (spirits, human beings, animals, nature)*.

The *Oraons* have a very familiar relationship with *Dharmes* as the *Grandfather* and themselves as His *grandchildren*. But probably because it is the father who provides for his children in a family, *Dharmes* is often addressed as *Father* in prayer: "God, *Dharmes* above… You *Dharmes* are *our Father*. You alone are *Father*, do Thou take care…".[99]

Tribals believe also in *spirits (Bongas)* which are supernatural powers. There are various kinds of spirits like *nature spirits* (e.g., forest or village spirits) or *human* spirits (e.g., *ancestral spirits*), *benevolent* or *malevolent* spirits. The *good spirits* are propitiated through sacrificial offerings but the *evil spirits* are scared away or exorcised by the diviner (*ojha*).

Jal (water), *jamin* (land), *jangal* (forest) belong to the *tribal community* (*not* to the individuals). Certain areas of the land are reserved for special needs/purposes e.g., *akhra* for dancing, *sarna* for worship, *sasan* for burial.

2)   Tribals' Negative Experiences

In the light of our discussion on the Tribals (in **2.2.** above), we may now highlight some of the *negative experiences* of the Tribals.

a)   Socio-Cultural Crisis due to Dikus (Outsiders)

Outsiders (*dikus*) like *Muslim kings* and the *landlords, jagirdars* (lease-holders of tribal land), *thekedars* (contractors), the *British traders and rulers/officers exploited* the Tribals and *marginalized* them so much that many of them had to *migrate* to other parts of the country like Assam, Andaman and Nicobar Islands, etc. Encounter with outsiders *alienated* the Tribals from their *culture* and they *felt inferior* to the others.

b)   Deforestation and Displacement

Thousands of hectares of *forest* have been *submerged/destroyed* and *lakhs* of Tribals (*Adivasis*) have been *displaced* from their land and forests due to so-called developmental projects like *mega-dams* and *mining, industrial establishments* (like TELCO, TISCO, HEC, Steel City, Bokaro, etc.) and *field-firing ranges* (e.g., at Netarhart in Jharkhand). At least *50% of the displaced people* in India are *Tribals* and many of them have never been properly *rehabilitated. Displacement* of Tribals not only *deprives* them of their *resources* like water, land, forest (*jal, jamin, jangal*) but also *destroys their community life* and *uproots* them from their *religion, culture* and *ancestors. The Adivasis* encounter the Supreme Being in nature and especially in all forms of life. They *worship God* in the natural setting of green trees (*Sarna*). Likewise, every tribal village has *akhra* for community dancing. Similarly, their *ancestors are buried* in *sasan* (reserved land for the burial of the dead).

c)   Naxalite Problems

Because of the perceived exploitation and oppression of the Tribals by governments, police and vested interests, Naxalite groups have been working in the tribal areas to fight for the tribal rights of land and forest, justice and equality. But the common people are caught between the devil and the deep sea! On the one hand, large numbers of armed Naxalite cadres come to the villagers at night and demand food; on the other hand, the village people are harassed, threatened and even arrested by the police who demand information about the Naxalites and their activities but any police-informer will be shot dead by the Naxalites!

d)   Massive Poverty and Emigration

Even seven decades after independence, the *economic condition* of many of the Tribals has become *worse* than before because of the *alienation of tribal land* and *lack of access to the forests* (taken over by the government). Thousands of Tribals, especially village women, come to megacities like Mumbai and Delhi looking for a livelihood.

> The loss of the best lands to land sharks, or the uprooting of the entire villages to make land available for industries or dams has resulted in the total breakdown of their economic system. As a result, a wave of emigration into other parts of the country has come about. Thousands of young tribal men and women, especially women, are pouring into metropolitan cities, which is one of the most catastrophic impacts of a massive assault on tribal land.[100]

e)   Violation of Human Rights

There are thousands of '*Tribal Domestic Working Women*' employed in the houses of the rich in the megacities like Delhi,

Mumbai, Kolkata, etc. They are abused by their employers in many ways:

> First of all, they are paid minimal salaries. Secondly, they have to work countless hours of the day. Besides, most of them become victims of sexual harassment in many households. In some cases, they are treated by their employers as bonded labour. In yet other cases, they are traded like cattle… many tribal girls have been forced into prostitution.[101]

Likewise, there are hundreds of tribal men and women who are hired by contractors for construction works (buildings or roads), quarrying, etc., but are paid very low wages and young women are exploited sexually.

f)   Fear of the Evil Spirits

Fear of the evil spirits is prevalent among the tribals because they have the superstitious belief that *sickness and suffering are caused by evil spirits.* "They believe that the evil spirits use the 'evil-eye' (*Najar-Gujar*) and 'evil-mouth' (*Bai Bhakh*) of the witches to spell sickness over someone they are not pleased with."[102] Often old women and suspected witches are brutally beaten up and even cruelly killed!

3)   Tribals' Understanding of Liberation and Salvation

a)   Liberation from Negative Experiences

Liberation for the Tribals means *deliverance from the negative experiences of life* (mentioned above), which may be summed up as freedom from material poverty, injustice, oppression, discrimination, dehumanization, socio-economic exploitation and land/forest alienation, political powerlessness, *dikus* (outsiders), sickness, fear of evil spirits, superstitions (like witchcraft), etc.

b)   Liberation from Sin

Sin is understood by the Tribals as *alienation* from *God, community* and *nature.* Sin *ruptures the order* established by Dharmes (God, the Supreme Being). The *primary sins* for the Tribals are *greed and pride,*[103] from which they have to be freed.

c)   Salvation as Prosperous, Happy and Harmonious Life in Community

The Tribals have a *pragmatic understanding* of '*life*' and for them, '*good life*' means *prosperity and happiness.* In the words of Boniface Tirkey S.J.: "Abundant harvests, numerous cattle-head, and healthy progeny are most highly valued possessions."[104]

Salvation for the Tribals means *a happy and harmonious life* (prosperity with land, cattle, children, etc.), *in their community on earth* and *immortal life with the ancestors after death.*

It is to be noted that the tribal concept of *salvation* is *not* centred on *the individual* but on *the community.* This is clear from the fact that *personal devotion to Dharmes* is *not* emphasized at the *individual level.* In short, Tribals believe in *communitarian salvation,* which has a *social* dimension (*happiness and harmony in society*).

4)   Tribal Myths about God's Protection and Liberation[105]

Tribal *myths* reveal *basic religious beliefs* and *guide their socio-cultural-religious practices.* Since the myths are transmitted orally, there may be variations in details but the basic elements and central message are the same.

Dharmes/Singbonga (God the Creator, Protector, Provider) and his *caring relationship* with the *Tribals* in this world and how he *liberates* and *protects* them are symbolically narrated in many of the tribal *myths*.

a)   *Khasra-Khusru Kukkos (Sore-Stricken Boy) (Xaddi Myth)*
Dharmes sent bird-messengers to the *iron smelters* (12 *Asur* and 13 *Lodha* brothers) and told them to stop bellowing the polluting furnace at night but they *refused to obey Dharmes* and *arrogantly* claimed themselves to be *gods*. This shows their *pride, greed* and *disobedience*. So *Dharmes* took the form of a *sore-stricken boy* (*Khasra-Khusru Kukkos, K.K.K.*). He asked the iron smelters and their wives for shelter but they chased him away! But he was warmly welcomed by a poor old widow and was lovingly looked after as her son.

When the smelting furnace stopped functioning due to some serious problem, the *Asur-Lodha* brothers were at a loss as to what was to be done. So they approached *K.K.K.* and he advised them to sacrifice a white fowl, a goat and a buffalo to placate the evil spirit causing the failure of the furnace. But, in spite of the animal sacrifice, the problem persisted. So a human sacrifice was suggested by *K.K.K.* and he volunteered to sacrifice himself and told them to bellow the furnace for seven days and seven nights. But on the 8th day *K.K.K.* came out of the fiery furnace unharmed but wearing a lot of silver and gold ornaments! Burning with greed for gold and silver, the brothers too wanted to enter the burning furnace for seven days and nights but all of them were reduced to ashes! By *destroying the proud and greedy Asur-Lodha men, K.K.K. freed* the Tribals from poisonous pollution. Thus *K.K.K.* (the visible image/symbol of *Singbonga*) is *a mythical liberator/saviour figure* for the Tribals. By cunningly *killing* the *greedy and proud persons, K.K.K. saved* the Tribals (and humanity) from deadly pollution and taught them *not to sin* through *greed* and *pride* but to obey *Dharmes*. Thus *K.K.K.* (God in human form) is a *symbol* of the *Saviour* of the Tribals.

b)   *Liti Bir (Dwarf Boy) & Sonu Giddhi (Giant Vulture) (Faggu Myth)*

A *giant vulture* (*Sonu Giddhi*) with sharp claws used to swoop down daily to catch human beings to eat them. It also carried away the ploughs and yokes from the fields to make its nest on the cotton tree. So the helpless humans prayed to *Dharmes* to save them from the murderous vulture. Therefore, *Dharmes* took the form of a *dwarf boy* (*Liti Bir*) and stayed in a widow's house. One day he went out with an iron bow and arrow, shot down *Sonu Giddhi* and saved humans from its sudden and deadly attacks.

c)   *Addo Xapu Kukkos (Bull Boy) (Sohrai Myth)*

Like the *Dwarf Boy* in the *Phaggu* myth, there is a *Bull Boy* (*Addo Xapu Kukkos*) in the *Sohrai* myth. He too was staying with a poor widow. There was a *man-eater monster* who had to be given a human being as its daily food. When the widow's turn came, the Bull Boy took her place, encountered and killed the fierce monster and thus saved the widow and others from a cruel death.

It is to be noted that *Khasra-Khusru Kukkos (Sore-Stricken Boy)*, *Liti Bir (Dwarf Boy)* and *Addo Xapu Kukkos (Bull Boy)* are *God (Dharmes) in human form* (boys) who *saved/liberated the Tribals* by killing their *enemies*, symbolized by the *Asur-Lodha iron-smelters*, the *vulture*, and the *monster*. To *free* the Tribals from their foes, *Dharmes*, the creator of the earth and humans, *becomes a poor human being (K.K.K., Dwarf Boy, Bull*

Boy) and lives with a poor widow and saves the humans from their enemies (life-threatening evil forces). Hence *Dharmes* is the *protector* and *liberator* of helpless human beings.

d)   *Karam Raja (Karam Tree) (Uraon Myth)*

According to this *Uraon* myth, the tribal ancestors lived a happy and prosperous life under their king. Their enemies attacked the king's fort and killed him and many others. But his queen and children and a few elders and others escaped through a secret underground passage. After traveling a long distance, they found *a mountain cave*. The mouth of the cave was covered by the leafy branches of a big *Karam tree* and so they took shelter in the cave. When their enemies came looking for them, they could not find them because they failed to notice the cave since it was covered by the Karam branches. The *Karam tree,* which *protected the tribals* from their enemies, is the *symbol* of *Dharmes, the Protector* of the Sarna people.

•   *Karam Festival:*

The *feast* of *Karam Raja* is celebrated every year on the 11th day of the lunar month of *Bhado,* when three branches of the *Karam* tree are planted by the tribal maidens in the middle of the *akhara* (village dancing ground). The *Pahan* (priest) anoints the *Karam Raja* with *sindur* (vermillion) and ties it with unbleached thread and pours milk on it as an offering. The *maidens* place their Karam-baskets (*dowra* containing some pearl rice and flat rice, a tender cucumber and maize shoots, an earthen lamp and flowers) at the foot of the Karam branches. Then they sit around the branches and listen to the *Karam Kahani (Karam Legend).* After this, the maidens and the boys *dance* around the *Karam Raja* the entire night. The next day morning the maidens (potential bearers of children) distribute *tender maize shoots* (*symbol of new life, Jawa Punp*) to their elder brothers, requesting their protection. Finally, the maidens take the *Karam branches* in procession to a flowing stream or a clean pond and immerse them in it. When they return home, they offer the *tender cucumber* (*symbol of children*) to their grandparents. In this festival, the *Karam branch* is the *symbolic protector of the life* of the Tribals.

3.2.1. Tribal Metaphors for Jesus

Just as in the Synoptic Gospels Jesus asked the disciples: "Who do *people* say that I am?" and "Who do *you* say that I am?" (Mk 8,27-28; Mt 16,13-15; Lk 9,18-20), so during the twenty years (1987-2007) of my teaching 'Christology' in *Vidyajyoti* (College of Theology, Delhi) and a few years in *Tarunoday* (Ranchi RTC), I used to ask the tribal students similar questions: "Who do *Sarna* Tribals say that Jesus is?" and "Who do *you* (*Christian* Tribals) say that Jesus is?" Some of them also wrote papers and/or dissertations on the tribal (Sarna & Christian) understanding and interpretation of Jesus. Based on these and on what tribal scholars have written on the above subject, I have already given above some of the major *tribal myths.* Now I would like to present some of the relevant *tribal metaphors for Jesus.*[106]

a)   *Karam Branch (Karam Raja) and the Crucified/Risen Christ*

Just as the *Karam tree,* which by covering the mouth of the cave saved the Tribals hiding inside from death, was a symbol of Dharmes' saving action, so Jesus' death on the *Cross* was God's saving deed on behalf of humankind. In the words of

Cornelius Ekka S.J.:

> This myth presents the *Karam tree* as a *symbol of salvation*. It resembles the Christian understanding of the *Cross* as the *symbol of salvation*. In both traditions, the symbols acquire salvific meaning because of their association with God/Jesus/ *Dharmes*...[107]

> The tribals could see the *Cross of Christ* as the *saviour tree* on which Jesus was hung to save humanity... Both, the *Karam tree* and the *Cross*, are just *instruments of God's saving action*. Ultimately, it is God himself who saves. But we believe that God and Jesus are one [because Jesus said: "I and the Father are one": Jn 10,30]. Hence it is Jesus himself whom the tribals worship on the occasion of *Karam* celebration.[108]

During the "Way of the Cross" Christians pray: "We adore you, O Christ, and we bless you because, by your Holy Cross, you have redeemed the world." It means that, because of his obedience to God the Father and his self-sacrificing love for the sinful humans, Jesus *chose* to die on the *Cross* to save humanity. Therefore, the *Cross* has become the *symbol* of *God's saving action* in *Jesus' redeeming death*, out of his great love for humans ("Greater love than this no one has than to lay down his life for his friends": Jn 15,13).

Since the Sarna Tribals consider the *Karam tree* (in the *Karam* myth) as a symbol of *Dharmes* (who is regarded as their *Grandfather* in God's affectionate relationship with them), *tribal Christians* may *integrate* their Christian faith in *Jesus, the Son of God,* with the Sarna myth in a *new way*, namely, by regarding the *Karam Tree* as *Dharmes* (God the Father) and the *Karam Branch* as *Christ* (the Son of God) through whom *Dharmes protected* His *grandchildren* (the Tribals) from death.[109] The *cutting* of the *branch* from the *Karam Tree* may be compared to the *cross* on which Jesus *died,* and its *planting* in the *akhra* (dancing ground) to his *resurrection.* This is the reason why the Christian tribal maidens and boys sing and dance around it. This may be a meaningful *tribal Christological interpretation* of the *Paschal Mystery* (death-resurrection) of Jesus through which he saved all and gave them new life (cf. Jn 10,10-11).

b)   *Sore-Stricken Boy (Khasra-Khusru Kukkos) and Jesus, the Suffering Servant*

Even though the "*Sore-Stricken Boy*" (in the original *Xaddi* myth) is *Dharmes, K.K.K.* may be considered as an *image of Jesus* in the Gospels, who was *prefigured* in the "*Suffering Servant*" in Isaiah (Is 50,6; 52,14; 53,1-12). Like the mythical hero *K.K.K.* who enters voluntarily the burning furnace but comes out resplendently transformed into gold and silver, *Jesus* willingly *suffers and dies on the cross* but *rose gloriously* from the tomb. But unlike *K.K.K.* who *deceived* the greedy and proud *Asurs/ Lodhas* and *destroyed* them, *Christ* did/does *not deceive* nor *destroy* the *sinners* but *dies for them* and *redeems* them *through his suffering and death on the cross.*

c)   *Dwarf Boy (Liti Bir) and Bull Boy (Addo Xapu Kukkos) and Jesus, the Liberator*

Both the *Dwarf Boy (Liti Bir)* and the *Bull Boy (Addo Xapu Kukkos)* took the form of a young '*boy*' and stayed with a *poor* widow and *freed* the Tribals from the deadly giant *Vulture* and the man-eating *Monster.* Similarly, *Jesus* was born in poverty, served the sick and poor and *liberated* possessed persons from the clutches of demons. Therefore, the *Dwarf Boy* and the *Bull Boy* may be regarded as *tribal images of Jesus, the Liberator.*

d)   *Jesus, the First Ancestor*[110]

According to the *Adivasi* understanding of *ancestors*, it is not *all forebears* who are "*ancestors*" but only those who were *persons of integrity* in their lifetime and who *bequeathed a good moral and spiritual heritage* to their descendants and who now *pray to God* for their total welfare on earth.

> Because of their spiritual state, the ancestors *mediate* between God and the living community. The ancestors attained spiritual state because of their exemplary life here on earth and now they mediate God's blessings onto the living. The ancestors remain exemplary because they lived the traditional virtues of anti-greed, anti-pride and anti-jealousy…[111]

According to the Gospel of John, God created all things through the eternal divine Word: "In the beginning was the Word, and the Word was with God, and the Word was God" (Jn 1,1). "All things were made *through* him" (1,3) and "That which became *in* him was life" (1,4).

Even though everything was created *through* the Word of God (1,3), *life* was created *in* the Word (as in the womb) (1,4a). Therefore, every *living* creature is a *revelation* of the Word of God to human beings (1,4b: "*life* was the *light* of men"). That is the reason why Tribals, who live in constant contact with various forms of life (plants, forests, animals, birds, humans), respect life and find God in all living beings.

It is this creative, revelatory and life-giving Word of God that became a human being in Jesus: "And the Word became flesh and dwelt among us…" (1,14). This is the *first time* that the *divine Word* has *become a human being* (Jesus). Hence *Jesus*, the *enfleshed Word of God*, may be regarded as the *First Ancestor.*

Jesus, the *First Ancestor*, came with the mission of imparting *fullness of life*: "I came that they might have life and have it abundantly" (Jn 10,10). He has revealed himself as "the resurrection and the life" (11,25) and continues to be "the way, the truth and the life" (14,6). He is the *mediator of eternal life* to all believers not only after their death but also during their earthly life (cf. 3,16.36; 17,2), and he sustains it through his self-gift of the "*bread of life*" (the Eucharist) (6,35.48.51-58).

Jesus, the *First Ancestor*, has also given a *new commandment of love*: "Love one another as I have loved you" (Jn 13,34; 15,12), that is, love each other generously, selflessly and self-sacrificingly. This is a *universal love* for all (not restricted to one's biological family, tribe or clan) and especially for all in need (e.g., the poor, the hungry, the thirsty, the naked, the sick, the prisoner or the stranger). This *law of love* is the criterion that *Jesus Christ*, the *ancestor-judge*, will apply to all on Judgment Day for admission to the kingdom of God (Mt 25,31-45).

The *divinehuman Jesus*, the *risen Lord*, the *First Ancestor*, promises his *perpetual presence*: "I am with you always, to the end of the age" (Mt 28,20). Jesus *Christ's presence* is not restricted to any particular village or tribe (like that of an Adivasi ancestor) but is *universal* (applicable to *all human beings* of all times and all places). In the words of Boniface Tirkey S.J.:

> Oraon Christology consists in Jesus, the Son, being the *First Ancestor*. The God-made-man has sacrificed himself and has been taken up into the world of Dharmes; and in that [he] has borne witness to and achieved man's incorporation into the ancestral community of the saved. He, the *First Ancestor*, is the Lord and Master of history and is God. The primordial leprous boy (Dharmes) has acted again definitively in Jesus the Son and has constituted a new 'tribe', which transcends all

times and peoples, through which man can be saved. The tribe is constituted both by the living and the dead.[112]

e)   *Jesus, the Servant Leader (Dangar-Agua)*

Jesus was anointed by the Holy Spirit not to be a political lord over others and to receive their service, but on the contrary *to serve* others especially the marginalized as a *Dangar-Agua (servant-leader)* (Mk 10,42-43; Lk 4,16-30).

> The *Adivasi model of servanthood* [*Dangar*] draws its inspiration from the *servant-God* who came to earth as a *leprous boy* as mentioned in the *Asur* myth… The Adivasi servant-God gets involved in ordinary human life to correct it. *Jesus* as the *self-emptying servant* enters human history to inaugurate God's reign by becoming a *model of service*, humility and suffering, even if it demands death.[113]

Unlike the *Adivasi* leaders whose feet are washed by *Adivasi* women, Jesus, "the *Lord and Teacher*," *washes the feet of his disciples* and asks them to follow his example of *servant leadership* (Jn 13,3-9.12-15). Jesus, the *Good Shepherd lays down his life* for the sheep (Jn 10,11; Jn 15,13). In short, *Jesus, the Servant Leader*, is an *inspiration* to all (especially *Adivasi* Christians and their leaders).

f)   *Jesus, Great Exorcist (Maha Devda), Divine Healer (Deonra) and Redeemer (Uddharak)*

As we have seen above, the *tribal mythical heroes* (Sore-Stricken Boy, Dwarf Boy and Bull Boy) took *human form* (a boy) to *destroy the evil forces* (represented by the Asurs/Lodhas, the Vulture and the Monster). Similarly, *Jesus, the Son of God*, has *become human* to *destroy the evil spirit* (demon) who cries out: "Have you come to *destroy* us? I know who you are, the Holy One of God" (Mk 1,24; Lk 4,34). Here and elsewhere in the

Gospels, Jesus is presented as a *powerful exorcist* because he *casts out the evil spirits* from the possessed persons with the power of his word (cf. Mk 1,25-26; 9,14-29; Mt 8,5-13; 9,32-34; 11,14-15; Lk 4,31-37.41). Tribals who are frightened of the evil spirits (which are supposed to cause sicknesses) are eager to welcome Jesus, the *Great Exorcist* (*Maha Devda*), empowered by *the Spirit of God.*

Jesus, the *divine healer* (*Deonra*) *of all illnesses*, is an appealing person to all the *Tribals* in India. *Tribal Christians*, who believe in the divinehuman Jesus, experience him as *the most powerful healer.*

Since Jesus in the Gospels *saves sinful people* from their sins by *forgiving* them (e.g., the paralytic: Mk 2,1-5; a sinful woman: Lk 7,36-50; the woman caught in adultery: Jn 8,1-11), Christian *Adivasis* acknowledge Jesus as their *Saviour/Redeemer* (*Uddharak*) and pray to him to *redeem/save* them from their *sins of pride, greed* and *jealousy.*

g)   *Jesus, the Itinerant Teacher (Gosain)*

Just as Abraham welcomed three strangers who were on their journey and served them with heart-warming hospitality and discovered in the process that it was God who visited him and promised him a son in his old age (Gen 18,1-15), *Adivasis* (e.g., *Kharias*) believe that God may visit them as an ascetic *Gosain.*

> A *Gosain* in the Kharia tradition is an itinerant ascetic teacher, a speaker and seeker of the truth, a prophet, a peaceful and nonviolent reconciler, a wonder worker, and ultimately the one who shows the way to liberation. He is an unknown yet clairvoyant person who has spiritual powers because of his intimate association with the divine. This *Gosain* offers a panacea for all ills.[114]

John the Baptist tells the people: "among you stands one whom *you do not know*" (Jn 1,26). Further, he testifies that he did not know him until he was revealed to him as "the Son of God" (1,34), "come from above" (3,31), and "he whom God has sent utters the words of God" (3,34). Therefore, *Jesus* who comes as an *"itinerant teacher"* among the *Adivasis* may be regarded as a *divine Gosain.*

> Jesus can be viewed as *Gosain* or a clairvoyant teacher who surpasses all others because he comes from heaven (Jn 3,31). … Because of his *Abba* experience (Mk 1,9-11; 1,35; Lk 3,21-22; Jn 1,31-34), he guides others to the Father; he speaks the Father's language. In India, a wandering guru in search of disciples would be under suspicion, but if understood to be a *Sakhi Gosain,* or a liberation-bestowing teacher would be well accepted among the Adivasis.[115]

h)   Jesus, the Great Priest (Maha Pahan)

The *Pahan* (priest) prays and offers animal/bird sacrifices for the wellbeing (health, wealth, cattle, crop, children) of the tribal family and community. Like the *Pahan,* Jesus also prays for his disciples of all places and times (cf. Jn 17,9-26) and offers a sacrifice for them. But, unlike the tribal *Pahan, Jesus, the High Priest, offers himself* for the salvation of humanity (cf. Heb 7-8). His *self-sacrificing death on the cross* (symbolized by *the white fowl* during the *Sarhul puja*) is for the forgiveness of sins (cf. Jesus' prayer from the cross: "Father, forgive them…" Lk 23,34) and for the human participation in the divine eternal life (cf. Jn 10,10-11; 17,2-3). Therefore, Jesus may be rightly called *Maha Pahan (Great Priest)* who *mediates forgiveness of sins and fullness of life* for all.

i)   Jesus, the White Cock (Pandru Xer) of God[116]

During the *Sarhul puja* (sacrifice) the *Pahan* (priest) offers to *Dharmes* a *white fowl/cock* (*Pandru Xer*) as *a sacrificial victim* (symbolizing the life of the Tribals), while reciting the following prayer (asking for God's forgiveness of their offences and his protection):

> O God [*Dharmes*], you are up above, and I [*Pahan*] and the *Panches* (elders) are here below. Your eyes see, ours can't. You know everything, we know nothing. I am offering this white fowl, which represents all of the young, the old and us. If knowingly or unknowingly we have offended you and the spirits, look not on them. And save us, our children and cattle, and the whole area of our village boundary from all harm and ill.[117]

John the Baptist proclaimed Jesus as "the *Lamb of God* who takes away the sin of the world" (Jn 1,29.36). Here Jesus is presented as the *sacrifice for the sins* of humankind. Tribals would find it more meaningful if Jesus is called "the *white Cock of God*" rather than "the Lamb of God".

j)   The Risen Jesus, the Flowering Sal Tree and New Maize Shoot (Jawa)

The *Sal tree* which *flowers* in the new year and the *Jawa* (*tender maize shoot*) are symbols of *new life*. Since Jesus has died like the grain of wheat/maize and has *risen* like the *tender shoot* (cf. Jn 12,24) and since he is the new "life" (cf. Jn 11,25; 14,6), *the risen Jesus* may be called *the flowering Sal tree* and *Jawa* (*new shoot*). These are similar to *Jesus* being "*the Vine*" (Jn 15,1).

k)   Jesus, the First Fruit

Just as the *Tribals offer* the *first fruits* to *Dharmes* out of *gratitude* for the gifts of all the fruits (food for human life and nourishment), *Jesus, the incarnate Son of God*, is *God's greatest gift* to humankind so that humans may have eternal life: "For God so loved the world [of humanity] that he *gave* his *unique Son* (*ho hyios ho monogenês*) so that those who believe in him may not perish but may have eternal life" (Jn 3,16). So the Tribal Christians offer the *incarnate-risen Jesus* as *the First Fruit* to God the Father (*Dharmes*) during the celebration of the *Eucharist* (a *communal* meal and '*thanksgiving*' sacrifice).

l)   The Risen Jesus, the Rising Sun

Just as *the rising sun*, which dispels the darkness of night and enables humans to see at dawn, is admired and accepted by the tribals as God's gift, so *Jesus*, the *incarnate Son of God*, who revealed himself as "*the light of the world*" (Jn 8,12; 9,5; cf. also 1,4-5; 3,19; 12,36.46), continues to enlighten every human being (cf. 1,9) like *the rising sun* every day. Hence the tribal Christians may regard the *rising sun* as the *symbol* of the *risen Jesus*, who was *seen* by Mary Magdalene and another Mary at the first Easter *dawn* (Mk 16,9; Mt 28,1.9; Jn 20,1.18) and later by other disciples (Jn 21,4-7).

m)   Jesus Christ, the Divinehuman Drummer and Dancer

On feast days the *sound of the mandar* (*Adivasi* drum) invites the tribal community to gather at the *akhra* (dancing ground) for singing and dancing. Similarly, the *Word of God* (the divine sound of the drum) summons the believing *Adivasis* to assemble around *Jesus Christ, the divinehuman Drummer and Dancer*, to celebrate salvation joyfully with songs and dances.

> God's Word made flesh *dances* to the rhythm of every culture and also tunes and intones every culture to God's design. Jesus beckons every culture to drum, dance and sing according to

God's message manifested in the *adi-drummer* and the *dancer-Jesus Christ*.[118]

3.2. © Conclusion

Keeping in mind the *tribal context, world-view* and *understanding of life, liberation and salvation*, and making use of the *tribal myths* (e.g., Sore-Stricken Boy, Dwarf Boy & Giant Vulture, *Karam Raja*) and *interpreting* them in the light of the Gospels, we (together with tribal Christian theologians) have discovered *new tribal faces of Jesus Christ* as *the First Ancestor, Karam Branch (Karam Raja), Great Exorcist (Maha Devda), Divine Healer (Deonra), Liberator/Redeemer (Uddharak), Itinerant Teacher (Gosain), Great Priest (Maha Pahan), White Cock (Pandru Xer) of God. The (risen) Jesus Christ is also symbolized by the tribal metaphors like the Flowering Sal Tree, New Maize Shoot (Jawa), First Fruit, Rising Sun, Divinehuman Drummer and Dancer.* They manifest the *salvific significance of Jesus Christ for the Tribals.*

3.3. The Good News of Jesus Christ for Women (Feminist Christology)

3.3.0. Introduction

Our focus here would be on *Indian women's understanding and faith interpretation of Jesus Christ* based on their *experiences* in the *light of his revelation in the Gospels. Indian feminist Christology* is *not* an *exclusive woman-centred* but an *inclusive Christology.*

Indian feminists are *not anti-male* but *anti-patriarchal.* They are aware of women's marginalization, subordination, subjugation, suppression and dehumanization in the Patriarchal Indian family, society and religions.

3.3.1. *Indian Women's Experiences of Oppression in the Patriarchal Context*[119]

In *Indian patriarchal society, men are regarded as superior to women* and so *women experience* every day various kinds of *male domination, discrimination, dehumanization, subordination, subjugation, oppression and violence.*

> Manifold are the ways in which *violence* is perpetrated *against women* in this country. It includes selective female foeticide, infanticide, discriminatory practices against the female child as well as the widows, wife battering and sexual abuse of various kinds. Women, on the whole, receive less of everything - less food, less medical care, less educational and job opportunities and less rest and leisure time. The *strong patriarchal bias* of Indian culture continues to *dehumanize women.*[120]

a)   *Oppressive Situation of Women in Indian society and Hinduism*[121]

Despite the *deification of woman* (as *Lakshmi, Parvathi, Saraswati, Durga,* etc.) in Hindu Scriptures and festivals, the *woman* is *oppressed from the womb to the tomb* in *Indian patriarchal family and society:* female foeticide and infanticide, denial of food, freedom and education to girls, child marriage, sexual exploitation and rape, trafficking of girls and women, sex tourism, sexual slavery as *devadasis* in temples or as prostitutes in brothels, arranged marriage (against the woman's will), the practice of dowry and dowry-death, physical violence against women (wife-battering), acid attacks and honour killings, sexual harassment of women at work-places, gender-based discrimination (e.g., lesser wages for women for equal work in farms and factories).

There are also *patriarchal stereotypes of woman* as *inferior to man* and as *his possession/property, male domination* of woman at home *as wife and mother.* All the *decisions in a traditional family* are taken *by the father or husband.* The woman has a *subservient status as wife to her husband. Wife* is expected to be always *pleasing to her husband* and *not vice versa!* Wife has to *do all the domestic work* (cooking food, cleaning the house, washing clothes, etc.,) which is not recognized as productive labour! *Mother* is "like a tree producing fruits" and a *childless married woman* is considered as "*a barren tree* or *waterless river*"! *Mother is blamed* for *not bearing male* children! *Widows* are *barred from remarriage.* Women (of menstruating age) are *banned from entry into temples* like Sabarimala. The list of *patriarchal negative attitudes and atrocious acts of female oppression* in Hinduism and Indian society is endless!

b)   *Subjugating Situation of Women in Islam*

In *Islam,* there are also other *forms of subjugation and oppression of women,* e.g., *polygamy, divorce* through *triple Talaq* (even though recently it has been banned legally), *purdah* (a male imposition on women to deny them equality and freedom) and *Khatna* or *Khafz* (Female Genital Mutilation).

c)   *Discriminatory Situation of Women in Male-Dominated Christianity*

In *Christianity* too, *women* experience various forms of *patriarchal domination and discrimination* e.g., branding of *woman* as a *temptress* (Eve as the cause of Adam's fall! cf. Gen 3), *incest* and other forms of *sexual exploitation of girls, sexual abuse of women* at work-places (e.g., offices, factories), prevalent practise of *dowry, wife-beating, denial of equality and freedom* to women, *secondary roles* of women in the Catholic Church (scant representation in decision-making bodies like parish councils and diocesan councils, etc.). *Awakened Indian Christian women* have begun to *claim their rights to liberty, equality and dignity* as the daughters of God.

3.3.2. Situation of Women at the Time of Jesus

There was a *patriarchal anti-woman bias* at the time of Jesus. Jewish Rabbi Judah ben Elai used to pray: "Blessed be God that he has not made me a Gentile or a woman or a slave." The woman was considered *inferior* to man. The woman was always *under the control of man* (daughter by father, wife by the husband, mother by adult son). A *menstruating woman* was treated as *polluting* (a taboo of purity and pollution as in Indian caste system). The woman was spoken of as a *seducer* (cause of sin) and as an *unreliable witness*. Women had a *segregated* place in every Jewish synagogue and the Jerusalem Temple ("the court of women").

3.3.3. Prominence of Women in the Gospels of Luke and John

Even though women are mentioned in all the four Gospels, *women* are given much more *prominence* in the *Gospels of Luke and John* than in those of Mark and Matthew.

a)   Women in Luke's Gospel

Many women play *important roles in Luke's Gospel* right from the *annunciation* of Jesus' birth (1,26-38) till his *resurrection* (24,1-11).

(i)   Mary, Mother of Jesus

In Lk the angel Gabriel *announces Jesus' birth to Mary* (*not* to Joseph as in Mt), tells her about the child's mission in the future, and she gives *her fiat (free consent) to God's plan of salvation* after *dialoguing* with the messenger of God (to clarify her doubts about how she was going to conceive) (Lk 1,34-38). She does not put any condition to be *the mother of the Messiah*. She consents to it without even consulting Joseph to whom she was betrothed. In Lk it is *Mary* (*not* Joseph) who is asked by the angel to *name* her child *"Jesus"* (1,31).

Mary takes the *initiative to visit* her expectant kinswoman *Elizabeth* (1,39-45), who, like a Spirit-filled prophetess, proclaims Mary as "blessed among women" and the child in her womb as "blessed" and praises her faith in the Lord. Mary's *Magnificat* is *a song praising God for the salvation and liberation* of the hungry and *exaltation* of the lowly (1,46-55). Mary *serves* her pregnant kinswoman for three months (1,56).

Mary is a *contemplative woman* who *keeps in her heart*[122] and *prayerfully ponders* over the shepherds' memorable words about her new-born son (2,19) and later her twelve-year-old son's mysterious words about his "Father's house" (2,49-51).

(ii)   Widows and Jesus

Several *widows* are presented in Luke's Gospel. For instance, *Anna*, an old widow, a praying and fasting prophetess, comes up to the Temple at the hour of Jesus' presentation and *recognizes* him (like Simeon) as the *redeemer* and speaks about him to others (2,36-38). Again, Jesus has *compassion* for the *weeping widow of Nain* and raises her dead son (7,14-15) and thus gives her *a new life of hope*. Watching *a poor widow* putting two little copper coins into the Temple treasury, Jesus praises the destitute *widow's offering* as very valuable in the eyes of God because she has "put in all that she had," indicating her *self-sacrificing generosity in giving* (21,1-4). To persuade his disciples to *persevere in prayer,* Jesus tells them the *parable of the persistent widow and the unrighteous judge* (18,1-8).

(iii)   Sick/Suffering Women and Jesus

Jesus' *healing of the bent woman* on a Sabbath reveals his *compassion* for the *handicapped woman* (Lk 13,10-13). But his ensuing discussion with the indignant ruler of the synagogue who objected to Jesus' curing her on a Sabbath shows his priority of woman's wellbeing over Pharisaic observance of the laws. *Laws* that *discriminate against women* must be challenged and changed.

(iv)   Women Disciples of Jesus

It is noteworthy that, unlike Jewish Rabbis, Jesus had *women disciples* (Lk 8,1-3) who *followed him from Galilee to Jerusalem and also to Calvary*, where they were *eye-witnesses* to *his crucifixion and burial* and later they became *messengers of his resurrection* to the male disciples (the Eleven and others) (cf. 23,49.55-56; 24,1-12).[123] Whereas all his male disciples (except the Beloved Disciple) have deserted him and his relatives (except his mother) stand away from the crucified Christ, his *women disciples silently see* (contemplate) whatever happens to him (23,49). The Galilean *women followers* of Jesus observe how his body is laid in the tomb and they go back and prepare spices and ointments to anoint his body after the Sabbath rest (Lk 23,54-56), which highlight how the *women disciples love Jesus even after his death and burial.*

Lk 8,1-3 is an excellent example of the *inclusive* nature of the *Christian community* of believing and caring, *female and male disciples*. Any discrimination against women in the Church is the expression of an anti-Christ attitude. Such a Church cannot be called 'Christian'!

(v)   Women Friends of Jesus

When Jesus was a *guest* of *Martha and Mary*, one *served* him and the other *sat at his feet as a disciple* and *listened* to his teaching (Lk 10,38-39). The *same Guru-shishya relationship* exists between Jesus (*Sadguru*) and all his disciples (*male or female*). This is *a revolutionary idea* in a *patriarchal country* like India, where *women* are regarded as *subservient to men* and in *patriarchal religions* like Hinduism, Islam and Christianity, which treat *women* as *second-class members* of the respective communities.

b)   *Women in John's Gospel*

(i)   Mother of Jesus

In the Gospel of John "*the mother of Jesus*" is introduced at the *Cana-wedding* (2,1-5). Here she has important roles of *caring presence* (2,1), *trusting prayer* (2,3) and *gentle persuasion* (2,5), which are typical of every woman/mother in a family and society. The active presence of Jesus' mother at the beginning of the wedding at Cana may recall the presence of "the Spirit of God brooding over the waters" at the beginning of creation (Gen 1,2; cf. also Prov 8,22-31). Just as the Holy Spirit "will glorify" Jesus before the disciples (cf.16,14), the timely intervention of Jesus' mother helped him to do the miraculous *sign* of changing water into wine and "manifest his glory" to his disciples (2,11). "Hence 'the mother of Jesus' at Cana seems to be the *symbol of the Holy Spirit...*"[124]

Similarly, *"the mother of Jesus"* is described as *standing,* together with the Beloved Disciple, *under the cross of Jesus at Calvary* (19,25-27). Jesus' words to his mother ("Woman, behold *your son!*" 19,26) and to the Beloved Disciple ("Behold *your mother!*" 19,27) manifest their *new spiritual relationship* as *mother* and *son*. Here too *"the mother of Jesus"* is *the symbol of the Holy Spirit/Paraclete* who will remain with the disciples (as promised by Jesus at 14,16-17), who are represented by the Beloved Disciple.[125]

> "The mother of Jesus" is also the *symbol* of every *caring "woman"* (2,3-4), who is the face of the life-giving Spirit on earth. The mothers who give birth to their children and suffer for their welfare and the persons like Mother Theresa who care for the poorest of the poor, the most deprived and the destitute, mirror Jesus' mother, the symbol of the *"Mother Spirit"*.[126]

(ii)   The Samaritan Woman

It is very significant that in John's Gospel it is only to *a Samaritan woman* (who expresses her expectation of the Messiah: "I know that the Messiah is coming": Jn 4,25) that *Jesus explicitly reveals himself* as *the Messiah* ("*I am*, the one speaking to you": 4,26). And just as the *first Jewish disciples* (Andrew and Philip) who discovered Jesus as the expected Messiah and proclaimed the good news to others and led them to him (1,35-45), so the *Samaritan woman* announces him as the Messiah and brings her townsfolk to meet him (4,29-30), because of which they believe in him (4,39). Thus in the Fourth Gospel, *both men and women* are *missionary disciples of Jesus* on an *equal* footing (cf. 4,36-48).

(iii)   Spirit-filled Women Disciples

According to Jn 19,30, realizing that Jesus' mission "is accomplished" (*tetelestai*), "he bowed his head and *handed over the Spirit*" (*paredôken to pneuma*).

> The question may be asked: "*To whom* did the dying Jesus hand over the Spirit?" The immediate context of 19,30 points to the persons who "put a sponge full of vinegar on hyssop and held it to his mouth" (19,29). But to whom do "they" refer in 19,29? In the immediately preceding scene (19,25-27) Jesus' mother, her sister, Mary the wife of Clopas, Mary Magdalene and the Beloved Disciple were "standing by the cross of Jesus" (19,25). Therefore it is reasonable to believe that they (who were standing close to the crucified Christ) were the ones who offered him a drink when he cried out: "I thirst" (19,28). But if the Beloved Disciple had taken Jesus' mother to his home (19,27), the *three women* still *standing under the cross* of Christ are most probably the ones who *gave the thirsty Jesus a drink* and *to whom he gave the Holy Spirit*. This means that those who respond positively to a needy, suffering person receive the life-giving Spirit. (In Jn 4,7-14 the thirsty Jesus, who had asked the Samaritan woman for a drink, promised her "living water," the symbol of the Holy Spirit. Now the women who offered a drink to the crucified Christ who cried "I thirst," are given the Holy Spirit.)[127]

It is noteworthy that the *women disciples* received the Holy Spirit from the *crucified Jesus* at the moment of his death on *Good Friday*, whereas the *risen Jesus* "breathed" on the *male disciples* and said to them "*Receive the Holy Spirit*" on *Easter Sunday* (20,22).[128] If the same (crucified and risen) Jesus has conferred the Holy Spirit on the disciples (female and male), *women disciples* must be treated as *equal* to the *men disciples* in the *Church today*.

(iv)   Jesus' Friends: Martha & Mary and Mary Magdalene

Jesus "loved" not only Lazarus but also Martha and Mary of Bethany (Jn 11,4-5). Seeing the weeping sisters, the loving and compassionate Jesus not only wept (Jn 11,33-35) but also called the dead Lazarus out of the tomb (11,43-44) and gave their brother back to them, thus revealing to them "the glory of God" (God's saving presence) (11,40). Jesus' *love* for his *friends Martha and Mary* (Jn 11,5.20-35) will evoke sentiments of *love and gratitude* in their hearts and will inspire them to *serve* him and *anoint* him with a very precious ointment (12,1-8).

Mary Magdalene's love for Jesus was manifested by *her standing under his cross* (Jn 19,25) and her *coming to his tomb early in the morning* while it was still dark (20,1) and *her running* to Simon Peter and the Beloved Disciple to report the sad news of the empty tomb (20,2). *Her* grief-stricken *weeping* and persistent *search* for Jesus and her affectionate address *Rabbouni!* ("*my* Teacher") and her "*holding on*" to him are all *unmistakable signs* of *her love and affection* for him (20,11-17). He *commissions her* to announce the good news of his resurrection to his other disciples and she *accomplishes her mission faithfully* (20,17-18).

> She [Mary Magdalene] becomes the first witness of the great news of the resurrection of Jesus. That among all his disciples *a woman disciple* is made by Jesus *the first witness of the risen Lord* is very significant in the Jewish context where the witness of a woman has been undermined. By making a woman his first witness, Jesus upholds the worth, dignity and importance of women who were marginalized and treated as second rate citizens.[129]

These loving *women friends of Jesus* draw many *Indian women* towards Jesus who, out of *self-giving love (agapê)*, are ready even to lay down their life for their friend (cf. 15,13). They can never find a more *faithful friend* than *Jesus*, with whom they have "fallen in love."[130] This experience of love transforms them (like Mary Magdalene) into *faithful witnesses* to the risen Lord.

3.3.4. Indian Feminist Christology

a)   Jesus, an Integrated Person

Jesus in the Gospels is an *integrated person* who has *both masculine (animus) characteristics* (e.g., assertive, courageous, critical) *and feminine (anima) traits* (e.g., caring, nurturing, consoling and compassionate),[131] which are revealed in *his tenderness towards children, his caring love for the sick and the suffering, his love and compassion* which impelled him to *weep with Mary of Bethany* over his brother *Lazarus' death* (Jn 11,35) and to *weep over Jerusalem* (Lk 19,41). Jesus has also affirmed that *his mission* is one *of service*: "The Son of Man has come not to be served but to serve, and to give his life as a ransom for many" (Mk 10,45; Mt 20,25).

Incarnation means the *divine becoming human* to save all human beings (men and women). The Gospel of John describes the *incarnation of the Word of God*: "The Word became flesh" (*sarx egeneto:* Jn 1,14), which highlights the divine Word *becoming a weak and mortal human being* in solidarity with humanity. The *emphasis* here is on God's becoming a *human being, not a male*.[132]

The *risen Jesus transcends his maleness* and represents a *new humanity of caring love and service*, which was manifested by addressing affectionately his disciples in the boat and asking them: "*Children*, have you anything to eat?" (*paidia, mê ti prosphagion echête;* Jn 21,5) and *cooking fish* on charcoal fire

(21,9), and inviting them: "Come and *have breakfast*" (21,12) and *serving* it to them lovingly (21,13).

b)   Jesus's Inclusive Mission

Jesus' *mission* was meant *for all* but especially for the poor, the weak and the marginalized (like the sick, the prisoners, the women) (cf. Lk 4,16-20). Jesus came *to give (eternal) life, abundant life i.e. life in its fullness/wholeness to all who believe in him* (cf. Jn 10,10; 20,31).

The '*Kingdom of God*' (*basileia tou theou, the reign of God*) *belongs to all* (cf. the *Beatitudes* in Mt 5,3-10 and Lk 6,20-23). Jesus used some *feminine similes* (e.g. woman in *labour-pain*: Jn 16,21) and *parables* (a woman searching for the *lost coin*: Lk 15,8-10, a woman adding *yeast* to the flour: Mt 13,33) to explain the mysteries of the Reign of God. It is noteworthy that *man and woman* are *paired* in the *two parables* of the *mustard seed* and the *yeast* (Mt 13,31-32.33), indicating that Jesus draws *inspiration* for his parables of the kingdom from the *experiences of both man and woman*. All disciples (men and women) must contribute to the reign of God through their transforming ministries in today's world.

c)   Jesus' Positive Attitudes and Relationships vis-a-vis Women

The greatest mysteries of the *conception of Jesus* (Lk 1,26-38) and *his resurrection* were communicated to *women* (Jn 20,11-18; Mt 28,1-10), which highlight the *privileged position of women* in the *salvific plan of God*.

Jesus *respected* all *women as human persons* with *dignity* (e.g., he *called the bleeding woman* "*daughter*" (Mk 5,34). He *forgave* sinners like the *woman caught in the act of adultery* (Jn

8,2-11) and the *sinful woman of the city*, who kissed his feet and anointed them, and he publicly acknowledged *her great love*: "for she loved much" (Lk 7,36-38.50).

Jesus was *compassionate to all women* especially *to those in need or in distress*. He *opposed divorce* because it went against the original divine plan (Mk 10,6-12; cf. also Mt 19,3-9). Jesus was kind and forgiving to the woman caught in adultery and prevented her from being stoned to death by the scribes and Pharisees (Jn 8,3-11).

Jesus' heart was moved to *compassion* when he saw the plight of *widows*. So when he met the *weeping widow of Nain* who had lost her only son, "he had *compassion on her* and said to her, 'Do not weep'" (Lk 7,13). Out of his initiative, Jesus *raised the dead son to life* and gave him back to the widow/mother (7,14-15). He was *compassionate* even to *Gentile women* in their helplessness. For example, he heard the prayer of the *Syrophoenician woman* to heal her possessed daughter (Mk 7,24-30).

Jesus *touched women to heal/raise them* (e.g., Simon Peter's mother-in-law: Mk 1,29-31; the bent woman: Lk 13,10-17; Jairus' dead daughter: Mk 5,35-43; Mt 9,18-26).[133]

Jesus also allowed himself *to be touched by women* (e.g., by the *bleeding woman*: Mk 5,25-34; Mt 9,20-22). Jesus is not concerned about his being polluted by the touch of the woman with a haemorrhage (cf. Lev 15,25-27) but he interprets her touch from the *faith* perspective of the suffering woman.[134]

Jesus *defended* both the *sinful woman* (Lk 7,36-50) and *Mary of Bethany* who *anointed his feet* (Jn 12,3-8). Jesus *gratefully acknowledged* an unnamed *woman's anointing* his head/body as *a beautiful and prophetic act* ("She has done a beautiful thing to me": Mk 14,6; "she has anointed my body beforehand for burial": 14,8; "wherever the gospel is preached in the whole world, what she has done will be told in memory of her": 14,9).

Jesus *related to women* as *responsible persons* and accepted them as *partners in his ministry.* So *some women accompanied him* from Galilee to Jerusalem as "he was going through cities and villages, proclaiming and bringing the good news of the kingdom of God" and the women "were *ministering* to them (*diêkonoun autois)* out of their means" (Lk 8,1-3). We find these *female followers/disciples* standing under his cross and present at his burial (Lk 23,49.55), and some of them are privileged to be the *risen Lord's witnesses:*

> As it goes in the narration of Jesus' story, Jesus was rejected by his family and home town folks, by the religious authorities, by the crowds, and then by his male disciples, while the *women disciples* remain as the *faithful* remnant at the cross. The *women* are among the *first witnesses to the resurrection* who bring the good news to the male disciples closeted in the upper room (Mk 15,40; Mt 27,56; Lk 23,49; Jn 19,25). In the Gospel stories, *Jesus* not only played *positive role* towards women, but *women* also played *important roles* in his life as well.[135]

Jesus had *women* with whom he *dialogued* on theological/ spiritual issues and to whom he *revealed himself* as the "*Christ*" who gives "*living water*" (to the Samaritan woman: Jn 4,7-26) and as "*the resurrection and the life*" (to Martha of Bethany: 11,20-27). It is also worth noting that *a Gentile (Syrophoenician) woman challenged Jesus' narrow vision of his mission* (limited to the Jewish people: "I was sent only to the lost sheep of the house of Israel": Mt 15,24) and persuaded him to expand his missionary vision (to include the Gentiles) (15,26-27). Seeing her great faith, he *responded* to her request *positively* by curing her possessed daughter (cf. 15,28).

d)   *Jesus, the Liberator and Saviour of Women*

From the above discussion it is evident that, unlike the Jewish rabbis of the time, Jesus had *women disciples* whom he allowed to *accompany him* and to *support* him financially (Lk 8,1-3). He held *dialogues with women in public* (Jn 4,7-26; 11,20-27). Thus Jesus *freed women* from their limiting patriarchal socio-cultural conditioning which prevented them from being on an equal footing with men.

Jesus, the *prophet*, preached and practised the *humanizing, liberating and empowering message* of justice, dignity, equality, freedom and fellowship of the *reign of God*, equally applicable to all women and men. Jesus, the *liberator*, took the side of the marginalized, despised and oppressed, especially *women*, and *freed* them from the cruel clutches of men (cf. the woman caught in adultery: Jn 8,2-11).

> He [Jesus] honoured women, and he has affirmed women in the masculine roles (public confrontation of Syrophoenician woman), anointing Jesus (woman anointed the head of Jesus) and he as a man assumed feminine characteristics of kindness, obedience (for death), fear, helplessness, and so on. He has challenged the men of high social status and affirmed women. Thus Jesus re-defined the values of honour-shame, and broke the rigid stereotyping gender ideology.[136]

Similarly, by asking for a drink from a *Samaritan woman* at Jacob's well, Jesus *challenges* the *socio-cultural prejudices* of the Jews against the Samaritans and especially against the *presumed ritual impurity of Samaritan women* (Jn 4,7-9). "Jesus as a Jew dared to drink from the utensil of the Samaritan woman and thus defied a discriminatory social practice [Jn 4,7.9]."[137] Through this unconventional meeting and dialogue with the *marginalized sinful Samaritan woman*, Jesus *transforms* her into *an effective missionary* to her townspeople (4,7-30).

> *Jesus' enabling and liberative interaction* with *the Samaritan woman is a prototype of the liberation of Dalit women*, who, though more oppressed in today's society, are also seen as the *agents of liberation*. The Dalit women by their God-experience and thirst for humanism, by their active struggle for humanizing themselves and society and by their resilience and determination to usher in a society of freedom, fellowship and equality become *co-partners* in the project of building up a just and equitable society.[138]

Jesus is a *committed liberator* and *compassionate saviour* who helps *Indian women to come out of their oppression and stand with dignity.*

> *Who is Jesus for Indian women?* He is one who *challenges* them *to come out* of the space of *impurity and pollution* to which they are confined physically and mentally by the *patriarchal culture...* Jesus considers *a menstruating or a bleeding woman* not as an impure being but as *a close relation,* a 'daughter' (Mk 5,24-34). And this man is not just an ordinary human person but he is *the true image of God*, who came to reveal the nature of God through his words and deeds.[139]

> Like the *crippled woman* in the Gospel (Lk 13,10-17), *Indian women* are *bent* over under the weight of multiple oppressive forces... Even though the bent woman did not seek Jesus' help, Jesus took the initiative to unburden her and *to help her stand straight*. Thus, Jesus desires the wellbeing of women and takes steps to *liberate them from all sorts of bondages*. For the millions of women who are under bondage, *Jesus* comes across as a *liberator* and *saviour*.[140]

e)   Jesus, the Friend of Women

Jesus had some *women friends* whom *"he loved"* (e.g., Martha and Mary of Bethany: Jn 11,5) and who *loved Jesus* (e.g., Mary Magdalene and Mary the mother of James and Joseph: Mt 27,55-57).

The *two Marys* "were there, sitting opposite *the sepulchre*" of Jesus even after the departure of Joseph of Arimathea (Mt 27,60-61). On early Easter Sunday morning, they *return to Jesus' tomb* (28,1). This reveals *their deep love and affection for Jesus.* This manifests the *faithful friendship* of the *female disciples* of Jesus, which even death cannot destroy. Jesus *sent* them as *his* heralds and *trusted* them as his *witnesses* to announce to his male disciples ("brothers") the *Easter news of his resurrection* (Mt 28,9-10; cf. also Jn 20,17-18).

> Jesus cultivated good friendships with women. He enjoyed family meals with them and he even shared his thoughts with them (Lk 10,38-42). His relationship with women did not come to an end with his violent death but continued. Women were the first ones to go to the tomb and they were the first ones to receive the good news of his resurrection. He trusted women to be his witnesses (Mt 28,1-10; Mk 16,1-8; Lk 24,1-12; Jn 20,1-18).[141]

f)   Jesus, the Suffering Servant?

The Gospels often present Jesus as *"the Suffering Servant,"*[142] the significance of which has been differently interpreted by modern Asian/Indian feminist theologians.

> Women across Asia have experienced the *image of Jesus, the Suffering Servant as a double-edged sword.* While for many it has been *a source of comfort* as they journeyed painful paths of suffering, it has also equally been *a source of abuse, violence and subordination.* The problematic element of the suffering servant image is the *glorification of suffering* as necessary and the claim

that *suffering in itself* can be *redemptive and salvific.*"[143]

Today some of the *Indian Christian feminists interpret* the traditional image of *"Jesus, the Suffering Servant" in a new way.* For instance, they regard him, *not* as a *passive sufferer* but as *a courageous protestor against injustice.* Jesus *protested against the officer* who *slapped* him in the court of the chief priest (Jn 18,22-23), instead of suffering the insult silently (like battered Indian wives)! Similarly, Jesus was *angry at the merchants* (who desecrated the Court of the Gentiles in the Jerusalem Temple) and *drove them out with a whip* in his hand (Mk 11,15-18).

Jesus *questioned* the *unjust authorities* of his time (the scribes and the Sadducees, the chief priests Annas and Caiaphas, and the Roman governor Pilate) and *challenged* those who exploited the poor and the marginalized. He *suffered and died on the cross in solidarity* with those *struggling against injustice* and *fighting for their liberation.* "Jesus resisted the powers and principalities of injustice during his time… Jesus' body was torn and tortured and killed, yet his struggle lived on after him, because it was a struggle against injustice…"[144] "The cross symbolises not a one-time event in which the sufferings of the world are forever taken up in the life of Jesus, but concrete historical situations of oppression that we continue to experience today."[145]

We may ask the question: "*Why was Jesus crucified?*" It was because he struggled *for justice* for the poor, the exploited and the marginalized, and because he *challenged and criticised the religious leaders* (the chief priests, the teachers of the law and the Pharisees).

> Jesus challenged the ethical-social-cultural barriers of his time. He redefined what holiness meant. Jesus showed that touching the dead and raising them by his hand did not pollute him. Neither

did the touch of the haemorrhaging woman contaminate him. Pollution happened only on account of evil thoughts and deeds. It was this resistance and challenge that led him to the cross.[146]

The *risen Jesus, the victor* (who has won the victory over suffering and death), is a *source of hope* especially for *women* who are *struggling* to attain *human dignity and equality, freedom and fellowship*. He *empowers* them to *become daughters of God* ("He gave them the power to become children of God" (Jn 1,13). *Christ (the Anointed One)* also enables them to become *"Christs"* (*anointed ones* by the Holy Spirit, the Spirit of Christ). When they are in the process of becoming *"human"* they are becoming *"Christs"* as well.[147]

g)   Jesus, Motherly Emmanuel

Jesus is *not* a *master* who *dominates* others but one who *serves* others *lovingly like a mother* (cf. *Jesus' washing his disciples' feet*: Jn 13,5-15 and *his preparing breakfast* and *serving* them: 21,9.12-13).

Jesus is *compassionate to the hungry* (Jn 6,5) *like a mother* eager to feed her hungry children (21,12). He compares himself to *a hen* which wants to *protect her chicks* by *gathering them under her wings* and, like a *loving mother*, he *laments* over the hard-hearted people of Jerusalem (Mt 23,37). *Jesus' suffering is like a mother's travail of childbirth* (Jn 16,21). *His death on the cross* may be likened to a *mother's life-giving death during delivery*.[148] The *"blood* and *water"* from the pierced body of Jesus (19,34) are like the blood and amniotic fluid from the mother's womb after childbirth. Jesus' offering his own *body and blood* as *food and drink* in the *Eucharist* (6,51-58) may be compared to the *breast-feeding by a mother. The motherly image of Jesus modifies* the traditional *male image of Jesus* into *a maternal loving life-giver.*

Jesus, Emmanuel ("*God-with-us*": Mt 1,23) is not passively but actively *present among all his* (male and female) *disciples* because the risen Jesus assures them: "Behold! *I am with you all the days, to the end of the ages*" (Mt 28,20). It is noteworthy that Jesus promises his disciples that "*another Paraclete,*" whom the Father sends them, also "*remains with you* and *will be in you*" (Jn 14,15-17). The *Paraclete's presence with* and *within* the disciples is *like* that of a *loving mother with her children.*

If *Jesus, Emmanuel,* manifests many *motherly qualities* (as we have seen above), it is because he was "*conceived*" (*gennêthen*) in Mary's womb "*from the Holy Spirit*" (*ek pneumatos hagiou:* Mt 1,18.20). Like Jesus, the *enfleshed Son of God* (cf. Jn 1,14), all the "*children of God*" (*tekna theou:* 1,12), who are "*born from God*" (*ek theou egennêthêsan:* 1,13), "*born from above/ Spirit*" (*gennêthê anôthen/ek pneumatos:* 3,3.5), all the *sons and daughters of God,* must *integrate* in their lives the *fatherly, motherly* and *filial qualities* of the *Triune God* (the *Father,* the *Spirit* and the *Son*).

3.3.5. Relevance of Jesus Christ for Indian Women

For the *Indian women* who experience manifold layers of oppression, *Jesus Christ of the Gospels* offers *hope.* He is the one who *accepts them, respects them and treats them as dignified human beings.* He helps them to *stand erect* free of every burden. He enters into a *relationship of equality and mutuality* with them. He is the *compassionate one* who understands even the erring ones, the discarded ones and the 'inauspicious' ones. He *challenges* them to come out of their restricted spaces and to accept their 'polluting and impure' *bodies as sacred.* He *invites* them to enter into *friendship* with him and *collaborate* with him in his *mission* of establishing *God's reign* which is characterized by *equality, freedom, friendship, peace, joy, fellowship, brotherhood and sisterhood.*[149]

3.3.6. Indian Feminist Creeds[150]

a)   *An Indian Woman's Creed*

I believe in *God, Father and Mother,* who *created man and woman in their image and likeness* and who gave them the *stewardship of the earth.*

I believe in *Jesus,* the *Child of God, born of the woman Mary* who said *yes to God.*

I believe in Jesus who *preached the good news to the poor and the oppressed.*

I believe in Jesus who had *compassion on a widow* and *raised her son to life.*

I believe in Jesus who *healed a bent woman* and made her *stand straight with dignity.*

I believe in Jesus who *touched women to heal them* and let them *touch him.*

I believe in Jesus who *asked for a drink from a Samaritan woman* and *manifested his Messiahship* to her and *enabled her to become his missionary.*

I believe in Jesus who respected *women, stayed in their homes* and *spoke about the reign of God* with them.

I believe in Jesus who *allowed women disciples to follow him* and *to support him.*

I believe in Jesus who *appreciated his anointing by women* and *defended them* from men's negative criticism.

I believe in Jesus who *spoke of God as a woman* who *looks for the lost coin* by sweeping the floor and on finding it *rejoices* with her neighbours.

I believe in Jesus who *regarded labour-pain* with reverence – not as punishment – but as *giving life* in anguish and joy.

I believe in Jesus who *spoke of himself* as *a mother hen*, who *gathers her chicks under her wings.*

I believe in the *risen Jesus* who *appeared first to Mary Magdalene* and sent her as *his apostle to the apostles.*

I believe in the Holy Spirit, the motherly Spirit of God, who gives us rebirth as the children of God, who remains with us and within us forever. Amen.

b)   *Indian Women's Creed*

We believe in *God, our Father and Mother,* creator of heaven and earth and all women and men.

We believe in *Jesus, the Word become flesh, born of the woman Mary and brought up by her.*

We believe in *Jesus who is fully human, an integrated person with feminine and masculine qualities,* who accepted graciously *the love and care of women.*

We believe in *Jesus* who was *a friend of women* who affirmed their trustworthiness and capability to be *disciples, witnesses, missionaries and apostles.*[151]

We believe in *Jesus* who treated *women and men* with *equal dignity and great respect,* who challenged the existing oppressive structures of his time.

We believe in *Jesus* who *sided with poor and oppressed women* and who *cared for the marginalized women.*

We believe in *Jesus* who *had compassion for the woman caught in adultery and rescued her* from the snares of wicked men.

We believe in *Jesus* who was *supported and consoled by women* on his way to *Calvary* and even at the *foot of the cross.*

We believe in *Jesus* who *rose from the dead and appeared to a woman first.*

We believe in *Jesus* who has *promised fullness of life to all* who believe and love.

We believe in the *Holy Spirit through whom the Church was born and is sustained.*

We believe in the *communion of Saints,* who are *holy women and men. Amen.*

c)   *Indian Women Religious' Creed*

We believe in *Jesus,* the *enfleshed Son of God,* who has *freed us* from *gender discrimination and male domination,* who *treats us* as *daughters of God* and as *equal members of his community of disciples.* We cherish *his love and friendship* and are happy to be *his faithful friends and messengers of integral liberation and holistic transformation.*

3.©. Conclusion: Jesus Christ, Liberator of Dalits, Tribals and Women

3.©.1. *Jesus Christ, Liberator of Dalits*

Even though *Jesus* was *not* a *Dalit by birth* but *by choice,* the *divine Son of God* who *became human identified himself with the marginalized from his birth till his death,* indicating *his solidarity with and a preferential option for the poor and the oppressed* (Dalits).[152] He was *born in a stable* (like the Dalits living in huts outside the caste village). The good news of the *birth of the Messiah* was announced to the *marginalized Shepherds,* who recognized him (*wrapped in swaddling clothes and lying in a manger*) as *their Saviour.* His parents had to *flee to a foreign land* to save the child from the murderous plan of king Herod (like the Dalits who have to run away from their villages to distant slums to escape the upper caste oppression). As an adult, Jesus lived as a *hard-working carpenter* for many years in Nazareth.

Before starting his public ministry, *Jesus identified himself* with the *ordinary people* and was *baptized* with them in the River Jordan. There he was revealed as the *beloved Son of God*. Yet he was *tempted/tested*, like other humans, by Satan in the wilderness. But he overcame the tempter by being an *obedient Son of God* who was determined to do the *will of God the Father*. The *Dalits* too must also *be attuned to the will of God* in order not to fall into the *temptations of greed, pride and power* in today's world.

It is noteworthy that Jesus started proclaiming the good news of *the imminence of the "reign of God"* in *"Galilee of the Gentiles"*. The Jewish elites in Jerusalem looked down upon the Galileans (constantly exposed to the Gentile culture), just as the privileged upper castes in India despise the "polluting" Dalits forced to live outside the caste village. Therefore, Jesus' good news (gospel) of the nearness of God's reign has *special relevance to the segregated Dalits*.

It is also significant that *Jesus chose* some lowly *Galilean fishermen* to be *his first disciples* and he included a despised *tax collector (Matthew)* to be *one of the Twelve* Apostles. This clearly shows *Jesus' preferential option for the Dalits*.

In the synagogue at Nazareth Jesus refers to himself as the *prophet anointed* by the *Spirit of the Lord* to *bring good news to the poor*, to *proclaim release to the captives, freedom to the oppressed* and *sight to the blind* (Lk 4,16-21).

The *"reign of God"* that Jesus proclaimed was *"good news"* particularly to *the poor, the oppressed*, the *marginalized* (like the blind and the imprisoned). His *parables* highlighted the *kingdom/ Gospel values* of *love* and *forgiveness, freedom* and *fellowship*. He had loving *compassion* for the *despised* (prostitutes, the woman caught in adultery) and *tax-collectors* (cf. his table-fellowship with them) and he gave them human *dignity* and true *liberty* as the children of God. Most of his *miracles* were in favour of *the poor and the needy* (e.g., the hungry crowds), *the sick* (the blind, the deaf, the dumb, the cripple), and *the outcasts* (the lepers, the demoniacs). He also gave *life to the dying and the dead* as a response to the pleading or weeping relatives.

Jesus' healing touch of an "untouchable" *leper*, his *taking by the hand* the "polluting" *dead body* of the synagogue official's daughter to bring her back to life, his *healing the "bleeding" woman* who touched him are instances of *his limitless compassion for the rejects of* society. He dared to *heal the lame and the blind even on Sabbath days* in the synagogues and the Temple, even though it brought him into the bad books of the Jewish leaders. These miracles disclose Jesus' special concern for the *liberation of the helpless and the marginalized*, who are like the *Dalits* in Indian society.

The *divinehuman Jesus* realized that to be an effective *liberator* of the suffering people he had to be the *Servant of God and the people* and must be *the suffering Son of Man*. He is *an inspiring leader* to the *suffering Dalits* because he *laid down his life voluntarily* for the *liberation/salvation* of others particularly the outcasts and the oppressed, and so he was *glorified by God*. The *passion-death-resurrection of Jesus* gives the *suffering Dalits hope* that they too would be *vindicated by God.*

The *Christlike trust* in God will be possible for the *suffering Dalits* only if they realize, like *the beloved Son of God*, that God is "*our Father*" who *loves* and *cares for his children.* Jesus, the *divinehuman Teacher*, has revealed that all humans and especially the *Dalits* are called to become the *humandivine sons and daughters of God.*

Jesus' liberative preaching and practice in favour of the poor and the oppressed and *his prophetic critiquing* of the socio-political-religious authorities of his time enraged them and they plotted against him and put him to death on a cross. But *God raised him*, which gives the *Dalits assurance of a new life* of dignity, liberty and equality, *as the sons and daughters of God.* But for this new life to become a reality in the lives of Dalits, they too must *be ready and willing to suffer and die like Jesus*, the "*Suffering Servant*," the suffering "*Son of Man*," for the liberation of others. To enable them to accomplish this *liberating mission*, the *risen Jesus empowers* them with *the Holy Spirit* and the *ascending Jesus* assures them that he, *Emmanuel* ("God-with-us"), would be *with them* till the end of the world. *Jesus, the Liberator of the Dalits*, wants them to be his *co-liberators.*[153]

3.©.2. Jesus Christ, Liberator and Life-Giver of Tribals

We have examined earlier the *tribal world-view* (holistic vision of God, community and nature) and the *Tribals' negative experiences* (*socio-economic-cultural crisis* caused by outsiders, deforestation and displacement, Naxalite problems, massive poverty and emigration, violation of human rights, fear of the evil spirits),[154] the *tribal understanding* of *liberation* (as deliverance from the negativities of life and the sins of greed and pride) *and salvation* (as prosperous, happy and harmonious life in community), and *tribal myths of liberation and protection.*[155] In the light of the above, *two important tribal titles* for Jesus Christ seem to emerge: *a) Jesus Christ, the Liberator* and *b) Jesus Christ, the Life-giver.*[156]

a)   Jesus Christ, Liberator of the Tribals[157]

Since *liberation* for the Tribals means *deliverance from* sickness, evil spirits, superstitions, ignorance, poverty, socio-cultural-economic exploitation, marginalization, oppression, premature death, and *emancipation from sin* (especially *greed* and *pride*), a very meaningful *tribal Christological title* would be "*Jesus Christ, the Liberator of the Tribals*" which includes other *designations* like *Healer (Deonra), Great Exorcist (Maha Devda), Sore-Stricken Boy (Khasra-Khusru Kukkos), Dwarf Boy (Liti Bir)* and *Bull Boy (Addo Xapu Kukkos)* (who *freed* the Tribals from life-threatening situations).

b)   Jesus Christ, Life-Giver of the Tribals

Since the Tribals understand *salvation* as '*a happy and harmonious life in their community*' (here on earth and hereafter with the ancestors), another very significant *tribal title* for *Jesus* would be *Life-Giver*, various aspects of which are highlighted by the *titles* like the *First Adivasi Ancestor*, the *Friendly Stranger (Sakhi Kosain)*, the *Great Priest (Maha Pahan)*, the *White Cock (Pandru Xer)*, the *Flowering Sal Tree*, the *New Maize Shoot (Jawa)*, the *First Fruit*, the *Rising Sun*, the *Drummer* (all of which are related to *new life*).

c)   Jesus Christ, Liberator and Life-Giver of Tribal Christians

The oppression of the Tribals by the landlords and moneylenders was on the increase when *Christian missionaries* like Constance Lievens S.J. and Hoffmann S.J. came to Chhotanagpur to serve the subjugated Tribals with great personal sacrifice. Through them, *Jesus* came as a *light to dispel the darkness* of the Tribals and *to give new hope* for their survival, because Lievens fought in the courts to get back the Tribals' land and Hoffman and other Jesuits aided the Tribals to form village cooperatives which helped them to be freed from the clutches of the moneylenders and to make economic progress. But after Indian independence, successive *governments* have *taken over much of the tribal land* for building damns and industries or for mining minerals, and they have been displaced without proper rehabilitation which has destroyed their culture and community life. *Christian* Tribals (like the Jesuit missionaries) must join hands with the *Sarna* Tribals to fight for their rights through non-violent means.

The *tribal Christians* in responding to the "vision and mission of Jesus"[158] are often *faced with opposition* but the *crucified-risen Jesus* is *their hope*. If they *believe in him* as their *Liberator and Life-giver*, they must be *committed to continuing his liberating and life-giving mission*.

3.©.3. *Jesus Christ, Liberator and Friend of Women*

In the Indian *patriarchal* society and religions, *women* are treated as *inferior* to men and so they are marginalized, dominated, dehumanized, discriminated, despised, degraded and oppressed in many ways. They are denied dignity, liberty and equality. They are subjected to various forms of violence (physical, sexual, etc.). In this context of their many *negative experiences*, Indian women find *Jesus' positive attitudes and relationships to women* in the Gospels very *attractive* and *liberative*.

Jesus Christ of the Gospels who has *integrated both masculine and feminine qualities* is quite appealing to *Indian women.* Jesus, who *respects the dignity, equality and liberty* of women and *accepts* them as *his disciples and witnesses,* is very meaningful for the women. Jesus, as the *courageous liberator and compassionate Saviour* is indeed relevant to them. Jesus, *the faithful friend* who *suffers in solidarity with the suffering women,* is an inspiring guide to them in *their struggles for justice and equality, freedom and fellowship* of the reign of God here on earth. In short, *Jesus Christ is the liberator and friend of women.*

Chapter 4

THE GOOD NEWS OF JESUS CHRIST FOR HINDUS, MUSLIMS AND SIKHS

Indian Dialogical Christologies

4.0. Introduction

Since the *purpose of this Chapter* is *to enter into a fruitful dialogue* between *Christians* and *the People of India of diverse faiths* (especially *Hindus, Muslims* and *Sikhs*), we keep in mind the *lessons* learned from history and the *new guidelines* for a mutually enriching dialogue.

4.0.1. *Levels of Dialogue between Christians and People of Diverse Faiths*

At what *levels* do Christians *dialogue* with Hindus, Muslims and Sikhs on Jesus Christ?

Founders of religions, like Siddhartha, Mahavir, Guru Nanak, have enriched the religious and spiritual heritage of humanity. *Buddha* has taught humankind "the Four Noble Truths"[159]. *Mahavir* has qualitatively contributed to human civilization by his concern for all living beings (*bhutdaya*). *Guru Nanak* stands tall among *margadarshaks* (path-finders) of the world through his teaching on the oneness of God and equality of all human beings. It is in the company of people with such traits that we can locate the great name of *Jesus Christ*. He is a unique person who has been accepted as *a symbol and embodiment* of *integral service of the people* that gives *lasting peace*.

Almost at the beginning of Jesus' public life, he gave indications of the kind of *human relationships* all are expected to foster. In the course of imparting that most civilizing of teachings, namely, the wisdom-filled "*Sermon on the Mount*" (Mt 5-7), Jesus gave the following advice to his eager listeners: "Do not lay up for yourselves treasures on earth, where moth and rust consume and where thieves break in and steal, but lay up for yourselves *treasure in heaven*, where neither moth nor rust consumes and where thieves do not break in and steal. For where your treasure is, there will your heart be also" (Mt 6,19-21). There has been no mention as to where that "heaven" is, or what that "treasure" is. If we look back at the last two millennia, the verdict of history undoubtedly is that the "*treasure*" *Jesus Christ* talked about is *himself*. It is to that *Treasure of treasures* that the following pages are devoted. The people of India interacting with Jesus Christ, that universally treasured and historic personality, is the subject matter of this Chapter.

Jesus Christ has presented before all life-pilgrims the *six-fold expressions of charity*, wise injunctions that can guide them in their life-struggles and help them to reach their destination. They are: *feed the hungry, give water to the thirsty, offer shelter to the stranger/migrant, provide clothes to the naked, assist the sick and comfort the prisoners* (Mt 25,34-36). Compliance with these six-fold criteria might appear akin to the *visa* requirements for entering a foreign country. This validation certificate to "inherit the kingdom prepared for all from the foundation of the world" (Mt 25,34) is placed towards the end of Jesus' public life.

It is envisaged that *dialogue* between *Jesus Christ* of *Semitic lineage* and *the people of Indic lineage* (Indians) will be free, creative, open and unreserved. The *main tributaries* to the *rich Indic heritage* are the *tribal traditions* and the *Indic religions*. The contribution of *auxiliary* components like *ethical-moral resources* ought to be duly recognized. *Satyameva jayate*[160] ("Truth alone triumphs") is the *national motto* of India. *Sarvodaya* through *Antyodaya* ("the rising of all" through "the rising of the last") is the *goal* of Indian democracy (cf. Preamble of the Constitution of India).

When Jesus was in Jerusalem on the occasion of the Jewish feast of the Passover, some Greeks (Gentiles) came to Philip and Andrew asking for an audience with Jesus and they were led to him by the two disciples (Jn 12,20-21). Today too there are many Indians of different faiths longing to meet Jesus Christ. Are his *Indian disciples* ready to accompany them to a meaningful meeting with him? Or are we *exclusivist* towards them (like the *blinkered* disciples John and others who forbade a stranger from casting out demons in Jesus' name because "he was not following" them (Mk 9,38)? Jesus appeals to our common sense: "Do not forbid him… for he that is not against us is for us" (9,39-40). Jesus Christ challenges us to *give up* the old *exclusivist* understanding of salvation (*"Outside the Church, there is no salvation": extra ecclesiam nulla salus!*) and to welcome whole-heartedly the *"ray of that truth which enlightens all men [and women]"* of all religions.[161]

The *Semitic-Indic dialogue* could be based on several factors. Some of these we have just recalled above. A mysterious text that occurs in the nativity narrative of the Gospel draws our attention. The text tickles our imagination and curiosity. It needs exploration. Having seen an unusual star in the East, *wise men* (*magoi*, astrologers) come to Jerusalem enquiring about the place of birth of the new-born king (Mt 2,1-2). Having been informed that Bethlehem is the birthplace of the Messiah (2,4-6), they are led by the star (of the East) to the place (house) where the child was. The *Satpurush* was *welcomed and honoured* by *the representatives of the East. Gifts* of *gold, frankincense and myrrh* (the most valued materials proper to the East) were offered to the *divine Guest* (2,9-11). It was a gracious and symbolic gesture shown to *Jesus* soon after his arrival on earth. The so called *wise men from the East* did it. We Christians of our generation should *build up our inter-faith dialogue strategies* on that symbolic gesture.

4.0.2. *Lessons from History for a Fruitful Dialogue*

Plato in and through his writings, especially in *The Republic*, has attempted to delineate the *art of friendly conversation*. He has used the word *'dialogue'* (in his native tongue Greek it is *dia-logos: words shared, exchange through words*). It is a friendly exchange of thought, feelings and perceptions between friends or equals in an atmosphere of confidence and trust.

In such conversations there is *respect* for and recognition of *equality* of *dialogue partners*. There is *free, frank and fearless sharing* marked by *deep listening*. There is no high-low consideration among the dialogue partners. There is unhindered and frank flow of communication. When these *essential requirements* are complied with, the *outcome* can be *mutually enriching. Dialogue-Partners* are enriched and enthused because it is *a sharing of souls*!

It is now seen as regrettable that these refined requirements for inter-faith dialogue were not at work in many of the interactions between Christians and the people of India in the past. Despite *historical mistakes and errors*, blunders and violations of basic rules befitting civilized cultures, the exercise is now seen worth resuming. We know that much will be lost if the rules of engagement are ignored. Both the parties will lose in the process. Renewed attempts could commence with full acknowledgement of the missteps adopted by the dialoguing parties in the past in India. *Learning from errors and mistakes* also makes us *wise.*

Recalling the *lessons from the history* of the encounter between Hinduism and Christianity in India, there were at least *four different kinds of exchanges* between Christians and Hindus.

a) The *first* was *positive acceptance* by some Hindus of Travancore-Cochin Kingdoms when Apostle *St. Thomas* and later a certain 'Thomas from Cana' contributed significantly to the presence of Christianity in the first and fourth century respectively. The lifestyle of the Christians in Kerala, some of the traditions and practices, do provide evidence of a creative interaction between Christianity and Hinduism.

But during this first phase of interaction, only the so-called *upper castes* in the hierarchically organized Kerala society were *beneficiaries.* The biting power of the Gospel to blast away social evils like *caste inequality* was not released. What is now known and recognized as the most discriminatory social practice of *caste-system* was blindly followed even by those who responded creatively to the message of Jesus, known as the Good News. And the economic, social and political structures continued without much change. The *deprived* continued to be deprived. The practice of *untouchability* persisted unmitigated even within the Christian community. The *disruptive teachings of Jesus* continued to remain *locked up in the Gospels*!

b) The *second* kind of *interaction* was *resistance* to or *rejection* of Christianity in some parts of India. Certain kings in the early days had strongly opposed the presence of the new religion. The cases of blessed Devasahayampillai and of St John de Britto in Tamilnadu are illustrations of the kings' rejection of the new religion. (Today we have RSS ideologies like *Hindutva* that regard *Christianity* as a *foreign religion.*[162])

c) The *third* mode of *response* was *indifference* to or *tolerance* of Christianity by the big majority of the Hindus. The Christian community was allowed to exist and function as a distinct identity subscribing to the tradition of Jesus Christ. This was what the rulers of petty kingdoms of Kollam (present-day Quilon) and Kochi did to the Christians.

The attitude of *indifference* or *tolerance* had *reasons. Hinduism* is a *well-developed religion* with great *self-confidence* and even a *sense of sufficiency.* For example, the idea of God as *anandam* (bliss) in the Upanishads and the rather well-developed concepts of God as *Maha Vishnu* in Vaishnavism and *Lord Siva* in Saivism, availability of ancient *Scripture*, belief in *avataras* (Vaishnavism), and variety of *rituals* attending to practically all the main phases of the life of a believer could be considered among some of the factors responsible for such indifference and tolerance. A healthy well-established community may not perceive any threat from other such communities around. Psychological self-confidence may not generate fear of a possible rival. Therefore, Christianity was seen as not holding any major challenge to Hinduism.

d) The fourth was a *suspicious response* to 'colonial Christianity'. *Conquerors and colonizers* from the West landed in India who unwittingly represented Jesus. To the *conquered people* of India, they were *conquerors* who happened to be Christians. But the motive of these colonizers was seeking *political power* to facilitate and achieve *economic benefits*. Consequently, *Jesus* was seen by many as the *endorser of the exploits of the conquerors*! Native wealth was the prime target of the conquerors. Therefore, the interaction between the people of India and the colonizers who were Christians was of mixed benefit. The reality of the *true person of Jesus was veiled* by the 'enemies of the land'. The *conqueror-conquered relationship* is ever distorted, vitiated and strained. At the political level, the reign of the conqueror was imposed and established with much economic, political, cultural and religious damage to the native peoples. For the greater part, India fell to the conquerors, sometimes by fraud, mostly by military conquest and in a few cases due to the betrayal by narrow-minded native rulers or advisers.

Since the *missionaries* went about under the shelter of the colonial rulers, a fair degree of indirect pressure or inducement/persuasion also could be at work in the responses. The late Sardar K. M. Panikkar in his book *Asia and Western Dominance*[163] has expatiated on the *suspicion* raised by the presence of *western Christianity in India*. That image still haunts.

The *worst part of that East-West interaction* was the *deep wound inflicted* upon the *host culture.* For instance, some from among the conquerors made *adverse observations* about *India's religions, cultures and mores.* James Stuart Mill, Thomas Babington Macaulay and such 'educated' among the conquerors figure in the list of those whose *disparaging remarks* about India showed ignorance of the rich cultural heritage of India and *arrogant contempt* for it by them. Many of them, ill-informed about the rich heritage of India, *maligned* the land and its people!

The *ideology of the current regime in India* is rooted in the insensitive *onslaught on Indian heritage* and the disturbing *entry of Semitic heritage via the West.* It has been held by scholars that it is comparable to the German reaction under Adolf Hitler to the country's defeat and treatment by the Allied powers after the First World War. In sum, the *conquerors' ignorance/arrogance* led to the *vilification of the heritage of the conquered peoples* of the subcontinent. This *prevented healthy interaction.*

However, it should be remembered that *Christianity* is not a packet of non-living faith but a package that has ingredients *to attend to the body, mind, soul and life beyond.* Therefore, attending to the bodily and community needs is part of the package. *Humanitarian service* to meet the *needs of the body* by the *Christian community* is always accompanied by attention to the *needs of the soul.* It is *an integral approach. Proclamation of the truth of God's becoming human* in *Jesus Christ* to *give abundant life to all* is *part of the service* which the Christian community renders to all men and women of goodwill.

4.0.3. New Guidelines for a Fruitful Dialogue

For sailing safely without the above-mentioned pitfalls, it is hoped that the following *guidelines* could *safeguard* future *inter-religious dialogues:*

> First a believer should guard against the tendency to defend his or her convictions and experiences at any cost.[164] Second, respect for the sentiments and convictions of the other is a fundamental requirement. There should be no preconditions that would interfere with honest dialogue. Third, the integrity of dialogue should not be compromised by hidden or ulterior motives. In Christian circles, inter-religious dialogue is often considered a dimension of evangelization. This may be permissible since the growing Christian sympathy for other religions guarantees the integrity of the religions as well as of the dialogue. Fourth, debates, argumentation or controversy can damage the very spirit of fraternal dialogue. Fifth, dialogue is not apologetics. The innate desire to defend one's own belief and practice should be checked. Sixth, equality that also respects diversity should be observed. The manifestation of a feeling of superiority can adversely affect the spirit of inter-religious dialogue. Finally, self-criticism will further help both partners in the dialogue.[165]

To avoid the above-mentioned *dangers* in 'inter-religious dialogues' in India, the *emphasis* today must be on '*inter-faith dialogue*' between followers of different religions. *Open, free and friendly sharing* by the *dialogue partners* of their *faith experiences, faith visions and convictions,* will *enlighten* one another, *lead* them to *mutual enrichment and fraternity.* In the words of Pope Francis:

> The different religions… contribute significantly to building *fraternity* and defending *justice* in society. *Dialogue between the followers of different religions* does not take place simply for the sake of diplomacy, consideration or tolerance. In the words of the Bishops of India, '*the goal of dialogue* is to establish *friendship,*

peace and harmony, and to *share* spiritual and moral values and experiences in a spirit of truth and love'.[166]

[S]ince the important things that we *share* are so many, it is possible to find a means of serere, ordered and peaceful coexistence, accepting our differences and rejoicing that, as children of the one God, *we are all brothers and sisters*.[167]

Just as Jesus genuinely *appreciated the faith of all* those who approached him to heal them of their illnesses, whether they were Jews or Gentiles or Samaritans, so we must *respect and acknowledge the faith of all* (e.g., Hindus, Muslims, Sikhs).

4.0.4. *Creative Dialogue between the Indic and Semitic Traditions Today*

A significant challenge to the people of India today is the call to *greater and deeper dialogue* and *integration* of the *two major world traditions coexisting in India*, namely, the *Indic* and *Semitic* strands. The *Semitic religions* include *Judaism, Christianity, Islam, Bahaism* and *Zoroastrianism*. The *Indic* religions include the many *indigenous religions* known as *tribal religions*, besides *Hinduism, Buddhism, Jainism* and *Sikhism*.

Both the *Indic and Semitic traditions* of historic antiquity have made *significant contributions* to the *creative dialogue* between *cultures and civilizations*. India's heritage and its resources have been highlighted by perceptive historians of different religions, cultures and anthropologies, with genuine appreciation. They have critically considered the dynamics of that interaction and paid rich tribute to the major contributing sources.

To the *Semitic* tradition belongs *Jesus Christ*, originally referred to as "Jesus of Nazareth," and popularly known as *Jesus*. His message and life, death and resurrection, had and still have both *Indian and global impact*.

To the *Indic* belong a large number of *sages and seers* whose *insights* were further elaborated and systematically structured as *systems of philosophy* by *Sankara, Ramanuja* and others, all of whom have been shaped by a fairly rich common heritage. And the *Indic tradition* has been acclaimed for its *deep probe into the mystery of God* in a variety of ways from historic times.

An *open, creative and free dialogue* between the *Semitic heritage* and the *Indic heritage* is sure to be *very beneficial* for both the *dialogue-partners*. This is the dominant concern of this Chapter. *One of its purposes* is *to knit all the peoples together*, both *Indic* and *Semitic*, to facilitate the *collaboration of all* to build a *united multi-cultural and multi-religious community* based on *the deepest yearning of every Indian*, expressed in the ancient *prayer*:

> From untruth lead me to *truth* (*asato ma sad gamaya*).
> From darkness lead me to *light* (*tamaso ma jyotir gamaya*).
> From death lead me to *immortality* (*mrtyor ma amrtam gamaya*).[168]

The Gospel of John begins with the *Prologue* which affirms the *divinity* (Jn 1,1), *creative role* (1,3) *and regenerative power of the Word of God* (1,12-13). "Those who welcome the *Word of God* in their hearts, those who believe in the Word that has been revealed to them, are enabled by God's Word to be *born from God* and to become *children of God* (1,12-13)."[169]

In the Gospel of John, *Jesus' first round of ministry* was from "Cana in Galilee" (to Capernaum, Jerusalem, the Judean countryside, Samaria, and back) to "Cana in Galilee," thus manifesting himself to be the *universal Messiah/Saviour* of the *Jews, Samaritans and Gentiles* (Jn 2,1-4,54).[170]

According to the Gospel of Mathew, Jesus started his public ministry in "*Galilee of the Gentiles*" (Mt 4,15-17) "and went about all Galilee," preaching and teaching, and healing all the sick (Jews and Gentiles) (4,23) who followed him "from Galilee and the Decapolis and Jerusalem and Judea and from beyond the Jordan" (4,25). It means that Jesus' ministry of proclaiming *God's reign* was *for all* (Jews and Gentiles).

Jesus was always *kind-hearted* and *magnanimous* towards *Gentiles* who came to him for help, for example, the *Canaanite woman* whose daughter was possessed (Mk 7,24-30), the *Roman Centurion* whose servant was paralysed (Mt 8,5-13; Lk 7,1-10), the *royal official* whose son was dying (Jn 4,46-50).

The *faith of the followers of other religions* inspires us to *accept* the *universal salvific plan of God* and to *respect* it during the *inter-faith dialogue with all*. Jesus tells us: "They will come from east and west, and from north and south, and sit at table in the kingdom of God" (Lk 13,29). For instance, the *Khristbhaktas (devotees of Christ)* in Varanasi are not members of any official Church but are *Hindu believers in Jesus*, the *Sadguru* and *Saviour*.[171] Similarly, *Muslims believe Jesus* as "*a prophet of God*," "*the Messiah*," and "*the word of God*," although they may *not* accept him as "*the Son of God*." Likewise, *Jesus Christ* in the Gospels is often addressed as "*Rabbi*" ("Teacher", which is the equivalent of "*Guru*" in Sikhism) and so *Guru Nanak* and *Jesus Christ* may inspire us to move "*towards Sikh-Christian dialogue*" for mutual learning, spiritual enrichment and fruitful collaboration in the loving service of the poor and the needy.

4.1. The Good News of Jesus Christ for Hindus (Hindu-Christian Dialogical Christology)

4.1.0. Introduction

Honey bees feel free to go to any flower, whether it be a rare flower in the Mogul Gardens of Rashtrapati Bhavan or a wild flower growing by the wayside. Poet Shelley aptly lamented: 'many a flower is born to blush' un-noticed! The bees enter delicately and collect gratefully whatever the flowers have to offer them. But there is an underlying exchange: in return, the bees render the service of pollination, for which all the flowers long. These service providers tell us that, despite the differences in colour, shape, size or beauty, there is a common treasure in every flower, namely, nectar, the nourishment of life. The nectar processed into honey by the honey bees is used by all, being treated as a universal gift from the bees and the flowers. And the claims like 'mine' and 'thine' disappear when the honey is on the dining table for all.

Much wisdom is provided by the bees for those living in inter-faith dialogical contexts. Inter-religious interaction is a similar exercise that enhances the quality of civilization and enriches inter-faith projects.

One could presume that it is with such convictions that the late Professor Raimundo Panikkar wrote a book entitled *The Unknown Christ of Hinduism.*[172] That was the time when organized interaction among adherents of the different religions in India began to be attempted. Indian theologians went further and theologizing in India, especially "theology of religions" and "inter-religious dialogue," were beginning in some centres.

Reactions to Panikkar's book were quite interesting: welcome, commendable, timely, mutually beneficial, on the one hand, and apprehensions and accusations of plunder, etc., on the other hand. Some even saw in it an effort to enter into another religious heritage to appropriate for one's interest what properly belongs to another tradition. However, the merit of the venture needs appreciation.

Similar were the reactions when Dr. Ishanand Vempeny S.J. published his book *Krishna and Christ*[173] (the fruits of years of research in Hindu-Christian religious heritages). These attempts have been rated as frontier efforts to break isolated existence and as helpful sharing between Hindu and Christian fellow-pilgrims on the way to the Supreme.

In these attempts, one can notice the desire to affirm the sense of the divine in all religions and to contribute to the emergence of authentic human communities, rid of vestiges of prejudice against others. National integration has been another overall concern, since pilgrims from linguistically different locations assemble and mix with similar and dissimilar linguistic-cultural groups. The values religions impart and inculcate in the society have a major role to play in that project. And the ancient poem appears pertinent to this role of integration: "If all the trees were one tree, what a great tree that would be." In that strain one could wish, if all values and spiritualties in all the religions in India were integrated, what a great force that would be to respond to the groans of the people of India today!

a)   *Who are Hindus?*

Distinguished spiritual-political leaders like Mahatma Gandhiji, Jawaharlal Nehru, mystics like Ramakrishna

Paramahamsa, mystical poets like Rabindranath Tagore, Tiruvallur, Manikkavacakar, philosophers like Sankara, Ramanuja, Dr. Radhakrishnan, revolutionary social reformers like M. N. Roy, Jotirao Phule, sages like Vasista, Visvamitra, religious-social reformers like Swami Vivekananda are some of the figures that pop up prominently when the word '*Hindus*' is heard. Saffron clad men and women with a garland of *rudraksha* beads around the neck, with lips moving inaudibly as a sign of uttering some *mantra*, men and women in their hundreds on the move any day of the year from one holy place to another, give us another picture. Places like Mathura, Varanasi, Haridwar, Rameswaram, Tirupati with historic temple complexes further enhance the image. Mahabharata and Ramayana, the great religious epics, loaded with ethical-moral precepts, may seem to complete the picture of Hindus.

On the contrary, there is *another side* to the picture of the '*Hindu*' people of India. *Apartheid* is a word detested by civilized society. But it was practiced more rigidly in India than in South-Africa. *Untouchability* has been abolished by an act of the Indian Parliament, but the social practice continues. A human person is reduced to a polluting material to be avoided! It is part of '*Hindu*' caste heritage!

Similarly, equality is promised in the Preamble to the Indian Constitution, but gross *inequality* is part of the '*Hindu*' hierarchical social structure. Higher in the graded caste hierarchy, the greater one's worth as human; lower in the scale, the less. Indians known as '*panchama*' ('*outcasts*') are kept outside of that structure. Just as a *cat* keeps the *captured rat* alive but under the grip of the claws, so *Hindus* have been keeping the '*untouchables*' under their feet for millennia!

Originally, '*Hindu*' simply meant the people beyond the River Sindhu or present-day Indus. The eminent Hindu scholar Shashi Tharoor gives the following description of *Hinduism*:

> It embraces an eclectic range of doctrines and practices, from pantheism to agnosticism and from faith in reincarnation to belief in the caste system. But none of these constitutes an obligatory credo for a Hindu: there are none. We have no compulsory dogmas.[174]

The word '*Hinduism*' is not a monolith. Indeed, the term itself is an Iranian construct. Rather *Dharma* was the designation from early times. This *Dharma*, often rendered as *Sanatan Dharma*, had several spiritual-cultural lineages that were rather independent. But these could be grouped and considered under *four main sects*. These are *Vaishnavism*, quite strong in the north, often called Sanskrit tradition, and *Saivism*, which originated from the Agamas in the south mostly, and *Shaktism* and the *Smartha* traditions, found in the north-eastern part of the subcontinent. All these are part of 'Hinduism'. (Today the Sanskrit-Agamic Hindu integration has been taking place significantly across peninsular India.)

b)   *The 'God-ward Thrust' of Hindus*

Pope Paul VI testified in 1963 that the Hindus are 'a people that sought God with a relentless desire.' Twenty-three years later (1986), in the course of the homily at Mass in the Indira Gandhi stadium, Pope John Paul II drew the attention of all to the deepest aspirations of the people of this ancient land and culture, and especially of the Hindus:

> Your ancient sages have expressed the anguished cry of the soul for the Absolute. There is indeed an age-old yearning for

the infinite, a constant awareness of the divine presence and endless manifestation of the religious feelings through popular feasts and festivals.[175]

The '*God-ward thrust*' has been a very distinctive feature of the Hindus from ancient times. The conviction that everything/everyone has originated from God and lives in and through God and will go back to God on cessation of life on earth has been a deep-seated belief of the Hindus. The Hindu Scriptures teach that the entire creation has been from God (Brahma) and longs to go back to God: "That, verily, whence beings here are born, that by which when born they live, that into which on deceasing they enter – that be desirous of understanding. That is Brahma" (Tat Up 3.1.).[176]

c)   Ways of Dialogue between Hindus and Christians
The initiative to have a *dialogue* with the people known as '*Hindus*' raises an important question: "What are the ways of facilitating a *fruitful dialogue* between Hindus and Christians?"

(i) One is the *Scriptural approach:* to *study* the *Hindu Scriptures* and *Christian Gospels* and *compare* and *contrast* their understanding of God, humans, cosmos, ethical-moral principles, spiritualities, etc.

(ii) The second is the *Experiential approach*. It is by getting immersed in the world of Hindu religious *practices* provided by the countless rituals, observances, festivals and celebrations, including the daily or periodic or annual events. Jostling with simple and educated believers at mammoth gatherings like Kumbh Mela that comes once in twelve years will give one unique opportunity to know the Hindus. Momentous celebrations like Kumbh Mela bring to one spot millions of devotees from diverse contexts. Their hearts are filled with deep feelings of simple piety, devotion and faith. The mini-ocean of the conjunction of the rivers Ganga and Yamuna beckons the devotees from across the subcontinent and beyond every 12th year.

There are similar festivals that recur regularly providing us with an opportunity for such interaction. For example, the vast concourse of devout pilgrims trekking their arduous yet devotion-evoking pilgrimage to Sabarimala in Kerala provides another fruitful scene for consideration. Opportunities abound for such immersion experiences.

The daily *puja* at home, the waving of lit lamps for *arati* in the evening, the offerings of flowers in the temple, the ritual of ablution in a temple pond or river, all are expressions of their faith and religiosity.

This is known as the realm of *popular Hindu religiosity*. Popular *festivals* that dot the Hindu calendar complete the phenomenal aspect of Hinduism. The village deity, the regionally worshipped deities and the national deities do contribute to the religious need of the people.

(iii) *Integral approach to dialogue between Hindus and Christians. Both* the *Scriptural* and the *Experiential* approaches are inter-related and beneficial *to fulfil the religious aspirations* of Hindus and Christians. They *complement* and *complete* one another. Therefore, we have to *integrate the two approaches* to have a *meaningful and innovative inter-faith dialogue* between Hindus and Christians.[177]

Christianity is not a package of beliefs and rituals but *a living faith* that attends to the needs of body, mind, soul and community here and now and points to life beyond. Hence *humanitarian service* by the Christian community is always accompanied by attention to the *human needs beyond life on earth*. It is an *integral approach*. God became incarnate in Jesus Christ in history so that all may have the *fullness of life* here on earth and hereafter; that is the service in which the Christian community is involved.

4.1.1. *Areas of Creative Dialogue between Hindus and Christians*

1)   *Presence of God in Creation in Hinduism and Jesus Christ, the Creative Word of God, in John's Gospel*

a)   *Presence of God in creation in Hinduism*

Hinduism pays special attention to the reality of God in the cosmos, in nature, and particularly in human life. *God's presence in creation* is affirmed by many sacred texts in Hindu scriptures. Everything in creation is marked or sealed by the presence and action of God: "By the Lord (*Isa*) *enveloped* must this all be — Whatever moving thing there is in this moving world" (Isha Up. 1).

The Taitiriya Upanishad categorically affirms: "Brahma is bliss (*ananda*). For truly, indeed, beings are born from bliss, when born they live in bliss, on deceasing they enter into bliss" (Tait. Up. 2.6). It is a beautiful and hope-generating affirmation. It is truly the fountain of spring for the ever-seeking human spirit. One may recall to mind the philosopher St Augustine who in his *Confessions* resonated with the groan of the human heart (expressed above) confessed: "Our hearts are restless until they find their rest in you (God)".

This view is further *elaborated* by Uddalaka Aruni, the sage of the Chandogya Upanishad, when he teaches his son Svetaketu, the earnest and inquisitive student: "In the beginning, my dear, this world was just Being (*sat*), one only, without a second" (Chand. Up. 6.2.1). "All creatures here, my dear, have Being as their root, have Being as their home, have Being as their support" (*ibid.*, 6.8.4). "That which is the *finest essence* – this whole world has that as its *soul*. That is the reality. That is *Atman* (Soul). *That art thou*, Svetaketu" (*ibid.*, 6.14.3).

b)   Jesus Christ, the creative Word of God, in John's Gospel (Jn 1,1-3.11-14)

The *Gospel of John*, taking the reader back to the primal phase of creation, refers to the presence of the *Word of God*: "In the beginning was the Word [*Logos*], and the Word was with God, and the Word was God. He was in the beginning with God. All things were made through him and without him not one thing was made" (Jn 1,1-3). It means that God created everything through His Word (cf. the repetitive refrain: "God said…" in Gen 1,3-31). Again, the presence of the Word of God not only in creation but also especially among human beings is emphasized: "He was in the world, and the world was made through him, yet the world did not know him" (Jn 1,10, where "the world" refers especially to the human beings). His people, however, failed to welcome him: "He came to his own but his own did not receive him" (1,11). And yet the divine Word became a human being to dwell with them: "And the Word became flesh [weak and mortal human being] and dwelt among us…" (1,14).[178]

2)   Pilgrimages to Holy Places by Hindus and Jesus

Arjuna in the Bhagavad Gita expressed his heart's longing to have a vision of Lord Krishna in his "imperishable form" (BG, 11:4). It is with deep-seated longings of the soul to have a personal experience of the Divine that pilgrims flock to well-known pilgrim centres in India. There is a need to respond to this hunger today.[179]

a)   Pilgrimages to holy places by Hindus

The intensity of the divine presence and action is believed by Hindus to be more in certain places than in others. Such places are known as *pilgrim centres*. A high degree of manifestation of the divine is considered specific to such places. The devout pilgrim's access to such places is considered highly beneficial and satisfies the spiritual thirst of earnest believers.

One should visit *Puri* when the three chariots are being pulled by zealous devotees to feel the religious fervor of the millions. Alternatives too are there. *Sabarimala* in Kerala provides an opportunity to experience the religious fervor of the 'Ayyappa' pilgrims with the prescribed load on their heads. The faces of the pilgrims show contentment and satisfaction as they retrace their steps after the momentary *darsana* of Lord Ayyappa after climbing the eighteen holy steps.

Varanasi became a pilgrim centre because the left bank of the north bound stretch of the holy Ganges provides the required spot for entry into the holy water to offer homage to the rising sun in the east by ablution with both the feet in water.

Sacred mountains play a similar role to demonstrate in practical ways what Hinduism is offering. Honoured as the abode of Lord Siva and Parvathi, his spouse, and held as the sacred haunt of thousands of ascetics living in their hermitages or shrines, the Himalayas provide the occasion for religious fervour to those who assemble there. Hindu devotees visualize mountains with a religious perception.

b)   Pilgrimages to holy places by Jesus

We recall how John the Baptist was standing in the *Jordan river* and baptizing people (by immersing them in the water) (Lk 3,21; cf. Mt 3,5-6). Jesus, the sinless one "who takes away the sin of the world" (Jn 1,29), was also baptized by John in the Jordan. Immediately after his baptism, he had a deep *spiritual experience* of being the *beloved Son of God* ("You are my beloved Son; with you I am well-pleased": Lk 3,21-22; Mt 3,13-17).

In the Old Testament Moses and the Israelites experienced God on Mount Sinai (cf. Ex 3, 1-6; 19,1-25). Jesus often went up to the *mountain to pray* and sometimes he spent whole nights in prayer (Lk 6,12), for instance, before choosing the Twelve (cf. 6,13-16). Jesus preached the "*Sermon on the Mount*" (Mt 5-7); he was *transfigured on Mount Tabor* in the presence of his chosen disciples Peter, James and John (cf. Mt 17,1-9).

Jesus also used to go to the *Jewish synagogues* not only to take part in the Sabbath services but also to preach and to teach (cf. Mk 1,21; Lk 4,14-16; Mt 4,23; etc.). He visited the *Temple in Jerusalem* on the occasion of the *major Jewish feasts* like the Passover, the Tabernacles and the Dedication (cf. Jn 2,13; 7,14; 10,22). Thus Jesus joined the Jewish devotees in the annual celebration of the religious feasts.

*3)   River Fronts as Moksha Dwars (Door-Ways to Salvation)
and Jesus Christ as the Door of Salvation*

a)   River fronts as moksha dwars (Door-ways to salvation)
Hari-dwar, where the river Ganga touches the vast plain in the
State of Uttarakhand, had been a sacred '*door*' for entry in and
out for devotees and gods for centuries. Its geographical location
is the sub-Himalayan plain where sacred Ganga descends from
the upper regions of the Himalayas and is received by the
plains. The entire Himalaya mountain ranges are sacred for
the worshippers of Lord Siva and Parvati. Millions of pilgrims
flock to the water-front to be cleansed by the heavenly water,
the gift of Lord Siva and Parvati.

Blessings of the celestial powers are sought on similar riverfronts further downstream or in other fronts hallowed by sacred
memories. In the Hindu religious calendar (*panchanga*) sacred
riverfronts are marked and these have become part and parcel
of Hindu religiosity.

The *Sangam* (confluence) at *Prayag* (Allahabad) where the
two sacred rivers *Ganga* and *Yamuna* meet and merge is doubly
sacred. Every 12th year, when planet Jupiter is in Aquarius and
the Sun enters Aries, the great *Kumbh Mela* is celebrated. The
pilgrims in their millions rush to the waters for their *Shahi
Snan* ('*royal bath*') when *Makara Sankranti* is celebrated. The
rare occasions like the great *Kumbh Mela* beckon all to come
and be beneficiaries.

There is yet another reason for the auspiciousness of the
Kumbh celebration. A large number of religious leaders assemble
for the major event, whose *pravachans* (religious discourses) are
occasions for the pilgrims from far off lands to deepen their

faith and religiosity. Thus instructed by their venerable religious leaders and having participated in the prescribed rituals, they return to their homes enlightened and rid of their various kinds of karma impact. *Darsan* of the genuine *sadhus* and *sanyasis* provide for the pilgrims inspiring opportunities of blessings which they cherish very much.

Ardh Kumbh is celebrated at Ujjain or Haridwar. Kaveri river in South India is regarded as the *Dakshin Ganga (Ganges of the South)*. Also, river Narmada is held as another sacred river.

b)   Jesus Christ as the door of salvation (Jn 10,7.9)

In the allegory of the Good Shepherd, Jesus reveals himself as "the *door* of the sheep" (Jn 10,7). And he explains it by adding: "*I am the door;* if anyone enters through me, he *will be saved…* (10,9)." It is a symbolic way of saying that Jesus is the *mediator of salvation.* And *salvation* in John's Gospel is understood as "*eternal life*" (3,16.36) or "*abundant life*" (10,10), life in its fullness. This qualitatively new life that Jesus gives cannot be destroyed even by physical death (cf. Jn 11,25).

4)   Fire in Hinduism and in Christianity

a)   Fire in Hinduism

A most striking truth that is conveyed by the hymns of the *Rigveda* is the esteem and veneration accorded to nature's elements like fire, wind, sun, water and the juice of the Soma plant.

For example, the element of 'fire'! One is struck by the nature and function of fire. Fire is accorded almost a priestly role because of the service it does to living beings, especially to humans. Treated almost as a non-terrestrial being, high respect and homage are accorded to *fire* (*Agni*). Therefore, depositing selective materials like ghee in the *sacred fire* (*havan*) was considered as the privileged means *to be in touch with the powers of heaven*, the Power beyond the skies, because it is quite natural for the flames of the raging fire to move upward, heavenward. Hence Vedic religiosity was expressed by putting offerings in the fire. The fire will carry them to the heavenly Power. "O Agni, the worship and sacrifice that thou en-compassest on every side, that same goes to the gods" (RV 1.1.4). (The universal appeal of the element of fire to direct the human mind to the celestial powers/Power is reflected in the role of fire in Zoroastrian religion.)

b)   Jesus Christ and fire in Christianity
John the Baptist told the Pharisees and Sadducees: "I baptize you in water (*en hydati*) for repentance ... but he who is coming after me... will baptize you *in Holy Spirit and fire*" (*en pneumati hagiô kai pyri*: Mt 3,11). "*Fire*" in the preaching of the Baptist may be a reference to God's final *judgement* of unrepentant sinners (cf. Mt 3,10.12). This is similar to *Jesus Christ's judgement* of "unloving" humans to "eternal *fire*" (Mt 25,41).

However, *Jesus Christ* associates "*fire*" with the accomplishment of *his mission*: "I came *to cast fire* upon the earth; how I wish it were already kindled!" (Lk 12,49).[180] In Acts, Luke connects "*fire*" with the *Holy Spirit* that was given to the disciples as "*tongues of fire*" which enabled them "to speak in tongues" on Pentecost (cf. Acts 2,3-4.17-18). Jesus' baptism in suffering and death (Lk 12,50) *kindled the fire of the Holy Spirit in human hearts* (Lk 12,49). Therefore, *Jesus Christ* is *the kindler of the "sacred fire"* (the Holy Spirit) that enables all believers (Hindus, Christians, etc.) to ascend to the divine domain.

5)   Avatara in Hinduism and Incarnation of Jesus Christ

a)   Avatara in Hinduism

This has been a much-discussed issue in philosophy and religion. It is about the actual relationship between the visible universe and the invisible God.

Everything in creation is traced to God. Some hold it is due to a *creative act of God*. Others consider it is an *evolution of God* from an original common substance.

Avatara, though popularly rendered as "incarnation", literally means '*descent*' (from a higher situation or locale, to a lower one). *Matsya* (Fish), *Kurma* (Tortoise), *Varaha* (Boar), *Narasimha* (Lion-Man), *Vamana* (Dwarf), *Parasurama* (Lumberjack), *Rama*, *Krishna*, *Buddha* and *Kalki* (Horseman) are the *ten avatars (dashavatara)* of Vishnu among the many similar other versions at the popular level.

At the philosophical level, we have texts like Chandogya Upanishad which would hold that in the beginning there was just Being and everything in the manifold creation came out of it (Chand Up 6.3.1). In recent times Sri Aurobindo Ghosh has built up the philosophical rendering of *evolution*.

Yet, there is still the belief that the godhead seeks to be in and with the people in a more manifest way. This *religious belief* in Hinduism is rendered through the phenomenon of *avatara* of the godhead in human history. It is part of the *philosophy of Hinduism* which is *evolutionary and cyclic*.

Bhagavatha Purana has treated the belief in the *avatara of Krishna* extensively. The birth of Lord Krishna and its purpose is further treated in the *Bhagavad-Gita* as follows: "Whenever there is a decay of righteousness, O Bharata, and there is an exaltation of unrighteousness, then I Myself come forth" (BG IX,7).

b)   *Incarnation of Jesus Christ (Jn 1,14)*

The mystery of the incarnation of Jesus Christ is revealed in the Gospel of John: "And *the Word* [of God] *became flesh* and dwelt among us, and we have seen his glory, glory as of a *unique Son from the Father* full of grace and truth… Grace and truth came to be through *Jesus Christ*" (Jn 1,14.17).

'Incarnation' literally means *'en-fleshing'* (the divine assuming 'flesh', a weak and mortal human being), that is, *God becoming* truly *human.* The *crucial difference* between the *incarnation* of Christ and the *avatara* of Krishna consists of the *'once-and-for-ever'* efficacy of incarnation/redemption by Jesus Christ versus the *repeated* occurrence of *avatara.* Secondly, whereas Christ *suffers* the excruciating pain of the crucifixion and death and is raised, *avatara* is *unaffected* by suffering. Hence we cannot equate *incarnation* of Christ with *avatara* of Krishna.

An ever-recurring prayer of the sages/prophets in the Semitic religions has been: "Shower, O heavens, from above, and let the skies rain down righteousness; let the earth open, that salvation may sprout forth." (Is 45,8). *Isaiah* is vocalizing the eternal and ceaseless *hunger and thirst for God by all humanity.* Every man and woman has an *inherent desire for God-realization.* The destiny of everyone is treated as God-realization. *Jesus Christ* is presented as the *great facilitator* for the realization of that inherent destiny through his incarnation.[181]

The regrettable act of disobedience by Adam, the head of the human family, and the great promise thereafter described in the

Book of Genesis (3,1-22; cf. also Rom 5,12-21) are considered as expressions of humankind's deeply felt need for God. *Search for the path to God* had been a distinctive yearning of all. Much of prophecy in Israel contained this idea.

Often, *Jesus' life and actions* are interpreted by the Evangelists as the *realization of prophecies*. For instance, Matthew interprets the *virginal conception* of Jesus in Mary's womb as the *fulfilment of the prophecy* ("All this took place *to fulfil* what the Lord had spoken by the prophet": Mt 1,22), for *Isaiah* had foretold: "Behold, *a virgin shall conceive* and bear a son, and his name shall be called *Emmanuel*" (which means "*God with us*") (Is 7,14; Mt 1,23).

The Hindus' belief in *avatara* may be regarded as the expression of their *longing for God becoming truly human* so that they may experience God-realization. Therefore, it may be a *good starting point* for a fraternal Hindu-Christian dialogue on *Avatara* of Krishna and *Incarnation* of Christ.

6)   *Lord Krishna of Bhagavad Gita and Jesus Christ of the Gospels*

a)   *Lord Krishna of Bhagavad Gita*

The prolonged conversation between Krishna and Arjuna in the first ten chapters of the Gita is a *graded revelation of the true identity* of the charioteer, *Lord Krishna*. The horse-cart driver begins to be seen as a good *friend*, then a well-informed *teacher*, then a highly proficient *scholar*, a wise *philosopher* well versed in many branches of human knowledge. *The climax* is reached when the charioteer claims to be the *creator of the world*, of the cosmos, nay, the *final destination of the human family*. Moved by the self-disclosure of Krishna as Lord and destiny of everything and everyone (Gita 10.32), the warrior Arjuna is awakened. The revelation of the person and works of Lord Krishna prove so truly ravishing to the heart of Arjuna, so much so that he would like to see his full divine form: "If, Lord, thou thinkest that I can look upon it, then do thou, Lord of Power, reveal to me thy divine Self immutable" (XI.4). It is almost like the prayer of Moses to Yahweh: "I pray thee, show me thy glory" (Ex 33,18).

The great Teacher Krishna informs the earnest seeker Arjuna that the *finite eye* cannot behold the *Infinite Form*. But he assures Arjuna that he will remedy the handicap: "I give thee an *eye divine*" (BG 11:8). It is like Yahweh enabling Moses to have a glimpse into His nature (cf. Ex 33,19-23).

Krishna's *Visvaropa darsana* (*cosmic manifestation*) takes place (BG, 11). An awe-inspiring description of the origin of the cosmos by Krishna, its marvellous maintenance by him and its eventual return to the Lord follow (*samahara*). It was a colourful and remarkable rendering of the central Hindu philosophical view of creation: Brahman is "That, verily, whence beings here are born, that by which when born they live, that into which on deceasing they enter -- that be desirous of understanding, that is Brahma" (Tait. Up. 3.1.).[182]

The impact of the theophany on the eager petitioner Arjuna is such that he confesses that his despondency is gone. He falls at the feet of Krishna, offering himself as a pliant disciple to do his bidding in whatever way it comes to him. The simplicity of the language, elegance and attractiveness of the description of devotion in a humanly accessible form, the vision of the cosmos emanating from the Lord of the universe functioning most marvelously and finally being absorbed into the Lord himself, is truly great.

b)   *Jesus Christ of the Gospels*

Jesus reveals himself gradually to his disciples from the time of his calling them to follow him.[183] They accompany him throughout his ministry. They listen to his preaching and teaching and sees the miracles of healing, casting out demons, raising the dead, feeding the hungry crowd, calming the stormy sea, etc. Towards the middle of his ministry, Jesus asks his disciples: "Who do you say that I am?" And they answer: "You are the Christ/the Son of God" (Mk 8,29; Lk 9,20; Mt 16,16). After they confess faith in Jesus as the Messiah/Son of God, he takes three of his disciples Peter, James and John to a mountain and he is transfigured before them (Mk 9,2-8; Lk 9,28-36; Mt 17,1-9), when his garments become dazzling white, his face shining like the sun and a heavenly voice from the cloud announcing, "This is my beloved Son; listen to him" (Mk 9,8; Lk 9,35; Mt 17,5). In short, *Jesus Christ's glorious transfiguration* (as the *beloved Son of God*) before his chosen disciples in the Gospels is almost like *Krishna's cosmic manifestation* to his dear disciple Arjuna in the Bhagavad Gita (11.9).

7)   *Sacrifice in Hinduism and Jesus Christ's Sacrifice*

a)   *Sacrifice in Hinduism*

(i)   *Vedic rituals and sacrifices*

The '*Godward thrust*' mentioned above had taken *concrete shapes* in multiple forms of *Vedic rituals* and *sacrifices*. Sacrifice began to be accepted as a means of communion with the godhead or to placate gods and goddesses or to secure benefits like protection from hostile forces. The rite of 'sacrifice' has a far wider dimension than what the empirical performance communicates. To attest to their prayers and praises of the deities, *offerings* like Soma juice, cakes cooked in milk, etc. were made to them. These actions were later known as *sacrifices*. These were daily or weekly or monthly or annual. The early Hindu mind travelled with the *rhythm of the cosmic rotation* of the innumerable functionaries like the sun, the moon, the stars, the planets, the constellations, all of which were considered affecting their life for good or evil. What is now known as *panchanga* (the Hindu calendar) was the manual to assist them in their monitoring of the cosmic phenomenon to perform their *religious rituals* including *sacrifices* to gods and goddesses. Innumerable are these observances and celebrations.

(ii)   *Purusha Sukta in the Rig Veda and the cosmic sacrifice (RV. X.90.1)*

A most significant hymn where a *cosmic yajna* (*sacrifice*) is presented is *Purusa-Sukta* (X.90). In it, Rig Vedic sages conceived the *gods* as *agents of creation*, while the *material* out of which the world is made is nothing but the *body* of the *Primeval Man* named 'Purusha'. *Creation* is the *outcome of a sacrifice* in which this *Purusha* was the *victim*: "*Purusha* is this all that has been and that will be" (X.90.1). In other words, the *whole creation* is from the *body* of *Purusha*. Here the religious view is *pantheistic*, but the wish contains much that is desirable. It was *a form of sacrifice* the *outcome* of which was the *manifold universe*. The dismembered parts of *Purusha* became portions or regions of the universe. It is interesting to note that such a great Being is described as a *victim* in a cosmic sacrifice. Thus *sacrifice*, especially *cosmic sacrifice* is *foundational* in the Rig Veda:

In Vedism there is a close relationship between God, sacrifice and the cosmos. The universe takes its birth from the divine sacrifice and remains in existence thanks to it. This cosmic dimension is often not sufficiently stressed when we speak of the purpose of the Vedic sacrifice."[184]

(iii)   *Bhagavad Gita and the cycle of sacrifice ('yajna chakra')*

Bhagavad Gita has further elaborated this insight of sacrifice at a cosmic level in the form of a *yajna-chakra* (*wheel of sacrifice*) (BG, Chapter 3). It is conceived as a mode of relationship between the gods and the cosmic goods like fruits, juice of selected plant-leaves, cereals, etc. and mutuality between gods and the grateful humans who are the beneficiaries. Rains from above lead to the fruitfulness of plants and cereals on earth. Out of gratitude, the labouring humans select the best fruits and offer them to the gods. Pleased at this benign gesture, the heavenly powers continue to send down rain. Rain is considered as the response of the gods to the gifts offered to the gods in the fire (BG, 3:24 passim). This mutuality between the humans, the heavenly powers/gods and goddesses is held as a sign of collaboration between God, nature and humans.

b)   *Jesus Christ's Sacrifice (Pain, Suffering and Death) in the Gospels*

It is a common phenomenon that the *shadow* of everyone follows her/him even when one walks at mid-noon. At noon it is short but at dawn or sunset, it is long. The popular sentiment sometimes expressed, other times implied, is an unspeakable unease which had been accompanying everyone from the prehistorical time of the *first parents* in Judeo-Christian tradition or that of the *primal couple* who began to walk and look around for food or water as in the evolutionary theories (propounded by

Charles Darwin, Teilhard de Chardin, Aurobindo Ghosh, etc.). All lament that some undetectable dark force shadows them. Philosophers like Kierkegaard, Alfred Camus, have expressed certain ever-present melancholy associated with human life. Novelist Thomas Hardy articulates this universal negative feeling in human life: "Something is amiss; this is not the situation that should have been." Who will free human beings from this mysterious gloom to begin a new way of being humans? That has been a universal anguish. "I fall upon the thorns of life and I bleed" was poet P. B. Shelley's melancholic strain in one of his poems.

One fine morning should *dawn* when the whole human family will be rid of that *un-severable shadow* – this was the hope of people. What light-house is for life-belt wearers in the risky mid-ocean after a ship-wreck, the word HOPE is for this struggling mass of humankind. Virtually that refrain is what a distant pole star is for sea-farers. The words like *mukti, moksha, nirvana,* have been such light-houses, kindling the HOPE and sustaining the life-struggles of peoples across ages or eons or *yugas.* That 'dawn' is dreamt of when humanity will be free of that '*something dark*'.

It is with such sentiments that the word '*Saviour*' is repeatedly used in the Gospels. For instance, the *name* of the son to be born to the Virgin Mary is "*Jesus*": "she will bear a son, and you [Joseph] shall call his name *Jesus*, for he will *save* his people from their *sins*" (Mt 1,21). When Jesus was born in Bethlehem, an angel appeared to the shepherds and announced to them: "I bring you *good news* of great joy, which will be for all the people, for to you is *born* today in the city of David a *Saviour,* who is Christ the Lord" (Lk 2,10-11). The birth of *Jesus,* the

Saviour, is "*good news* of great joy" not only for the shepherds but also "*for all the people*" because he is going to "*save*" them by *removing* the "*shadow*" *of* "*sins*" from their lives.

Again, when Jesus takes the initiative to invite himself to the house of *Zacchaeus* (a tax collector, a *sinner*), his entire household experiences salvation: "Today *salvation* has come to this house... For the Son of Man came to seek and *to save the lost*" (19,9-10).

Even though the *crucified Jesus* was mocked and challenged by the Jewish leaders, Roman soldiers, and even by one of the criminals, to "*save*" *himself*, he refused to come down from the cross (cf. Lk 23,35-39) because such was *not his Father's will* (cf. 22,42). *His will* was to "*save*" *the sinners* through the suffering, death and resurrection the Son of Man (cf. his Passion predictions in 9,22; 18,33).

c)   Comparison between Purusha's Cosmic Sacrifice and Jesus Christ's Self-Sacrifice

Purusha is, in general, the male principle in the creation and maintenance of all existence. In the *Samkhya* philosophy, it stands for the spiritual dimension and *prakrti* the material dimension of all existence. There are seven hymns dealing with *Purusha* in the *Rigveda*. Vedic scholar A. A. MacDonnell explains in the well-known hymn *Purusha-Sukta* (X.90) as follows:

> The gods are the agents of creation, while the material out of which the world is made is the body of a primeval giant named *Purusha*. The *act of creation* is here treated as *a sacrifice* in which *Purusha* is the victim, the parts which when cut up becoming portions of the universe.[185]

In Christian theology, *Jesus Christ* is *human and divine. His suffering and pain* are *truly human.* Jesus Christ is a *historical* person, born in a particular place and time, whereas *Purusha*, both in Samkhya philosophy and Rigveda, are *ahistorical* but regarded as belonging to *Puranic* literature where historical-mythological creative expressions are treated.

8)   Truth in Hinduism and Jesus Christ, the Truth

a)   Truth in Hinduism

Beneath the emblem of the Indian nation is the phrase "*Satyam eva jayate—Truth alone triumphs*" (Mundaka Up. 3.1.6). Because of the deep meaning and significance of truth in human life, it was accorded high recognition by people of all faiths and cultures. The full Upanishadic text reads as follows: "*Truth alone triumphs;* by truth is laid out the path leading to the gods (*devayana*)". The entire verse becomes a mighty declaration: *truth* is *the goal*, and the path to the world of gods and goddesses is made with fragments of truth. [Now *satyam* (truth) is related to *sat* (existence, reality, truth), and *asat* (non-existence, non-reality, untruth) is the opposite of *sat* (cf. Br. Up. 1.3.28: *asato ma sad gamaya…*).]

b)   Gandhi and truth as a moral force (for social regeneration) and Truth as God

The autobiography of the Father of the Nation is entitled *My Experiments with Truth.* Two reasons could be behind the title.

One is that Gandhi's autobiography is a truthful portrayal of the events in his life. He had recorded his early childhood experiences graphically. Even his relationship with his spouse he has described without withholding anything. There had been discord among the two. Even the bitter feud that occurred periodically he has placed before the reader.

Similarly, Gandhi has narrated in his autobiography a matter of fact portrayal of the tension between him and the leaders of the Congress and other parties. His decades-long leadership at the political level, his approach to communal harmony and the manner of his handling of the mighty imperial administration were riddled with tensions and disagreement. But he maintained his tested values of *ahimsa* (non-violence) and *satyagraha* (holding on to truth-force) along with his efforts at harmony and communion with all religions (*sarva dharma samababhav*). *Satyagraha* for him was the *method of applying truth-force at all levels*.

Gandhiji's decades-long campaign for the freedom for the country was a protracted and laborious one. A mighty colonial empire was his opponent. He held that domination of a people by another mighty force is unjust and against the truth. Britain had been economically and politically benefiting from this domination. It is not very easy for the mighty holder of beneficial booty to surrender it. Indeed, it is painful.

Satyagraha, the method adopted by Gandhi, was accompanied by '*fast*'. He had his reasons for that. Both *satyagraha* and *fast* are *moral forces*; there is no physical violence involved, nor use of force. Now *fast* is the infliction of some kind of physical pain and suffering by the *satyagrahi* on oneself. Gandhi argued that of his own free will, the pain that the holder of the empire would have to bear in giving away a huge colony, he is *vicariously* inflicting on himself. It is not only an act of civility but also a unique manner of releasing the moral force involving an act of the will, not an act of the hand by handling a deadly weapon.

Gandhi is here raising to an eminent height the *moral force* over the physical force in which the will and reason of rational human beings are used persistently. The method is certainly a befitting civilized human approach.

Gandhiji preferred to hold that "*Truth is God*," and not "God is truth." He has testified to the impact of the Sermon on the Mount on his life and perspectives. Certainly, he wanted to *highlight the importance of truth* and related values like *ahimsa* in human life. We know from later developments in India that the unique method Gandhi used to free the country from colonial rule was the *moral-spiritual force* generated by the unique weapon of *fast* and '*satyagraha*'. The world has recognized the *civilizing force* of *ahimsa* and *satyagraha*. The *message* is clear: *truth* must be the *distinctive criterion* for personal, communitarian, national and international relations and decision-making processes and transactions at all times.

This was the reason for Indian national leaders from Nehru onwards to follow the *policy of non-alignment* in dealing with international tensions and conflicts. The term communicates the message that this nation stands by *truth* and *neutrality* without yielding to the might of weapons. It is a very civilizing force supplied by religions.

Born a Hindu and quite influenced by multi-religious education, especially while in England, Gandhiji is quite an interesting phenomenon for inter-religious interaction and integration. The word *Sat* (Truth) is equated with the *Supreme* and the compound *Sat-Chit-Ananda* is used to address God. By identifying *Satya* ("Truth") with God, Gandhiji affirms that it is *by knowing the "truth" and living by it* that one can attain the *Supreme Saccidananda*.

c)   Jesus Christ, the truth (Jn 14,6)

About two millennia ago a very thought-provoking and categorical communication was made by a young sage to a small band of loyal friends in another part of the globe in west Asia. It was made while they were in a small upper room, chatting after a friendly and refreshing meal. But the impact was truly epoch-making. The ethos to which the assertion belongs was found to be charged with transformative potential. It indeed did contribute much to change the face of the world, as the late Professor Christopher Dawson in his book '*Formation of Europe*' has claimed in the book. For, *in Jesus Christ*, the *humans* became potentially *divine-citizens*, and the domain inhabited by them was expected to display characteristics of the '*Kingdom of God*'. The historic claim was: "I **am** the *path* and the **truth** and the *life*" (Jn 14,6). The statement was *not* 'I *have* the truth but "I **am** the truth".

The weightage of the assertion challenges every thinking person to investigate not only the *claim* but also the *person* to whom the assertion is attributed. One could wonder: 'what could be the nature of the young sage to place such a claim before the world!' It is spurred by such a challenge that exploration into the meaning of the mystery of his *claim* and *person* is undertaken here.

Jesus identifies himself with the *truth* (the *revelation of God* as "*Father*") since Jesus continues to say: "no one comes to the Father except through me" (14,6). It is by following the path of Jesus, the truth, that one can reach the Father. The *truth of God* as a *loving Father* and Jesus as his *beloved Son* was made known to him during his baptism (Mk 1,11: "You are my beloved Son with whom I am well-pleased") and to his disciples (Peter, James and John) during his transfiguration (9,7: "This is my beloved Son; listen to him"). It is this *loving God* whom Jesus always addressed in prayer as *Abba* (14,36), which is the Aramaic equivalent of *Papa, Daddy*. Jesus, the *incarnate Son of God*, is the *revelation of God* as *the loving Father* (cf. Jn 1,14.117-18; cf. also Mt 11,25-27). Jesus assures his true disciples: "you will *know the truth, and the truth will make you free*" (Jn 8,32), which Jesus himself explains as: "if the Son makes you free, you will be free indeed" (8,36). *Jesus*, the incarnate Son of God, is *the liberating truth*. Jesus' words and deeds manifest the truth of the *mystery* of the *mutual indwelling* of God, the Father, and Jesus, the Son ("I am in the Father and the Father in me": Jn 14,10.11).

9)   Three Margas in Hinduism and Prem Marga of Jesus Christ

a)   Three margas in Hinduism

The bounty and richness of God had been manifested and available to His children always in all places. All are equal beneficiaries of this Fatherly love and providence irrespective of climate, culture, racial differences. People respond first by organizing their lives according to the ethical, moral and religious prescriptions. Different religions assist them to live a godly life irrespective of diversity in race and culture.

Some among them may be moved by still greater gratitude. Some do feel the Providence intimately far more than what ordinary religious/ritual practices give them. These intense and focused struggles eventually got the name of approaches or paths. Over centuries these were classified and put under three broad categories. Eventually, these became known as *Margas* (paths). These are *Karma Marga, Jñana Marga* and *Bhakti Marga*.

(i)   Karma marga (path of action) in Hinduism

Historically the *first phase of religiosity* in India was marked by *rituals and sacrifices*. Right from the Vedic phase onwards, one or more gods or goddesses had been figuring. Awareness of one's dependence for everything on celestial powers was associated with the mindset of primordial inhabitants all over the world. Here in India too, symbolic rites were part and parcel of the culture of both the natives as well as of the immigrants who came and settled down here. An abundance of sacrificial systems grew around these celestial figures responsible for human identity, existence and all the available resources for living. Sacrifice to these 'gods/goddesses' was the earliest ritual system to originate and to grow diversified and it continues even to these days. Gradually, concern for rectitude in the performance of these rituals grew and led to various interpretations. A system of philosophy sprouted as a result, known as *karma marga*.

The word *karma* has many connotations. First, it refers to *any human action* which is preceded by deliberation or just an impulse. Second, it refers to an *ethical-moral action*, like service to a needy person. If human actions are not conformable to ethical-moral directives, one has to bear the consequences. This may be in this life or the next, depending upon the nature of the action. Third, the connotation of *karma* refers to a specific *ritual action* or *sacrifice (yajna)*. The latter actions are prescribed and enjoined on specific occasions.

Sacrifice is a central point in most religions. In fact, from Vedic times onwards a variety of sacrifices grew in India and a lot of interpretations were given to these sacrifices performed on prescribed modes. Eventually, the patterns of interpretations grew and developed. This is known as *karma or purva –*

mimamsa, which is one of the six systems of philosophy in India. Strict observance of ritual duties and caste regulations as a path to a happier life in an individual's next incarnation is enjoined upon the devotee. In other words, it is *salvation by works.* It is also known as *karma yoga.* Therefore, *Karma Marga* is popularly described as the *yoga of action.*

•   *Gita's nishkama karma (selfless action/service)*
It could be recalled in this context that *Bhagavad Gita* has further popularized and widened *karma* by attaching an *exalted ethical dimension to the human act* by adding the prefix *nish* ('without') to *kama* ('desire') *karma* ('action'). *Nishkama karma* may be rendered as *self-less action. Service* of another human person should not be motivated by any reward here in this world or the next. Such a *selfless service (nishkama karma),* however, assures *final liberation (mukti)* from the cycle of births and rebirths.

One may recall here the German Philosopher *Immanuel Kant's 'ethics of categorical imperative'.* 'An action is performed not because of fear or out of compulsion or expectation of reward but because in itself it is worth doing'. St Paul has *paraphrased* such actions in terms of *love* or *charity* (1 Cor 13,4-13).

(ii)   *Jñana marga (path of knowledge) in Hinduism*
The second *marga* in Hinduism is known as *Jñana marga* (the path of knowledge, the way of meditation or contemplation). Sankara, the great *bhashyakar* (commentator) of *Brahma sutra,* would interpret all life in terms of a journey to full awareness of one's identity with Brahman. For that discriminating knowledge between the temporal and the eternal (*niyanityavastuviveka*) is a requirement. It is supposed to be preceded by ethical-moral

aptitude to be able to focus on the supra-intellectual world of God who is pure Spirit.

Dissatisfied with the over-emphasis on the elaborate rituals in religion, dissenters began to seek alternate modes of achieving the goals of religion. Human life on earth was seen to be in a state of bondage. The cycle of birth-death-rebirth phenomenon began to appear counter to the longed-for peace and bliss consequent upon liberation. These experiences keep perpetually recurring. For life seemed subject to the many fluctuations that were seen as stemming from personal, communitarian and empirical miss-conceptions. Some of the sages of those days began to offer explanations and solutions too.

Thus, Uddalaka Aruni tells the truth-seeking young man: "Believe me, my dear, that which is the finest essence - this whole world has that as its soul. That is Reality. That is *Atman* (soul), *tat tvam asi* (That art thou), Svetaketu" (Ch. Up. 6.12.3).

Further explanations came. Life is in bondage because of ignorance of its essential oneness with Brahman. That ignorance is called *adhyasa,* (superimposition) which is responsible for the nescience experienced as bondage. Taking these reflections from the Upanishads, system builders in *Nyaya-Vaiseshika* constructed the *advaita siddhant* (philosophy of non-dual identity of God and soul) For them nescience is introduced as a key concept which consists in the *Jiva*'s (individual's) ignorance of oneness with the Supreme. The consciousness of one's true identity becomes central to this way of attaining liberation.

Besides, this *cyclic rhythm* appeared like a *mirage* or illusion. Only by penetrating the dense delusion or unreality can relief or truth be reached. And the truth is that, as expounded by

Sankaracharya, the classic expounder of the *advaitic* system, all these are *mithya* (transitory appearance of truth), the real truth is Brahman. Mental training employing meditation, etc. is required to penetrate the veil and attain the ultimate truth of Brahman. This is *mukti* or liberation.

It became increasingly clear that it is not ritual actions that will enable the seeker to come to the Supreme but by the removal of the *avaranas* (the veil). One is helped in this through correct knowledge, acquired through contemplative experience.

"By meditating on Him, by uniting with Him, by reflecting on His being, more and more, there is complete cessation from the illusion of the world" (Svet. Up.1, 1.). *Isopanishad* states: "With knowledge wins the immortal (*vidyaya amrtam apnute*)" (Is. Up. 1,1).

Sankara would propose the way of correct knowledge: *niyanityavastuviveka* (discriminating knowledge between the temporal and the eternal). The temporal needs are to be transcended to attain to the eternal.

Tanqueray S.J. in his book *The Spiritual Life* refers to the three phases of the spiritual journey, namely, the Purgative, the Illuminative and the Unitive way. Purification of the will is attained by repeated acts of self-control, disciplining the manifold negative tendencies, as has been described in Gal.5:19. It is almost a requirement for ridding the will and heart of all unruly desires. This is followed by the illuminative way in which one's love of God or Christ will be inflamed. Thirdly the unitive way where one's love of God is not for any other motive but God's own sake.

Hindu and Buddhist approach to spiritual liberation holds out the role of the purificatory phase. Bhagavad Gita in the first two chapters elaborately deals with the need for taming the *vasana*s (the expressions and drives of the five senses) to be free for divine communication treated in Chapter 11.

It is in this context that the Yoga tradition with the practice of yogic mediation was developed. The founder of the Yoga tradition is Patanjali. The starting point of the new spiritual school is one's experience of life as marked by *dukh/klesh* (sorrow, affliction). Patanjali developed his *astanga yoga* (yoga and the eight steps recommended for practice). According to Patanjali all life is marked by affliction or sorrow because the human person is unaware of what she/he truly is. Consequently, one experiences conflict arising out of attachment *(raga)* or hatred *(dwesh)* both of which would still cling on to such a life of incomplete identity.

To maintain true inner freedom, the practice of truth, detachment, etc. leading to disciplined meditation is recommended as steps helpful to attain true peace.

An encounter between the diverse traditions is underway. A deeper interaction can lead to their integration. A new phase in inter-cultural, inter-spiritual interactions augurs well for the different heritages.

(iii)   Bhakti marga (path of loving devotion) in Hinduism
Of the three *margas* developed by the ancients, probably the most popular and easy to practice has been the way of *loving devotion* to the Lord (*Bhagavan*). Visiting and paying homage to the Lord, singing *bhajans* or *kirtans* glorifying the graciousness of the Lord, are central to the spirituality of *bhakti*.

Derived from the root *bhaj* (to share, divide, participate, etc.) *bhakti* would imply *participation*. And in the religious usage *bhakti* came to mean 'faith in, love for, trustful surrender to' the Divinity. Louis Renou renders *bhakti* as "affective participation of the soul in the divine."[186]

The object of *bhakti* is the *Bhagavan* (the blissful One). All religions do testify that the Lord is the attraction of all human beings. A *Bhakta* is one who is therefore attached to the B*hagavan*. It is this aspect that had been exhibited with intellectual rigour by Neo-Hindu thinkers like Kesab Chandra Sen, Rabindranath Tagore etc. Bhakti affirms and even promotes theism.

The roots of *bhakti* are to be traced to the earliest phases of Hinduism. In the *Rig Veda* gods and goddesses are worshipped yet fondly beseeched for favours, protection, progeny, good crops, etc. There is a healthy fear of the gods' wrath. A true worshipper feels confident in the benevolence of God. One places one's faith and trust in God whom one profusely praises and confidently invokes in all one's needs. Through such gestures and expressions, the sage demonstrates that these are parts of *bhakti* in the Rigveda.

For example, *Agni* is 'beloved guest of men's home," "Father, brother, son, friend" (RV. 10.7.3). God Indra is "the most fatherly God," who is "like a mother, my friend". He is men's "helper, saviour, protector, guide." Pleased by worship "he dwells in the home "like a comfortably establishing guest…like a blameless wife beloved by her husband" (1.73.1-3). Again, *Indra* "is better than a father or a mother". "Be our saviour, thou who art recognized as our relation, who looks upon us and pities us, as a friend, a father, most fatherly of fathers" (4.17.17), is the prayer.

Rigvedic piety is best illustrated by the Varuna hymns. Varuna is the guardian of the Law, all-wise and all-knowing. Sin destroys that deep bond and "ancient friendship" between himself and the god (7.86.3-4; 88.5-6). He longs for reconciliation and reunion. Heaven is to be with Varuna.

In the Upanishads a new form of worship emerges, *upasana*, respectful pursuit of and worshipful meditation on the reality that is Brahman-Atman. *Bhakti* and *upasana* will be intimately linked. Ardent longing for the knowledge of the Brahman-Atman and life eternal is expressed here.

In conclusion it can be stated that, through *Svetasvatara Upanishad*, its teaching will become manifest only "to him who has the highest devotion (*bhakti*) for God and *guru* (6,23).

In the Vaishnava tradition, this grew further. Books like *Bhagavatha*, *Bhagavad Gita* and similar other religious books contributed to the growth of *Bhakti* spirituality.

b)   Jesus Christ's Prem marga in the Gospels
The three *margas (karma marga, jñana marga and bhakti marga)* are *implied* in Jesus Christ's Prem marga (path of love).

(i)   Jesus Christ's Karma marga
Submitting to the prescribed religious observances had been part of *Jesus Christ's manner of organizing his life*. In the infancy narratives, the parents of Jesus initiated the infant Jesus into these customary performances and rituals. We also find that as an adult, Jesus is seen as a participant in the customary practices

in and around the Temple. Indeed, his statement: "Do not think that I have come to abolish the law and the prophets; I have come not to abolish them but to fulfil them" (Mt 5,17) suggests that he *accepts the religious practices* of the Jewish community but *reinterprets* them in *a new and perfect way*, by fulfilling them according to *God's purpose* of promoting the holistic welfare of human beings (cf. Mt 5,20-48; 6,1-4).

After washing the disciples' feet (Jn 13,3-11), Jesus explains to them the meaning of his action and asks them to *wash one another's feet* (13,12-16) and he concludes by telling them: "If you know these things, blessed are you if you *do* them" (13.17). Washing one another's feet is a *selfless act of loving service*. Such *loving deeds for others* (especially the hungry and the thirsty, the sick and the strangers, the naked and the prisoners) qualify them to "*inherit the kingdom*" *of God*, final salvation (Mt 25,34). This is Jesus Christ's version of *Nishkama Karma*.

(ii)   *Jesus Christ's Jñana marga*

Water in a well in a desert land brought together two thirsty persons: one was Jesus, the Jew. The second was a *woman,* most probably of disrepute, hailing from Samaria, a region which the Jews scrupulously avoided in order not to have any interaction with the mixed-race Samaritans. Jesus asks her for a drink of water, which shocks her (because he seems to be breaking a social taboo). Then their conversation takes a plunge into matters spiritual. "If you *knew* the gift of God, and who it is saying to you, 'Give me a drink,' you would have asked him, and he would have given you *living water*" (Jn 4,10). Jesus points here to the depth of *spiritual knowledge* about the *Holy Spirit* (cf. Jn 7,37-39).

In Matthew's Gospel Jesus declares: "All things have been delivered to me by my Father, and no one *knows the Son* except *the Father* and no one *knows the Father* except *the Son* and anyone to whom the Son chooses to reveal him" (Mt 11,27).

One of the important aspects of *Jesus' mission* is *to make the Father known* ("No one has ever seen God; *a unique God/Son* [*monogenês theos/hyios*] who is in the bosom of the Father *has made him known*": Jn 1,18). Towards the end of "Jesus' farewell discourse" to his disciples, he describes *eternal life* in terms of *knowing God and Jesus Christ*: "Eternal life is to know you, the only true God, and Jesus Christ whom you have sent" (Jn 17,3).[187]

And looking back at *his revelatory mission*, Jesus tells the Father in prayer: "I have *manifested your name* ['Father'] to the men whom you gave me... Now they *know* that all things which you have given me are from you; for I have given them the *words* which you gave me and they have received them and *know in truth* that *I came from you*, and they have believed that *you did send me*" (17,6-8; cf. also 17,25-26). Jesus has communicated his *experiential knowledge* (*ginôskein*) of God the Father to his disciples and they have started walking on *Jesus' path of knowledge* (*jñana marga*).

Using the parabolic allegory of the *good shepherd and the sheep*, Jesus says: "I am the good shepherd; I know my own and my own know me, as the Father knows me and I know the Father" (Jn 10,14-15). The *mutual knowledge* of Jesus and his disciples is not only *similar* to but also a *participation* in the *mutual knowledge* of the Father and Jesus. This mutual knowledge is a *loving knowledge* like that of *friends*: "I have called you friends, for all that I have heard from my Father I have *made known to you*" (15,15).

Jesus tells the disciples: "I am *the path* (*marga*), the truth and the life; no one comes to the Father except through me" (14,6). Jesus, (the Son), is like the *mountain path* which enables those who follow the path (Jesus) to have an *experiential knowledge* of the mountain (the Father). By revealing himself to the disciples, he manifests the Father to them and so, by knowing Jesus, they know the Father also (14,7.9). It is an *intimate knowledge* of the *mutual immanence of Jesus and the Father* ("I am in the Father and the Father in me": 14,10-11*)*. In short, *Jesus* (the Son) is the *filial path to God* (the Father).

Just as *jñana marga* in Hinduism leads to *liberation* (*mukti*), so Jesus tells the disciples: "If you remain in my word, you are truly my disciples, and *you will know the truth* and *the truth will make you free*" (Jn 8,31-32). However, there is a *difference* between *Hindu jñana marga* and *Jesus' jñana marga. Jñana* according to *Jesus* is an *intimate knowledge of God* but *jñana* in Hinduism is an *identification* of the *individual self* with the *Ultimate Self: Aham Brahmasmi* ("I am Brahman") and *tat tvam asi* ("That thou art"). Jesus never says: "I am the Father" but only "*I and the Father are one*" (Jn 10,30), which indicates an *intimate union* but not identification.

Jesus, the *divine Word, empowers* the believers "*to become children of God*" by being "*born from God*" (Jn 1,12-13), but *not to become God.* Jesus Christ, the "*divinehuman being*" (Jn 1,14: the 'divine' who has become 'human' without ceasing to be 'divine') enables believing men and women to become "*humandivine beings*" (1,12-13: the 'human' to become 'divine' without ceasing to be 'human').[188]

(iii)   Jesus Christ's Bhakti marga

Jesus promises his *loving disciples* that there would be a *gradual loving manifestation of himself and the Father*: "he who loves me will be loved by my Father, and I will love him and manifest myself to him… If anyone loves me, he will keep my word, and my Father will love him, and *we will come* to him and *make our home* with him" (Jn 14,21.23).[189]

This *loving devotion to Jesus* is manifested by *Martha* and *Mary of Bethany* who welcome him in their home; while Martha serves him, Mary sits at his feet and listens to his words like a devout disciple (Lk 10,38-39). On another occasion (six days before the Passover) Jesus goes to Bethany and, while Martha prepares and serves supper, Mary anoints his feet with precious ointment and wipes them with her hair (Jn 12,3), which are signs of her generous love and affectionate devotion.

Mary Magdalene is another *devoted disciple* (*bhakta*) of Jesus, since she not only *stands under his cross* with his mother (Jn 19,25) but also comes to his tomb on Easter Sunday even before dawn (20,1) and, seeing it empty, she runs to inform Peter and the Beloved Disciple about it (20,2), and she keeps on standing outside the tomb weeping till the risen Jesus appears to her (20,12-18). These actions reveal *her affectionate love and faithful devotion* (*bhakti*) to Jesus Christ. Even death cannot separate her from her "*Teacher*" and "*Lord*" (20,16.18).

(iv)   Jesus Christ's Prem marga (path of love) (Jn 13,34-35; 15,9-10.12-17)

Jesus' path of love *(Prem marga) integrates* all the other three paths (*karma, jñana, bhakti*) since it involves *action* (selfless service), experiential *knowledge* and loving *devotion*. During the "Farewell Discourse" Jesus gives his disciples a *new commandment of love*: "A new commandment I give you, that you love one another as (*kathôs*) I have loved you so that you too may love one another" (13,34; 15,12). Whereas the *old* commandment of love was: "Love your neighbour *as yourself*" (Lev 19,18.34), Jesus' *new* commandment to his disciples is *new* because they are to love each other *as Jesus has loved them* (*kathôs* means not only *like* but also *because*). That is to say, *Jesus' love* for them is the *criterion* of judging the quality of their mutual love for one another. Now Jesus' love for them is an unconditional, enduring, forgiving, faithful, generous, selfless, self-giving, self-sacrificing love (*agapê*) (Jn 13,1: "having *loved his own* who were in the world, he [Jesus] *loved them to the end*"). *Jesus' love for his own* (his disciples) is *patterned* and *based* on the *Father's love for Jesus*: "As (*kathôs*) the Father has loved me, so have I loved you" (Jn 15,9). The Father's love for the Son has been repeatedly highlighted in the Gospel (cf. Jn 3,35; 5,20; 10,17; 17,23.26). God the Father's love ("God is love": 1 Jn 4,8) is experienced by the Son, and is, in turn, revealed through *Jesus' love for the disciples*: "Greater love has no one than this, that one *lays down one's life for one's friends*" (15,13). In short, Jesus' love for his disciples is limitless and unconditional and he commands them to continue loving one another in the same way. *Christlike mutual love* is *the only criterion* by which Christ's disciples are to be known (13,35: "By this all will know that you are my disciples, if you have love for one another"). This is *Jesus' Prem marga* (*path of love*).

Jesus' Prem marga may also be called "*The Dharma of Jesus*"[190] or *Khrist-Dharma* (religion of *Christlike* love). Jesus Christ *invites* followers of all religions (Hindus, Muslims, Sikhs, etc.)

to walk with him and his disciples on *the path of love (Prem marga)* which will lead all pilgrims to *God who is love.* During their life-pilgrimage, all have to learn to love one another and make progress on the path of Christlike love (Jn 13,34-35). *Love (agapê)* is the *only key* that *opens the door of salvation* at the end of the pilgrimage. To enter into ultimate union with the God of love (*agapê*), all have to become God's loving children and grow in the generous, selfless, self-giving, self-sacrificing love (*agapê*). *Jesus' Prem marga* ("path of love") leads us to the *loving heart of God* to enjoy the *eternal intimacy* with the infinite and ultimate Love (God).

4.1.© *Conclusion*

Globalizing is taking place in more areas than what is now imagined. A new perception, a new way of seeing with 'divine eyes', is what is taking place. Pope Francis' recent encyclical ('*Laudato Si'*) is an invitation to open our eyes more widely to see and appreciate the truth of the cosmos. Arjuna is given a new perception by Krishna in the Gita, as the three disciples were granted the vision of the transfiguration of Jesus Christ on Mount Tabor. The joy of being at the dawn of a new culture is mind-blowing and heart-warming. What we have seen above is the widening of the human perception of truth. The beautiful richness of convergence and divergence, of diversity and unity, is brought home by our brief journey above. *Avatara*-incarnation, the role of the flame of fire, of love and sacrifice, the holy rivers where millions come and experience something celestial by ridding themselves of the negative in their life, the Baptist's preaching for the conversion of heart and the voice from above ("You are my beloved Son") have all been high points of the pilgrimage. The three *margas* converge on the *Prem marga* of

Jesus Christ, which seems to be the culmination of our (Hindu-Christian) dialogical endeavour.[191]

4.2. The Good News of Jesus Christ for Muslims: Jesus of the Qur'an and of the Gospels (Muslim-Christian Dialogical Christology)

4.2.0. Introduction

A frank and fraternal *dialogue* between *Indian Christians and Muslims* on *Jesus* of the *Quran* and of the *Gospels* is the *focus* of this subsection. We try to recognise the *common threads* as well as the important *differences* in the Gospel and Quranic presentations of Jesus.

Jesus Christ is dealt with very extensively from the beginning to the end of the Gospels and the Quran mentions Jesus many times and speaks very highly of him with great reverence (e.g., as the prophet, Messiah, etc.), even though he is not recognized as "the Son of God." Because of this, unfortunately, there has been much polemics between the Christians and the Muslims in the past. In the words of Dr. Chris Hewer:

> The days of polemics are over. Polemics destroy three things: the people being spoken about, the people doing the speaking and the relationship between them. The way forward now must be through understanding one another both in the head and in the heart. I call this empathetic understanding.[192]

It is in the spirit of *"empathetic" inter-religious dialogue* between *Indian Muslims and Christians* that we would like to look at *"Jesus of the Qur'an and of the Gospels."*[193]

"Back to the Gospels" has been the guiding principle of this book. Following this approach and extending it to *"Back to the Qur'an,"* we would like to briefly *examine* and *compare*

the *Qur'anic understanding of Jesus* with the *Gospel revelation of Jesus Christ* with open minds and hearts in the spirit of a fresh, fraternal and fruitful dialogue between Indian Muslims and Christians today.[194] This is the right approach to start an *interfaith dialogue* since *faith* in *the word of God* revealed in the Qur'an and the *Gospels* are the *foundations* of the *Muslim faith* and the *Christian faith* respectively. "Dialogue requires only two things from each dialogue partner: to *respect each other*, and to *listen to each other*."[195] We are convinced that this is one of the "paths for mutual learning and mutual enrichment."[196]

Jesus Christ is the *central figure* of *all the four Gospels*. Even though there are 'four Gospels' (according to Matthew, Mark, Luke and John), there is only *one Gospel* (*euangelion:* "Good News", "Glad Tidings"), namely, "*the Gospel of Jesus Christ*" (Mk 1,1). The *four Gospels* are like *four portraits* of Jesus Christ.[197] They *paint four pictures* of *Jesus Christ* from *various faith angles*, as it were, to highlight his relevance to different Christian communities in their concrete contexts in the first century (65-100 CE). They *complement one another* and help us to have an *integral faith understanding of Jesus Christ* (*his person* and *his mission*).

Jesus is mentioned in *93 verses* in the *Qur'an*.[198] It contains *many positive aspects of Jesus*: e.g., the *annunciation of his conception and his birth* (3:45-47; 19:22-23), Jesus as *a messenger* to Israel (3:49), *sent* with the *Gospel* (3:48; 5:46) and power to do *miracles* (3:49-50), a *servant of God* and *righteous prophet* (6:85; 19:30-33), his *prayer* for a table of viands (5:114), *raised up to God* (3:55-58; 4:158; 19:33).

"The Qur'an gives a greater *number of honourable titles to Jesus* than to any other figure of the past."[199] The most *important titles of Jesus* are the following: "*Son of Mary*" (*Ibn Maryam*), "*Servant*" (*'abd*) of God, "*Prophet*" (*nabi*) of God, "*Messenger*" (*rasul*) from God, "*Word*" (*kalima*) from God, and "*Spirit* (*ruh*) of God" and "*the Messiah*" (*Al-Masih*).[200]

The Qur'an and the Gospels agree on many *aspects and titles of Jesus*, but there are some others on which they do *not agree*. We shall *examine: 1)* the *positive statements (common threads)*, and *2)* the *differences* in a spirit of mutual, respectful, attentive *listening* to one another and of *fraternal inter-faith dialogue* (without entering into any polemical or disagreeable argument).

4.2.1. *Positive statements about Jesus in the Qur'an and their parallels in the Gospels*

Both the Qur'an and the Gospels *agree* on the *fact* of the *annunciation and birth of Jesus* from the *virgin Mary*.

a)   The annunciation and birth of Jesus in the Qur'an and the Gospels

The *Qur'an* and the *Gospels* give *two accounts each* of *the annunciation and birth of Jesus*, which are given below (in *parallel columns*) for easy reference:

1) Qur'an **19:17-21** (tr. A. Yusuf Ali)	*1) Luke* **1,26-38** (RSV) *[(a) Annunciation]*
17 We sent to her [*Mary*] Our *angel*, and she appeared before her as a man in all respects. 18 She said: "I seek refuge from you to (Allah) Most Gracious: (come not near) if you do fear Allah." 19 He said: "Nay, I am only a messenger from your Lord, (to announce) to you the *gift of a holy son*." 20 She said: "*How can I have a son, seeing that no man has touched me*, and I am not unchaste?"	26 In the sixth month, the *angel Gabriel* was sent *from God* to a city of Galilee named Nazareth, 27 to a *virgin* betrothed to a man whose name was *Joseph…*; and the *virgin's name* was *Mary*. 28 And he came to her and said, "*Hail, O favoured one, the Lord is with you!*" 29 But she was *greatly troubled* at the saying… 30 And the *angel* said to her, "*Do not be afraid, Mary*, for you have *found favour with God*. 31 And *behold*, you will *conceive in your womb and bear a son*, and *you shall call his name Jesus*. 32 He will be great, and will be *called Son of the Most High*; and the Lord God will give him the *throne of his father David*, 33 and he will *reign* over the house of Jacob *forever*, and of *his kingdom* there will be *no end*."
21 He said: '*So (it will be)*: your Lord says, '*That is easy for Me*: and We wish to appoint him as a *Sign* unto men and a *Mercy* from Us': *it is a matter* (so) *decreed*."	34 And *Mary* said to the angel, "*How shall this be* since *I do not know a man?*"

	35 And the *angel* said to her, "*The Holy Spirit will come upon you*, and the *power of the Most High will overshadow you*; and therefore *the holy one to be born* will be *called Son of God*. 36 And behold, your kinswoman *Elizabeth in her old age* has also *conceived a son*... 37 For *with God nothing* will be *impossible*. 38 And *Mary* said, "*Behold, the handmaid of the Lord; let it be to me according to your word.*"
Qur'an 19:22-26 (tr. A. Yusuf Ali)	**Luke 2,1-7** (RSV) *[(b) Birth of Jesus]*
22 So she *conceived* him, and she retired with him to a remote place. 23 The *pains of childbirth* drove her to the trunk of a palm tree: she cried (in her anguish): "Ah! Would that I had died before this! Would that I had been a thing forgotten and out of sight!" 24 But (a voice) cried to her from beneath the (palm-tree): "Grieve not! For *your Lord has provided a rivulet beneath you*. 25 And shake towards yourself the trunk of the *palm tree*: it will let fall *fresh ripe dates* upon you. 26 So eat and drink and cool (thine) eye..."	1 In those days a decree went out from Caesar Augustus that all the world should be enrolled. 2 This was the first enrollment when Quirinius was governor of Syria. 3 And all went to be enrolled, each to his own city. 4 And *Joseph* also *went up* from Galilee, from the *city of Nazareth*, to Judea, to the *city of David*, which is called *Bethlehem*, because he was of the house and lineage of David, 5 to be enrolled with *Mary, his betrothed, who was with child*. 6 And while they were there, *the time came for her to be delivered*. 7 And she *gave birth* to *her first-born son* and wrapped him in *swaddling clothes*, and laid him in a *manger*, because there was *no place* for them *in the guest-room* (katalyma: cf. 22,11).[201]

2) *Qur'an* 3:42-47 (tr. A. Yusuf Ali)	**Matthew 1,18-25** (RSV) *[Annunciation &Birth of Jesus]*
42 Behold! The angels said: "O Mary! Allah has chosen you and purified you – chosen you above the women of all nations...." 45 Behold! The *angels* said: "*O Mary*! Allah gives you glad tidings of *a Word from Him*: his *name* will be *Christ Jesus, the son of Mary*, held in honour in this world and the Hereafter and one of (the company of) those *nearest to Allah*. 46 He shall speak to the people in childhood and in maturity. And he shall be (of the company) of the *righteous*." 47 She said: "O my Lord! *How shall I have a son when no man has touched me?*" He said: "Even so: *Allah creates what He wills*: when He has decreed a plan, He only says to it, 'Be,' and *it is!*	18 Now the *birth of Jesus Christ* took place in this way. When his *mother Mary* had been betrothed to Joseph, before they came together she was found to be with *child from the Holy Spirit*; 19 and her husband Joseph, being a just man and unwilling to put her to shame, resolved to divorce her quietly. 20 But as he considered this, behold, an *angel of the Lord* appeared to him in a dream, saying, "Joseph, son of David, do not fear to take Mary your wife, for that which is *conceived in her* is *from the Holy Spirit*; 21 *she will bear a son*, and you shall *call his name Jesus*, for he will *save* his people from their sins." 22 All this took place to fulfil what the Lord had spoken by the prophet: 23 "Behold, *a virgin shall conceive and bear a son*, and *his name* shall be *Emmanuel*" (which means, *God with us*). 24 When Joseph woke from sleep, he did as the *angel of the Lord* commanded him; he took his wife, 25 but *knew her not* until she had *borne a son*; and he *called his name Jesus*.

All the narratives of the annunciation/birth agree that *Mary* would *conceive, not* through *intercourse* with her husband but the *miraculous intervention of God/Holy Spirit*. This announcement was made by an *angel of God/Lord* to Mary (Lk 1,35) and Joseph (Mt 1,18.20). The explicit question of Mary in the Qur'an ("*how shall I have a son*, when no man has touched me?" 3:47) and in the Gospel ("*How shall this be*, since I do not know man/husband?": Lk 1,34) and the implicit question by Joseph in the Gospel (*how* his "*betrothed*" could be "*with child*"? Mt 1,18-19) are answered by the angel's reference to the *creative action of God/Holy Spirit* (Q 3:47; Lk 1,35; Mt 1,20-23). The final angelic reply to Mary's question is: "For *with God nothing will be impossible*" (Lk 1,37; cf. Q 3:47: "*Allah creates what He wills*: when He has decreed a plan, He only says to it, '*Be*,' and *it is!*").

Both the Qur'an (3:45) and the Gospels (Lk 1,31; Mt 1,21) *agree* that the *name* of the *child* will be "*'Isa/Jesus.*" But whereas the Qur'an gives the full name as "*the Messiah, Jesus, son of Mary*" (3:45),[202] the Gospel gives the God-given name as "*Jesus, Son of God*" (Lk 1,35).

The *angel from the Lord* in the Qur'an *announced* to Mary God's "*gift of a holy son*" (Q 19:19). Now, what does a "*holy son*" mean in the Qur'an? According to the Muslim understanding, "*holy son*" refers to *Jesus' sinless status* because God protected him from all sins.[203] In the Gospel, the explanation given to Mary by angel Gabriel is: "*The Holy Spirit* will come upon you, and the *power of the Most High* will overshadow you; and therefore *the holy one to be born* will be called *Son of God*" (Lk 1,35).

The *Qur'an* presents Jesus as a *creature* (a human being created by God: cf. 3:48) but the *Gospel believes him* to be *a divinehuman being* ("child conceived from the Holy Spirit": cf. Mt 1,18.20). Again, whereas Qur'an identifies "Jesus" with "son of Mary" (3:45), the name "*Jesus*" in the Gospel refers to his being the *Saviour* ("for he will *save* his people from their *sins*": Mt 1,21), which is also related to his being "*Emmanuel*" ("*God with us*": 1,23). Hence the name of "*Jesus*" in the Gospel *points* to his *humanity* ("son of Mary") and his *divinity* ("Son of God").

b)   Jesus, the Messiah (Al-Masih)[204]

The title "*the Messiah*" (*Al-Masih*) is given to Jesus *eleven* times in the Qur'an (3:45; 4:157.171.172; 5:17.17.72.72.75; 9:30.31). As we have seen above, "the Messiah" is used as part of Jesus' full name: "the Messiah, Jesus, son of Mary" (3:45). At times the title alone is used to refer to Jesus: "*the Messiah* said, 'O Children of Israel! Worship Allah, my Lord and your Lord'" (5:72). Sometimes Jesus, *the Messiah*, is mentioned as "*only a messenger of God*" (4:171; 5:75), which implies in the context that he is *not* "*God*".[205]

Even though the etymological meaning of the title *Masih* is not given anywhere in the Qur'an, it is related to the Hebrew *Mashiah* (which means the "*anointed one*"). Although the "*anointing*" of Jesus as the *Messiah* is *not* explicitly mentioned in the Qur'an, God says: "To Jesus, son of Mary We gave clear (Signs), and *strengthened him with the holy spirit*" (2:253) and "O Jesus the son of Mary! Remember *My favour to you* and *your mother*. Behold! I *strengthened you with the holy spirit…*" (5:110). The "*signs*" (*miracles*) that Jesus does (like making a *living bird* out of clay, *healing the leper and the blind*, and *raising the dead to life*: 3:49) *manifest Jesus* to be *God's Messiah*. Jesus, the Messiah, has been enabled to do all these miracles because he has been "*strengthened with the holy spirit*" (2:253; 5:110), which may be an allusion to the *anointing of Jesus* with the *Holy Spirit* at the time of his *baptism* in the Jordan (cf. Mk 1,10; Mt 3,16; Lk 3,21-22; Jn 1,32-33).

The Gospels refer to Jesus as "*Messiah/Christ*" (*Christos*, "the anointed one") *fifty-five* times (Mk 7x; Mt 17x; Lk 12x; Jn 19x). Sometimes "*Christ*" is used as an integral *part* of *Jesus' full name* ("*Jesus Christ*": Mk 1,1; Mt 1,1.18; Jn 1,17; 17,3).

The many *miracles* narrated in the Gospels (and a few in the Qur'an) reveal *Jesus* as *the Messiah/Christ* (Mk 1,40-45; 8,22-29; Mt 11,2-5; Lk 4,38-41; Jn 11,43-44; 20,30-31; etc.).[206] Even though many acknowledge him as the *Messiah/Christ* in the Gospels (e.g. Mk 8,29; Mt 16,16; Lk 9,20; Jn 1,41; 7,31.41; 11,27; 20,31), Jesus himself does *not* say: "I am the Messiah" (except once in Jn 4,25-26).

> This silence does not mean that he did not believe himself to be the Messiah… His unwillingness to use the title must mean that he repudiated the then-current nationalistic expectations associated with it, feeling the need for a name more suited to express the nature of his mission for men. Perhaps Jesus preferred the more enigmatic title Son of Man.[207]

c)   *Jesus, God's servant ('abd)*

The Qur'an presents Jesus the Messiah as a willing "*servant* (*'abd*) of God*: "*Christ* disdains not to *serve* and worship Allah" (4:172). Jesus himself says: "*I am indeed a servant of Allah*" (19:30). *Jesus' portrayal of himself* as "*God's servant*" in the Qur'an is like his declaration about the purpose of his 'coming' (mission) in the Gospels: "The Son of Man *has come not to be served* but *to serve …*" (Mk 10,45; Mt 20,25; cf. also *his washing his disciples feet*: Jn 13,2-17). Jesus' understanding of himself as *God's servant* in the Qur'an and the Gospels is similar to his mother Mary's description of herself in the Gospel as "*the Lord's handmaid* (cf. Lk 1,38).

"It is said that the title *'abd* shows the *humanity of Jesus* as a *servant*... The Arabic *'abd* is related to the Hebrew *'ebed*."[208] *Jesus, "servant of God," in the Qur'an (4:172; 19:30) may be compared to the figure of the Hebrew 'ebed Yahweh ("Servant of Yahweh/God") in Isaiah (42,1: "Behold my servant, whom I uphold, my chosen, in whom my soul delights; I have put my Spirit upon him"). God's conferring his Spirit upon his Servant* in Is 42,1 is echoed in God's *"strengthening him* [Jesus] *with the holy Spirit"* in Qur'an 2:253 (cf. 5:110). In the synagogue at Nazareth, Jesus reads prophet Isaiah 61,1-2 (*"The Spirit of the Lord* is upon me because he *has anointed me* to preach the good news to the poor. He has sent me to proclaim release to the captives and recovery of sight to the blind, to set at liberty the oppressed, to proclaim the acceptable year of the Lord": Lk 4,18-19) and applies it to himself: "Today this scripture has been fulfilled in your hearing" (Lk 4,21).

d)   Jesus, God's prophet (nabi) with the Gospel (Injil)
Qur'an acknowledges *Jesus* as a *righteous prophet* (6:85). There have been *many prophets* (from Adam/Abraham to Mohammad). *Every prophet* is *given a message from God* to be faithfully communicated *to the people*. So what is *Jesus' message* and where do we find it? Only part of it is found in the Qur'an, especially in the context of some '*disputed things*' which *Jesus* in his *wisdom* was expected to settle: "When Jesus came with clear signs, he said, 'Now I have come to you with *wisdom*, to *make clear* to you some of the things [points] about which *you dispute*: therefore, fear God and obey me'" (Q 43:63).[209]

Jesus admits that, even though he considers himself a servant, God has made him "*a prophet*" *(nabi)* with *the Book* (Q 19:30) and *the Gospel (Injil)* (5:46), and *instructed* in it *by God* (3:48;

5:47; 5:110). "*The Gospel (Injil)*", "the Good News," which Jesus preached and practised, lived and died for, is contained in the *four Gospels.*

> The Gospels then truly contain the word of God to men, given by Christ who is the 'Word from God himself' (Q 3:45), to whom God gave the Gospel. The Gospel still contains 'guidance and light', and it both confirms the Torah and gives 'admonition to those who show piety' (5:46). The revelation given to Muhammad and Muslims came to 'confirm the Book which was before it' and 'to act as a protector over it' (5:48).[210]

Jesus is mentioned as *a prophet* many times in the Gospels (e.g., Mk 6,15; 8,28; Mt 21,11; Lk 7,16; 9,19; 24,19; Jn 4,19; 6,14; 7,40; 9,17). "*The Gospel of Jesus Christ*" (*to euangelion Iêsou Christou:* Mk 1,1) is proclaimed by him as "*the Gospel of God*" (*to euangelion tou theou:* "*the good news of God*": Mk 1,14). Sometimes it is described as "*the Gospel of the Kingdom*" preached by Jesus (Mt 4,23; 9,35) or later by his disciples (Mt 24,14; 26,13). Often "*the Gospel*" (*to euangelion*) is used absolutely (without any qualifier) (Mk 1,15; 8,35; 10,29; 13,10; 14,9; 16,15). '*The Gospel (of God/Jesus Christ/Kingdom)*' is found in the *four Gospels* (Mk, Mt, Lk and Jn).[211]

4.2.2. Issues about Jesus on which the Qur'an and the Gospels do not agree

a)   Jesus, "Son of God"

The *most sensitive issue* in the Muslim-Christian dialogue about *Jesus* has been his *divinity* ("*the Son of God*") which *Qur'an* denies: "The *Jews* call *Uzayr (Ezra) a son of Allah,* and the *Christians* call *Christ the son of Allah*" (9:30). But these are said to be *baseless* and *untrue utterances* (9:30).

When Allah asks: "O *Jesus* the *son of Mary*! Did you say unto men, '*Worship me and my mother as gods in derogation of Allah?*' Jesus' answer is: 'Glory to You! *Never could I say what I had no right* (to say). Had I said such a thing, You would indeed have known it. You know what is in my heart, though I know not what is in Yours. You know in full all that is hidden' (5:116). Here Jesus *denies* that *he and his mother* are "*two deities besides God*".[212]

Again Sura 4:171 addresses the Christians: "O People of the Book! Commit no excesses in your religion: nor say of Allah aught but the truth. Christ Jesus the son of Mary was a Messenger of *Allah* and His Word...: so believe in *Allah* and His Messengers. Say not "Three"[213] ... for Allah is one *Allah*" (4:171).[214] No Gospel says that there are "three" gods. Jesus prays to "the only true God" (Jn 17,3). Jesus is dependent on God and he always does God's will for he says: "I seek not my own will but the will of Him who sent me" (Jn 5,30). Just as Muhammad and Muslims address God in prayer "*Allah*," Jesus and his disciples (Christians) pray to God "*Abba*, Father" (Mk 14,36) pleading for help *to do his (God's) will* ("not what I will, but what *you will*" (14,36). Hence Jesus, *the Son of God*, is truly '*one who submits to the will of God*' in life and death and has taught his disciples to pray to God: "*Your will be done on earth* as it is in heaven" (Mt 6,10). I am sure this will find an echo in every Muslim heart! A heart-to-heart sharing and listening by both the dialogue-partners can lead them to a deeper understanding of the faith of one another even on a *sensitive 'apparently irreconcilable' matter of faith.*

At the end of the Meccan narrative of the birth of Jesus from Virgin Mary through God's decree, the child *Jesus* says that he is *God's servant* and *prophet* whom God has blessed (Q 19:30-33). Then the Sura continues in verses 34-35: "Such (was) *Jesus the son of Mary*: (it is) a statement of *truth*, about which they (vainly) *dispute*. It is *not befitting to* (the majesty of) *Allah* that He should *beget a son*." Here the *dispute* among the people seems to be about the way *Jesus was 'begotten'* but the Qur'an *denies* that *Allah ever 'begets a son'* because it is 'a physical act' by which one *'becomes the father of a child' through sexual intercourse* (like the pagan gods who produced sons through sexual union with women), which would be 'derogatory' to Allah.[215]

It must be noted that the usual English translation of Jn 3,16.18 ("*ho monogenês hyios tou theou*" cf. also 1,14.18; 1 Jn 4,9) as "the only *begotten son* of God" may be misunderstood by ordinary readers as though God has *'begotten'* him *sexually*, which would be offensive to the Muslims! A better translation of the Greek expression *monogenês hyios* (*monos* + *genesthai hyios)* in the Gospel of John would be a "*unique son*" ("one of its kind"), which does not have any sexual 'begetting' connotation.

Qur'an affirms the absolute *unity (oneness) of God* in Sura 112:1: "Say, '*He is Allah, the One* and Only, 2 *Allah*, the Eternal, Absolute [*Samad*].[216] 3 He *begets not, nor is* He *begotten*; 4 and there is *none like unto Him*." From this, it is quite clear that there is *only one God* and *no plurality of gods*.

It is a denial of God producing offspring in the manner of human beings, and of God having any associates. It stresses the Unity of God and his difference from men. Since it is generally regarded as one of the earliest Meccan suras, it would mean that it was directed against the many gods of pagan Arabia, though later writers turned it also against the Christian doctrine.[217]

The title "*the Son of God*" occurs *29 times* in the Gospels (Mt 9x, Mk 4x, Lk 6x, Jn 10x)[218]. In the Synoptic Gospels Jesus never speaks of himself directly as "the Son of God" (and only rarely as "the Son"), even though the demons, disciples and others (like the high priest and the crowd) use the title "Son of God" for him. Jesus prefers to refer to himself as "the Son of Man".

God declares explicitly in the Qur'an: "We [God] sent Jesus the son of Mary, confirming the Law that had come before him; We *gave* him *the Gospel:* therein was *guidance and light,* and confirmation of the Law that had come before him: a *guidance and admonition* to those who fear Allah" (5:46). That is to say, *what is revealed in the God-given Gospel* is *true* and all ("God-fearing") people are expected to believe in it. God Himself instructs Muslims *how to resolve any doubt* about *what has been revealed* in the *Qur'an* and the *Gospel: "If you are in any doubt* concerning what We have sent down to you, then question those who have read the Book before you: the *Truth* has come to you *from your Lord,* so do not be one of the doubters" (M. W. Khan's translation of Q 10:94).[219] God tells Muslims how to *dialogue* with '*the People of the Book*' on any *disputed issue*: "Say, "*We believe* in *what has been revealed to us,* and *what has been revealed to you; our God and your God are one; to Him, we submit*'" (Q 29:46; cf. also 2:136). Since *God's Gospel* reveals that *Jesus* is "*the Son of God*" (Mk 1,1; 9,7; Mt 3,17; 17,5; Lk 1,35; 9,35; Jn 10,36; 20,31), all believers in God are expected to accept it as *true*.

However, *Jesus* being "*Son of God*" does *not* mean that he is 'another' God. This is made clear in the Gospel of John. When the Jews accuse Jesus of "making himself *equal* with God" (Jn 5,18), he tells them that he ("the Son") is *dependent* on God (cf. Jn 5,19-30), and therefore he is *not* claiming to be '*a second God*'. Similarly, Jesus did *not* ever say, "I am God" or "I am God the Father" but only "I and the Father are one" (Jn 10,30). When the Jews pick up stones to stone him to death "for blasphemy, because you being a man, make yourself God" (Jn 10,33), Jesus defends himself by showing that the *works of God that he does reveal* that he is "*Son of God*" and "that *the Father is in me and I am in the Father*" (Jn 10,34-38), that is, there is *mutual communion* between Jesus and the Father.

There is a *unique relationship* between Jesus and the Father. On the one hand, Jesus humbly *confesses his ignorance* of the '*day or hour*' of *the parousia* (Mk 13,32) and acknowledges *his total dependence on the Father*: "I can do nothing on my own authority" (Jn 5,30). He tells his disciples openly that "the Father is *greater* than I" (14,28) and he prays to the Father with gratitude in his heart: "*All things* that *you have given me* are *from you*" (17,7). He confesses that even *the disciples* are the *Father's gift* to him: "they were *yours* and you have *given them to me*" (17,6). Even the (eternal) "*life*" of Jesus is a *gratuitous gift* of the Father to him (5,26). On the other hand, Jesus teaches *with authority* (Mk 1,22; Lk 4,31-32). He *casts out demons* with a command (Lk 4,33-36) and *calms the stormy sea* (Mk 4,39). *Authoritatively he reinterprets the Mosaic Law* (about anger, adultery, divorce, oaths, retaliation, etc. cf. Mt 5,21-48: "you have heard... *but I say to you...*") and claims to be the "*Lord of the Sabbath*" (Mk 2,28). He even *forgives sins* (Mk 2,1-12; Mt 9,2; Lk 7,49). Finally, God himself has revealed to Jesus at the time of his baptism: "You are my *beloved Son*" (Mk 1,9-11; 9,7). All these disclose *Jesus' divinehuman identity* and *unique filial relationship with God*, which is the *basis of Christian faith* in *Jesus, "the Son of God"*.

We may *sum up* our short discussion on the *disputed issue* of *Jesus' divine sonship* by saying that the revelation of *Jesus* as "*Son of God*" in the Gospels does *not* mean that he is "*a second God*" but one who has a *filial relationship with God in loving communion.*

Despite the *differences* in the faith-understanding of the *person of Jesus* as the "*Son of God*" (in the Gospel revelation) and as the "Servant of God" (in the Quranic revelation), both the Gospel and the Qur'an agree that Jesus *submits his will to the will of God*, which we (Christians and Muslims) too are called to do.

b)   Jesus' crucifixion, death on the cross and resurrection
Jesus' death and resurrection are *two other connected issues* on which the *Quran* and the *Gospel disagree.* The Quran says in 4:157: "They [the Jews] *said (in boast), 'We killed Christ Jesus the son of Mary, the Messenger of Allah*'; -- but *they killed him not, nor crucified him*, but so it was *made to appear* to them, … for of a surety *they killed him not: --* 158 Nay, *Allah raised him up unto Himself*" (Q 4:157-158).[220]

It must be noted at the outset that these *two verses* are *an answer* to the *Jewish boasting* of *killing Jesus, Allah's Messenger,* which would be an *insult* to Allah and would imply that Allah *allowed his enemies to kill His Messenger*! So to safeguard *Allah's honour*, He saved His Messenger from inhuman shameful death on the cross by producing *an illusion* for the *boasting enemies.*

Lebanese Scholar and Professor Mahmoud M. Ayoub *interprets* the Qur'anic statements about *Jesus' death* on the cross in the following words:

> The *Qur'an ... does not deny the death of Christ.* Rather, it challenges human beings who in their folly have deluded themselves into believing that they would vanquish the divine Word, Jesus Christ the Messenger of God. The death of Jesus is asserted several times and in various contexts." (3:55; 5:117; 19:33).[221]

Now the Quran admits that "*the Gospel,*" which Allah gave to his Messenger Jesus, is "*guidance and light*" (cf. 5:46; 57:27) to all believers in God: "Let the *People of the Gospel* judge *what Allah has revealed therein*": 5:47; "believers, *believe* in what has been revealed to you and *what was revealed before you*": 4:162). Christians believe that since *Jesus' passion predictions* in the Gospels (Mk 8,31; 9,31; 10,33-34; Lk 9,22.44; 18,32-33; Mt 16,21; 17,12.22; 20,18; 26,2) reveal God's providential plan for Jesus to suffer and die on the cross in solidarity with the suffering human beings, it is part of "*the Gospel of God*". All are expected to believe what Jesus *revealed* as "*the Gospel* ['Good News'] *of God*" (Mk 1,14) and what *Jesus proclaimed* through his words and deeds (cf. Lk 4,18; 4,43; 7,22; 8,1; 16,16; 20,1). Furthermore, the Gospels narrate *Jesus' death* on the cross and *burial* in a new tomb (Mk 15,39.44-47; Mt 27,50.59-61; Lk 23,46.52-53; Jn 19,30.38-42) and the *risen Jesus' appearances* to many of his disciples (men and women) on various occasions (Mk 16,1-8; Mt 28,1-18; Lk 24,1-43; Jn 20,1-29; 21,1-14). They were *transformed* by their personal and communitarian *experience of the risen Lord* and they *bore witness* to him. Thus the *Gospel accounts* are *unanimous* in affirming *Jesus' death*, *burial and resurrection* as *true*. The *death-resurrection of Jesus* is the *foundation of the Christian faith*.

In the Qur'an God Himself promises Jesus to raise him to Himself: "Allah said, *'O Jesus! I will take you* and *raise you to Myself* and clear you (of the falsehoods) of those who blaspheme; I will make those who follow you superior to those who reject faith, to the Day of Resurrection" (3:55). Here the Qur'an expresses the *belief* in *Jesus' resurrection* as *an event in the future*. Thus we (Christians) *differ* from the Muslim view in the understanding of Jesus' death and resurrection and their theological meanings. In the words of Victor Edwin, "What underpins our faiths is, despite profound differences, that *Jesus was obedient to God* and *surrendered his will to the will of God*."[222]

c) *Jesus' promise about Paraclete/Spirit (Jn 14,16-17; 14,26; 15,26; 16,7-14) or Ahmad (Q 61:6)?*

One verse in the Qur'an mentions Jesus as saying: "O Children of Israel! I am the messenger of Allah (sent) to you, confirming the Law (which came) before me and giving glad Tidings of a Messenger to come after me, whose name shall be *Ahmad*" (61:6). But Jesus in John's Gospel had told his disciples about the *Holy Spirit*, the *Paraclete* (*paraklêtos*: Jn 14,16-17; 14,26; 15,26; 16,7-14). Never does the Gospel mention "Ahmad" or "*periklutos*" ("famous, renowned"). There is *no textual evidence* for *periklutos* in the Gospel!

If we examine in detail the *four Paraclete-promises* of Jesus in the Gospel of John, we find: 1) The Spirit is "*to be with* you [the disciples] *forever*" (Jn 14,16) and will "*remain with* you [them] and *will be in* you [them]" (14,17). 2) Jesus identifies "*the Paraclete*" with "*the Holy Spirit*" in Jn 14,26 and describes that one of the functions of the Paraclete/Spirit is "*to bring to your remembrance all that I have said to you*" (14,26). 3) Just as Jesus promised the disciples that "the Paraclete/Spirit of truth" "*will bear witness to me*" [Jesus] and will enable them *to testify to him* (Jn 15,26-27), they *did bear testimony to him* after he gave them the Holy Spirit (cf. Jn 20,22-23.24-25; cf. also Acts 2,1-4.22-36). 4) Jesus tells the disciples, "when he ["the Paraclete"] comes, he will *convince/convict* the world about the *sin*... because they do *not believe in me* [Jesus]" (Jn 16,7-9). "Unmistakeably, the promise is that of the Holy Spirit, the Spirit of truth, which was to come to the disciples from the Day of Pentecost onwards, bear witness to Christ and lead all of them into more truth."[223]

d)   Allah in the Qur'an or Triune God in the Gospels or both? Related to the themes of Jesus' divine Sonship and of the Spirit/ Paraclete (which we have seen above) is the issue of the *One* God (*Allah*) in the *Qur'an* and the *Triune* God ("Father", "Son", and "Holy Spirit") in the *Gospels*.

The mystery of the "*Triune God*" (revealed by Jesus in the Gospels) does *not* mean that there are "*three*" *gods* but that *God* is "*One*" (in existence) but "*Triune*" (distinct Persons in relationship with each other). Limited human beings cannot know the infinite God in Self-existence (as He is in Himself) but the believers in God are enabled to know *God revealed in relationships to human beings* (e.g., Creator, Saviour, Sanctifier).

Islamic faith in *Allah* emphasizes the *oneness of God* revealed in the *Qur'an* (2:163; 6,19; 16,22; etc.), whereas *Christian faith* in the '*Trinity*' stresses both the *oneness* of God and the *threeness* (Trinitarian aspect) within the *Triune God* and in God's relationship with human beings revealed in the *Gospels* (Jn 20,21-22; Mt 28,19: "the Father, the Son and the Holy Spirit").[224]

But the *Muslim faith* in the *one God* and *Christian faith* in the *Triune God* are *not exclusive* but *inclusive*. They are *not contradictory* but *complementary*. *God (Allah)* in the *Qur'an* is not an abstract transcendent Being unrelated to the cosmos and human beings. God is the *creator* of all things (Q 2:29; 6:73), the *revealer* of the Torah, the Gospel, and the Qur'an (3:38; 6:92; 45:2) and the *sender of the Spirit* (17:85).[225]

On the occasion of Jesus' baptism, it was revealed to him: God as 'Father', God as 'Spirit' and Jesus as 'Son' (Mt 3,16-17; Mk 1,10-11; Lk 3,21-22; Jn 1,32-34). Because of this revelation of the mystery of God, Jesus used to address *God* as '*Abba, Father*,' in his prayer (Mk 14,36) and he taught his disciples to *pray to God* calling him '*Father*' (Lk 11,2) or '*Our Father*' (Mt 6,9). He instructed them to *trust in God* as '*your Father*' (Lk 12,30). He also told them to be *compassionate like God their Father*: "Be merciful even as *your Father* is merciful" (Lk 6,36). Jesus proclaimed the good news of God's loving and forgiving mercy towards repentant sinners through his "parable of the prodigal father" (a father who is extravagant in loving as in Lk 15,11-24). The mystery of the Father-Son relationship is manifested throughout the Gospel of John (e.g., Jn 1,14.18; 3,16-18; 4,23; 5,17.19-30; etc.). Jesus concludes his 'farewell discourse' to his disciples (Jn 13-16) with a long prayer, addressing God as "Father" (Jn 17,1-26).

When the risen Jesus appeared to his disciples, he told them: "As the Father has sent me, even so I send you" (Jn 20,21) and breathing on them, he said to them: "Receive the

Holy Spirit" (20,22). And just before his ascension into heaven, Jesus instructed his disciples: "Go and make disciples of all the nations, baptizing them in the name of *the Father* and of *the Son* and of *the Holy Spirit…*" (Mt 28,19). Thus the *Trinitarian dimension* is *central* to the revelation of God to Jesus Christ and through him to his followers. Christian faith in *Jesus Christ* as the 'Son of God' is linked to the mystery of the *Holy Trinity*.[226]

4.2.©. We may conclude our short discussion on the *positive points* about Jesus in the Qur'an and the Gospels by stating that they *agree* on the following facts: *Jesus* was *born miraculously from the Virgin Mary*; he was a *sinless person and a faithful servant of God*; he was a *very great prophet* with the God-given *Gospel*, and he was *the Messiah empowered by the Spirit of God* to do *miracles*.

But the Qur'an *disagrees* with the Gospels that *Jesus* is "*Son of God*" because it seems to imply God's '*begetting*' a son sexually and to deny the *oneness (unity) of God*. Jesus in John's Gospel describes "*eternal life*" as knowing *the one true God* (*ho monos athêthinos theos*, "the only true God": Jn 17,3; cf. 1,17) and his "*unique Son*" (*monogenês hyios*: 3,16.18). Again, all the four Gospels are *unanimous* in affirming the *Christian faith* that *Jesus was crucified,* and *he died* on the cross and *was raised* by God.

A *meaningful way forward* for a *fruitful dialogue* on *Jesus Christ* between *Indian Christians and Muslims* is to *read* (without prejudices) and *study* (without preconceived ideas)[227] "*the Word of God*" revealed in the *Gospel* and the *Qur'an* and to *share* their *insights* (with trusting hearts). Then they/we will *discover* the true "*message of God*" in the Gospel and the Qur'an and will gradually learn to *recognize, affirm and appreciate the similarities and even the differences* and re-interpret *the revealed truth* (e.g., *the divinity of Jesus Christ*) relevantly in the multi-religious context in our country.

The *frank and friendly sharing* of "*the revealed truth*" will *deepen and strengthen our faith in God* and will *initiate and build up* the *inter-religious fraternal fellowship*. These, in turn, will *inspire* us to be the *leaven* and *light* in the multi-religious Indian society and will *enable* us to *fight against* every form of *social injustice* and *religious discrimination* in our country. Then we will be *true Christians* (who *love* like Christ) and *genuine Muslims* (who *submit* to the will of God) in our motherland.

4.3.   The Good News of Jesus Christ for Sikhs: Guru Nanak and Jesus Christ (Sikh-Christian Dialogical Christology)

4.3.0. Introduction

Sikhism was born out of the religious experience of Guru Nanak (1469-1539). At the age of 30, Nanak had a mystical experience after which he began his mission of spreading the message of the Name and calling disciples to the way of the Name. The work he began was gradually consolidated by his nine successors: Angad Dev (1504-1552), Amar Das (1479-1574), Ram Das (1534-1581), Arjan Dev (1563-1606), Har Gobind (1595-1644), Har Rai (1630-1661), Har Krishan (1656-1664), Teg Bahadur (1621-1675) and Gobind Singh (1666-1708). The final foundational structures were given to this religious phenomenon when the last Master, Guru Gobind Singh founded the *Khalsa* (1699) and installed the sacred book as the Guru of Sikhs for all times to come (1708), thus ending the line of personal gurus. Since then the sacred book is called the Sri Guru Granth Sahib (GGS). Today the Sikhs are present on all continents. It is not a missionary religion; its spread across the globe has been due to migration. Though Sikhism has many affinities with Hinduism and Islam, devout Sikhs consider Sikhism as a separate and independent faith. Although Sikhism and its faith, practices and community structures, continually evolved under the ten Gurus and were finally set with the tenth guru, the basic tenets and practices had already been established during the lifetime of Guru Nanak himself.

4.3.1. *Life of Guru Nanak*

Nanak was born on April 15, 1469, in the village of Talwandi in West Punjab, in Pakistan, 65 km southwest of Lahore, into a simple Hindu family. From an early age, Nanak made friends with both Hindu and Muslim children and was very inquisitive about the meaning of life. At the age of 13 Nanak was to be invested with the sacred thread according to the traditional Hindu custom but he refused to accept the sacred cotton thread from the Hindu priest. When he was only 16, he was married to Sulakhani and eventually they had two children, Sri Chand (b. 1494) and Lakshmi Chand (b. 1497). Nanak was thirty years old when he had *a mystical experience*, which completely transformed him and gave him his life's mission. He had been employed as the keeper of the government store in Sultanpur by Nawab Daulat Khan Lodhi. He had gone to River Bein for the morning ablutions as usual and then went missing. He was assumed to have drowned in the river. However, he reappeared after three days but as a changed man. He had had a mystical encounter with the Lord. The *Mūlmantra* which begins the Guru Granth Sahib reflects this experience of God. He received the commission to spread devotion to the Name of God.

During the next 24 years, Guru Nanak undertook four great missionary journeys (*udasis*) and spread his message through simple and beautiful hymns. To the south, he visited as far as Ceylon, to the north as far as Tibet, to the west as far as Mecca and Baghdad and to the east as far as Assam. Wherever he went, he set up missions. In the end, Guru Nanak returned home to Punjab and settled down at Kartarpur with his wife and sons, leading the life of a farmer. Pilgrims came from far and near to hear the Master. Here his followers would gather in the mornings and afternoons for religious services. He institutionalized the common kitchen called *langar* where all could sit together and share a common meal, whether they were kings or beggars. Before his death, Guru Nanak appointed Lehna, a devout disciple, as his successor and renamed him Angad. At his death, Guru Nanak left behind for his Sikhs (disciples) a tradition, a community and a Guru. Sikhism had already its basic elements.

Nanak's principal teachings included *unity of God* (*Ik Omkar*), devotion to the divine name (*naam simran*), the importance of the company of saints (*sangat*), moral pure living, honest work, charity and sharing, universal brotherhood and rejection of caste. He denounced idol worship, ritualism in religion, asceticism and monasticism. He believed in a *casteless society* without any discrimination based on birth, religion or sex. He taught that *all are God's children.*

4.3.2. God of Guru Nanak

The most popular *name of God* among Sikhs is *Waheguru*, which means *wonderful guru*. This name occurs in the Guru Granth Sahib, though not in the hymns by the Gurus themselves. Nanak's understanding of God can be gleaned from his numerous compositions spread throughout the Guru Granth Sahib (GGS). But we restrict ourselves to three compositions - *mul mantra*, *japu* and *Asa di var* - which are doctrinally dense and significant. The Guru Granth begins with the *mul mantra*. Transliterated, it reads as follows: "*1 (Ik) omkar sati namu karata purakhu nirbhau nirvairu akal murati ajuni saibhan gur parsadi*" which means: "There is but one God. He is all that is. He is the creator of all things and he is all-pervasive. He is without fear or enmity. He is timeless, unborn and self-existent. He is the Enlightener and can be realized by grace of Himself alone." In the Guru Granth, the *Japu* of Guru Nanak or the *Jap(u)ji* comes at the beginning itself immediately following the *mul mantra*. Godwin Rajinder Singh describes its basic theme: "to describe the nature of God and to demonstrate that with all the mystic ingenuity of the *Sadhus* and *Sufis* God may remain ineffable unless through *gur parsad* he chooses to reveal himself."[228] *Asa di Var* (GGS, P. 462 - P. 475)[229] is a long hymnal composition of Guru Nanak.

The theological insights in the three compositions are sufficient to give us a total picture of *Guru Nanak's concept of God*. We *summarize* them as follows:

a) The Supreme Being is One (*1 omkar*). He is Truth-Eternal (*sati namu*). He is formless (*Nirankar*). He is Unborn (*Ajuni*), Immortal and Timeless (*Akal*), Unseen (*Alakha*), Infinite (*Apara*), Unattainable (*Agamma*), Imperceptible (*Agocara*). He is without form, colour and outlines.

b) Without attributes (*Nirguna*) he was in formless ecstasy (*sunna-samadhi*). To be the Creator, the Unmanifest manifested himself as God-with-attributes (*Saguna*). In his Will (*hukam*) he created the Universe and everything in it by a Word.

c) Having made the Nature (*qudret*) he took his seat in it. He made it his home. The created world manifests the power of God. The Name is the ineffable Supreme Being who has become manifest. The Name pervades the whole world.

d) The creation is real because it is the home of the Creator. But it depends on the Will of God for its existence. God is not only the Creator of the world but also its Sustainer. He sustains it by the power of his Will. The ways of the Lord are inscrutable. When he withdraws his Will the creation ceases to be. God is thus Creator-Sustainer-Destroyer.

e) God's knowledge is infinite. He knows the limits of all the world. No one knows God's limits. He is limitless.

f) God is gracious. He loves what he creates. He provides for his creatures. His Name dwells in the hearts of human beings. The Lord is the redeemer who saves the devotees from the coming and going (*Avai jai*), from the bondage of the *sansara*. He commands our surrender in obedience. God is compassionate and merciful to the believers. He particularly attends to the needs of the poor. He may very well be called the benefactor of the poor (*Din daiala*).

4.3.3. *Theological Anthropology of Sikhism*

Guru Nanak subscribes to the "Theory of *Karma*" (which includes a belief in the transmigration of souls) as is explained in classical Hindu Philosophy. One is born in such a state because of past *karma*. The goal of human life is *samyoga,* union with or absorption into the Lord. It marks the end of the cycle of birth and death. Until then the individual experiences the pain of duality or separation (*viyoga*). Human life is a struggle until the person reaches *samyoga* with the Lord. Human birth is the highest form of life in this world and the Sikh gurus see human birth as a blessing, a grace from God, a golden opportunity to attain release.

Release from the *sansara* is open to people of all castes and genders. Gender and caste differences have no religious or salvific significance. Sikh scriptures strongly condemn caste practice in society. The community kitchens (*langars*) which Guru Nanak began were a practical step towards abolishing casteist thinking among his followers. Women are held in high esteem. Guru Nanak explains the irrationality of any discrimination against women. He says that everyone is born of a woman. The one exception is the True Lord. Man marries a woman; the family comes from a woman. When his wife dies, a man accepts a second woman as his wife. Guru Nanak further says that it is women who give birth to kings. Therefore, there is no reason to call a woman evil (GGS, P. 473).

Throughout the Guru Granth Sahib, we find the gurus speaking of two kinds of people: *manmukh and gurmukh,* that is, the self-centred and the God-centred. The *manmukh* are persons who indulge excessively in what the world filled with *maya* offers. The *manmukh* controlled by *haumai* (ego) is a slave to the six passions, namely, *kama* (lust), *krodha* (anger), *lobha* (greed), *moha* (attachment), *mada* (pride) and *matsyarya* (envy). The individuals engrossed in *haumai* are so pre-occupied with themselves, that they are unable to remember the Lord or to be concerned about the well-being of others. Their world revolves around their selfish interest.

The ideal persons according to the Guru Granth Sahib are the *gurmukh*, who are open to the guru and God's Word. They are devoted to the Name of the Lord. The Lord's Name is ever enshrined in their hearts. The *gurmukh* are religious persons, persons of faith. Having found the Name, they do not think of lesser things. The remembrance of the Lord brings fulfilment and joy to the soul of the believer. They are also persons of truth in thought, speech and action (GGS, PP. 1058-1059) because they have rid themselves of their ego (*haumai*). They accept and follow the progressive guidance of the guru and are thus helped to ascend to higher levels of spiritual life. Their conduct is pure as they follow the way of the Truth and reach the gate of salvation. The *gurmukh* do not withdraw themselves from the world but live in it with universal consciousness. They enter into the lives of people as liberated and liberating persons.

4.3.4. *Understanding of God's Grace in Sikhism*

There are numerous hymns in the Guru Granth Sahib which express an overwhelming awareness of God's grace. God is spoken of as *kirpala* (the merciful), *din daiala* (the benefactor of the poor), and *miharbana* (the compassionate). By the grace of the merciful Lord (*kirpala*) the earth receives rain everywhere. The poor receive kindness from the benefactor of the poor (*din daiala*). The Creator is ever-kind (*kirpala*) and so he looks after all his creatures. He is the giver (*data*) of food for them. He is the "dispeller of sorrow" and "ocean of peace." The presence of the compassionate one (*miharbana*) is seen everywhere, on land and sea. In his grace, the Lord manifests himself as the redeemer of the lowly and the liberator of the fallen. The devotees find in him their friend, bridegroom, master, dispeller of sorrows, protector, peace-giver, refuge, redeemer and the Provident Lord.

Without guru or grace, we continue to be *manmukh*, governed by *haumai*, caught up in the poison of *maya*, enslaved to the six enemies (*shadripu*) of lust (*kama*), avarice (*lobha*), anger (*krodha*), attachment (*moha*), pride (*mada*) and envy (*matsyarya*). Grace leads us to the guru and the company of the holy (*satsangati*). The congregation of the worshippers becomes an environment conducive to the showering of grace and its reception. The grace of the Lord frees us from all worries and anxieties. The guidance of the guru purifies our minds and frees us from *haumai*. From being *manmukh* we become *gurmukh*. With the help of the guru, we cultivate in ourselves a taste for the Name and the Word. This is the most precious gift that we receive from the Lord's grace. Dwelling on the Name of the Lord wipes away all our sins. The ultimate grace is *samauna* which is merging with the Lord or entering into communion with him. This, the Lord grants us even in this life. This is the bliss of *sahaja*.

4.3.5. Nama Marga

The Sikh way to salvation is the *Nama Marga,* the way of the Name. The first aspect of the way of the Name is *Nam Simran*, translated as "remembrance of the Name". Sikhs find in their lives, their whole being and the created world, the glory and majesty of the Name, and are filled with a sense of amazement and wonder. Repetition of the divine Name by the tongue will rid one of *haumai* and one will eventually taste the Nectar-Name. The Name will percolate into the heart. The devotees will live their entire life in awareness of the Name. Nanak is critical of anyone who presumes that mechanical repetition of a name of God brings salvation. "By mere utterance with the tongue, thy bonds are loosed not, for thy ego and doubt leave thee not" (GGS, P. 353). The utterance is fruitful when the Lord is enshrined in one's heart by the grace of the Guru. The utterances with the tongue should lead one to unuttered utterance (*ajapa japa*), the highest form of prayer, which is possible only if the Name becomes a habit with the devotee. The grace most excellent that the devotees may ask for is the gift to dwell on the Name (*Nam Simran*) forever.

Meditation on the divine Name affects one's whole being and all activities of life. *Nama Marga* affects one's entire life. For the Sikh it means: i) being attuned to the Word of the Guru and the Name of the Lord, ii) personal prayer and congregational worship, and iii) service of the Guru and God through service of the community. This then entails iv) purity of life and controlling of passions, while engaging with the world, v) truthful living by honest efforts, and vi) service of others who are poor or in need.

Nam Simran does not allow the Sikh to escape from the pain and suffering around. On the contrary, it keeps him/her engaged in the loving service of others in need. The path of the *sannyasi* who keeps away from the world and its pains and sufferings is not for the disciples of Guru Nanak. The Guru says: "I have learned by the light given by the Perfect Master: recluse, hero, celibate or *sannyasi*, none may expect to earn merit without devoted service -- service in which lies the essence of purity" (GGS, P. 992). Honest work and service of others are two practical aspects emphasised in the Sikh tradition. In the community of devotees (*sangat*), the Sikh learns to serve others in humility. The *Panth* (community) is the embodiment of the Guru and, therefore, the service of the *Panth* becomes the service of the Guru. Besides, in the *Panth* or *sangat* one learns to be responsible towards the needs of people in need, especially the poor. Sikhs are expected to share with others what they have acquired by honest work. Honest work and sharing of wealth in loving service are integrally related to dwelling on the Lord's Name.

There is a triadic formula which comes from Guru Nanak and is found in the Guru Granth Sahib which more or less sums up these: *nam, dan, isnan* or Name, alms-giving and pure living. Guru Nanak says: *gurmukhi namu danu isnanu* (GGS, P. 942). There is another triadic expression popular with the Sikhs: *nam japo, kirat karo, vand chhako*, which means repeat the divine Name, earn your livelihood by honest labour, share from what you earn. These three tenets are considered the basic commands of Sikhism, its pillars. If *Nam Simran* is to be authentic, it must express one's love for the Lord and must also lead, as Kharak Singh says, to altruistic deeds per His altruistic Will. And conversely, altruistic work is the worship of the Lord.[230]

4.3.6. *Jesus Christ and Guru Nanak: Some Dialogical Threads*

Christianity is the world's largest religion and Sikhism one of the smallest. Christianity is more than 2000 years old and Sikhism has just completed a little over 500 years. At the origins of the two faiths are two world teachers, Jesus Christ and Guru Nanak. There are some fundamental differences between the two ways but these differences do not wipe out the many similarities. The paragraphs below will bring out some of these similarities and differences, understanding which is vital in dialogical interactions between the two faiths.

a) For Jesus Christ and Guru Nanak, *God is one* and one alone, the sole Creator of everything that exists, formless spirit, eternal and beyond time. For Guru Nanak, God is without attributes (*nirguna*) and *impersonal* who becomes God with attributes (*saguna*) and manifests himself as *personal*. Unlike Guru Nanak, Jesus Christ did *not* speak of God in *impersonal* terms. For him, God is deeply *personal* and *relational*. God is his *Abba* ('Papa', 'Daddy'), his loving Father, with whom he shares an intimate relationship so much so that he says "I and the Father are one" (Jn 10,30). Guru Nanak's concept of 'personal' God and Jesus Christ's understanding of 'relational' God resonate with each other. For both Guru Nanak and Jesus Christ, God is *light* and *truth*. God is *eternal* truth and light. God is *loving, compassionate, merciful, forgiving and just*. For both, God is the *Saviour* and *Redeemer* of those who love him.

b) Both Jesus Christ and Guru Nanak affirm the *greatness of human life*. For Guru Nanak human birth is special and one attains it after wandering through several births. Human life is also a golden opportunity to attain salvation. Jesus Christ does not share in Guru Nanak's philosophy of *karma* and transmigration of souls. Jesus Christ's esteem of the human person and human life is grounded in the Jewish faith that God created human beings in *God's image and likeness* (Gen 1,26-27) and his awareness of the *supreme love* that *God has for human beings* (cf. Mt 6,26). Both Jesus Christ and Guru Nanak know that human beings are controlled by *sin* (*haumai*) and need *to be liberated from the bondage of sin by God's grace* to choose God and pure living. The *greatest treasure* that human beings can have is *God* for which they must be willing to sacrifice everything else.

c) *Jesus Christ's vision of society* is implicit in his message of the '*Kingdom/Reign of God.*' This vision sees the whole humanity as *one family of brothers and sisters* who have *God as their Father.* Jesus envisioned an *egalitarian society* in which *all are equal, as God's children.* That fraternal society can only be built based on the 'Kingdom' values of justice, truth, love, compassion, mercy and forgiveness. The ethic of Jesus Christ is summed up in the *double commandment* of *love of God and love of neighbour* (cf. Mt 22,34-40). Guru Nanak's vision of humanity also upholds these values and ethics. He believed in an *egalitarian society without discrimination* based on caste, gender and wealth.

d) Guru Nanak emphasized the importance of *service (seva) of the Guru and God* through the *service of the community* and *service of humanity.* The illustrious Guru in the Christian tradition, Jesus Christ, has raised to great heights the role and value of service done to people in general and especially to those in need. Indeed, Jesus Christ has *equated an act of service done to anyone in need as done to him.* "Truly I tell you, when you did it to one of the least members of my family, you did it to me" (Mt 25,40). Giving food to the hungry, drink to the thirsty, shelter to the homeless, comfort and relief to the sick, and rest to the traveller, are accepted as intrinsically religious acts. What is surprising is that Jesus Christ as

Judge at the ultimate reckoning time will accept such acts of service as capable of winning heavenly rewards.

e) Guru Nanak is a *monotheist* and his monotheism is *absolute.* But the life and ministry of Jesus Christ, as understood in the Christian community, reveal a *Trinitarian* pattern in God. God is *Father, Son and Spirit.* The Christian community coined the word 'Trinity' to speak of God as revealed in Jesus Christ. God is one but in *one God* there are *three persons* - Father, Son and Spirit - who are equal in divinity, glory and majesty and are equally worshipped. From all eternity, God is a *communion of love* among three equal and different divine persons. This Trinitarian faith is unique to Christianity. Jesus Christ is the incarnation of the Son, the second person of the Trinity and is truly divine and simultaneously truly human.

f) Both the Christian and Sikh faiths speak about the *Supreme Being* as a *Personal God* who is *full of love and mercy* and who graciously provides for the needs of his creatures. Before God, both the faiths affirm, *human beings* are *unworthy creatures.* Human beings wholly depend on God for their existence as well as for their ultimate salvation. *Grace* purifies us of our sins and *sets us free* to live transformed lives according to the Will of God. The Christian is freed from slavery to sin by God's grace and begins to live as the son or daughter of God. The Sikh is freed from *haumai* and is converted from the life of the *manmukh* to the life of the *gurmukh.* The *Spirit* dwells in the Christian and the *Name* indwells the heart of the *gurmukh.* According to Guru Nanak, without

God's grace human beings will remain in the bondage of sin and delusion (*haumai, maya*) and will not receive release (*moksha*) from the cycle of birth and death. The guidance of the Guru and participation in the *sangat* are essential for attaining the grace of God. The way of salvation is the *nama marga—nam dan isnan*: devotion to the Name, charitable works and pure living. The Guru and the *sangat* are aids for the devotees to practise *nama marga* and attain God's grace and salvation. The path of salvation that Jesus Christ places before us is the *path of love (Prem marga)*: *love of God and love of neighbour.*

g) Jesus Christ and Guru Nanak are two great figures in the history of religions. Although the concept of '*Guru*', which means a spiritual guide or preceptor or enlightener, had been there since long in different Hindu traditions, in Sikhism it has a special significance. The word is reserved for the ten founding masters and the Sri Guru Granth Sahib. The Guru is a vital guide in the spiritual progress of human beings, one who shows the way through his example and instruction, the voice of God, one who brings God's word and instruction to human beings. The title '*Guru*' encapsulates the *total religious significance of Nanak*. But in the Christian understanding, *Jesus Christ* is *Guru and much more.* Unlike Guru Nanak and the Sikh Gurus, who are all human beings, *Jesus Christ* is *both human and divine.* He is the *human incarnation* of the *divine Son* (Second Person in the Godhead). Jesus Christ is the *unique mediator* between God and human beings. Unlike the Sikh Gurus, Jesus Christ is the *intercessor* between God and us, and the *mediator* of the grace of salvation. It is his death and resurrection that has saved humanity. In this way, he is *the Saviour of humanity.*

4.3.©. *Conclusion*

Belief in one God, the role of the Word, the place of service as central to religion and the idea of an egalitarian and casteless society are significant dimensions of Sikh religion. Although practically every religion in India is socially affected by the caste culture, the theoretical affirmation of fundamental equality of all human beings by Sikhism is greatly to be priced.

Jesus Christ and Guru Nanak are revered not only in their respective faith communities but also universally. We have had a quick survey of the life and teachings of Guru Nanak. We have also highlighted the basic *similarities* and *differences* between their teachings. Both Jesus Christ and Guru Nanak emphasize the equality of all human beings (irrespective of caste, colour, creed or sex) as children of God and stress the necessity of lovingly serving all those who are in need. However, Guru Nanak and Jesus Christ differ significantly regarding how human beings relate to God and how they are saved. These similarities and differences must be taken into account when the followers of both the faiths come together and dialogue with each other. *God, the Saviour,* (who comes to save human beings in diverse ways and through various means) is *a Mystery of Love.*

4.©. Conclusion: Relevance of "the Good News of Jesus Christ" for Dialogue with Hindus, Muslims and Sikhs

The fraternal, free and friendly *dialogue on "the Good News of Jesus Christ"* with *Hindus, Muslims and Sikhs* has been the *focus* of this *Chapter.* By the symbolic act of opening the doors and windows for fresh air and wider vision, *Pope John XXIII,* inspired by Jesus Christ, gifted to the Church and thereby to the entire Christian world a globalising perception and a mandate to initiate a *friendly dialogical culture*. By opening the minds and hearts to the dialogue partners, the birth of an innovative inter-faith dialogue and spirituality took place.

The *new eyes* that were gifted to the *three disciples* on the Mountain of Transfiguration enabled them to be witnesses to a new transformed person in Jesus Christ. And the *divine eyes* bestowed on *Arjuna* qualified him to see God's presence in everything with new dimensions. The sacred rivers and the holy places to which pilgrims flock and the sacred *fire* that mediates the offerings to the deities helped them to discover a new spiritual dimension to their lives. The Indic religious phenomenon of *avatara* and the Semitic faith in the *Incarnation* do give a density and concreteness to the divine Presence in the creation and among human beings. The concept of *sacrifice* is almost a universal element in almost all religions. Sacrifice is gratitude, adoration, petition for favours and self-giving love, all in one offering to the divine. The power of the *truth of God* becomes all-embracing.

The journey from the Indic religious reflections to the Islamic faith reflections comes as a transition that is pluralistic and enriching. The Islamic monotheism and Christian experience of God in Christ highlight areas of convergence and at the same time divergence. In these developments, it is the *increasing friendly dialogue at the faith level* that contributes to *mutual trust and respect*. What was impossible in the days of rigorous intellectual acrobatics and fence-making in the name of God is emerging as possible, beneficial and worthy of authentic believers. *Respect and reverence for the One God* invite the believing communities to leave the limited world of early days and to enter into the fast-emerging new spheres. What is encouraging is the widening disposition of the believers in these traditions facilitating *creative interaction and fruitful dialogue.*

It could be recalled at this juncture that the social, cultural, political and spiritual exchanges have been indirectly contributing to this new culture. The *universities* have contributed immensely to the *widening of mind-sets among Hindu, Muslim and Christian communities.* For all these the roles of *Sufism* in Islam and of the different *schools of spiritualities* in Hinduism as well as the growth of *religious studies* in the different universities in the world need to be put on record. Knowledge is the levelling factor in these frontier developments. Serious and systematic studies of the sources of these faith communities have been playing the role of a master of skills and progenitor of a new world. It is up to believers in these traditions to further this cause with commitment worthy of a *new world order.*

Through *Sikhism,* further religious frontiers have been opening up in our country and in the world. The concept of *monotheism* is its forte. Consequently, the *Sikh new religious understanding* of *all men and women as equals in the human family* has further contributed to *universal brotherhood and sisterhood. Caring for the needy, the homeless and the hungry* (by providing *shelter* and "*langar*" to all) is both inspiring and challenging to all believers in God and all men and women of goodwill in the world.

The divinehuman Jesus Christ (who is God-centred and human-centred) in the Gospels is a trailblazer in inter-faith dialogue. All are invited to walk with him along the path of friendly and fraternal dialogue as believing and loving children of God.

©.

CONCLUSION: SIGNIFICANCE OF JESUS CHRIST FOR THE PEOPLE OF INDIA

©.1. Relevance of Jesus Christ's Person and Mission for the People of India

The *Gospels' diversity* in the *contextual faith interpretations* of *Jesus Christ's identity* and *mission* has encouraged us to attempt *Indian contextual Christologies*, namely, *subaltern* and *inter-faith dialogical Christologies. Jesus Christ, the prophetic liberator,* is very relevant to the *Dalits, Tribals* and *Women* in India. *Jesus Christ, the divine incarnation, the revelatory sage,* who has taught *Prem marga* (path of love) to *mukti* (salvation), is meaningful to the *Hindus; Jesus, the sinless son of Mary, God's prophet with the Injil* (Gospel), is revered by the *Muslims; Jesus Christ, the Guru,* who is similar in many respects to Guru Nanak, is attractive to the *Sikhs.* To sum up, the *humandivine Jesus Christ in the Gospels* is *the living liberator and the loving life-giver for all.* This is "THE GOOD NEWS OF JESUS CHRIST FOR THE PEOPLE OF INDIA."

©.2. Relevance of Jesus Christ's Vision for the People of India

Plato in his book '*The Republic*' elaborates principles of governance, his idea of *welfare of the people* through *democratic way life*. Abraham Lincoln in his *classic* description of democracy as "*the government of the people, by the people and for the people*" has almost put a seal on the ideal way of governance.

Jesus Christ, in announcing the "*Kingdom of God*" (God's reign), gave the people of God/India *a new vision and way of life of freedom, fellowship, justice and love for all*, irrespective of caste or colour, race or religion. He *empowers all the people of God to become children of God* and *enables all to live as brothers and sisters* in the *family of God (Vasudaivakudumbhakam)*. He *shows* the *path of faith and love* to *abundant life* ("eternal life") here on earth and hereafter.

It is quite appropriate, therefore, that the *Preamble to the Constitution of India*, in which the *quintessence of "the Good News" of Jesus Christ* is given a *secular rendering*, becomes increasingly *normative for organizing the life of the People of India*. The well-known "*Sarvodaya* through *Antyodaya*" will be the *pole star* of all our deliberations, decisions and developmental actions.

Epilogue

Sangam is a fascinating word applicable to many convergences. The sacred rivers *Ganga* and *Yamuna* won the glory and richness contained in the word since the many streams not only merge to flow down together but also stir up within the pilgrims the precious dimension of heaven on earth. For, rid of the many sins and blemishes, those who assemble there are facilitated to have their spiritual life to shine with a new glow. The *main thrust* of this small book is *to assist all the people of God/India to immerse themselves* in the *life-renewing Sangam of Jesus Christ.*

ENDNOTES

ACRONYMS of *Books* **by George Mlakuzhyil S.J. and T. K. John S.J.:**

AL   :   *Abundant Life in the Gospel of John* (Delhi, 2007).

BLG   :   *Be a Life-Giver: A Retreat on John's Gospel* (Mumbai 2012).

CLDS   :   *Christocentric Literary-Dramatic Structure of John's Gospel* (Second Enlarged Edition) (Rome 2011).

GJCS   :   *The Gospel of John: Commentary for Students* (Delhi 2013).

GNJCG :   *The Good News of Jesus Christ in the Gospels* (Delhi 2021).

IGL   :   *Initiation to the Gospel of Life: A Guide to John's Gospel* (Mumbai 2008).

DBCNT :   T. K. John S.J. & James Massey (eds.), *Dalit Bible Commentary: New Testament* (New Delhi 2010).

[1] Aloysius Pieris S.J., *Helping Francis Renew the Church* (Book internet version, Kelaynia, Sri Lanka, 2019), 9-10 [*italics* and ***bold italics*** added]. (Cf. Pope Francis' *Evangelii Gaudium* for his vision of ecclesial renewal and reform.)

[2] Cf. Aloysius Pieris, *op. cit.*, 11-12.

[3] Cf. George Mlakuzhyil S.J., *The Good News of Jesus Christ in the Gospels [GNJCG]*.

[4] A new word *'divinehuman'* has been coined by me to point to the mystery that Jesus Christ is an *integral person* who is *both divine and human* (*not* a hyphenated ['divine-human'] being).

[5] From the historic "Tryst with Destiny" of Jawaharlal Nehru, India's first Prime Minister, broadcast to the nation at the hour of its becoming free on August 15, 1947, in the Central Hall of the Indian Parliament.

[6] *Preamble to the Constitution of India.*

[7] George Mlakuzhyil S.J., "Importance of Experience in Indian Contextual Theologizing," *Theologizing Today: Voices of Indian Theologians,* edited by Raj Irudaya S.J. & Roy Lazar, (Bengaluru 2019), 79-84 [*italics* added].

[8] *Fellowship of Faiths and Unity of Religions,* ed. Professor Abdul Majid Khan (New Delhi 1990), 2 [*italics* added].

[9] Romila Thapar, *A History of India,* Vol 1, 29-30.

[10] Cf. "Oxfam Report 2019," reported in *The Economic Times* (20 January 2020).

> "India's current rank on the *Global Hunger Index* (GHI) of 117 countries is at an ignominious 102. The Food and Agriculture Organization (FAO) data seems to doubly rub it in, emphasizing that upwards of 19 crore Indians currently suffer from malnutrition and hunger" (Editorial, *The Sunday Statesman,* 20 October 2019, p. 8).

[11] Institutionalized inequality and injustice are rampant in our country. For instance, compared to the *fat monthly salaries* (besides other allowances) of the Indian *President* (Rs 5 lakhs), *Vice-President* (4 lakhs), *Governor* (3.5 lakhs), *Prime Minister* (3.75 lakhs), etc., the minimum monthly wages for *unskilled workers* in the Capital is only Rs 14,842, which is a pittance!

While the President, Vice-President, Governors, Prime Minister, MPs and MLAs, etc. live in luxury at the taxpayers' expense, the poor labourers and their families are forced to live in poverty in the largest democracy in the world! While millions of "unemployed" and "underemployed" poor Indians and their malnourished children go to bed on empty stomachs at night, rich powerful politicians and their crony capitalists feast in five star hotels in India and abroad! Seven decades after India became a democratic Republic, what has happened to the *"justice"* and *"equality"* promised to *"all its citizens"* by the Preamble of the Indian Constitution?

[12] Satish Deshpande, *Dalits in the Muslim and Christian Communities, A Status Report on Current Social Scientific Knowledge,* (New Delhi 2010), 37 [*italics* added].

[13] *Ibid.,* [*italics* added].

[14] Samarendra Saraf, *Hindu Caste System & The Social Idiom* (Delhi 1986), 54.

> [15] 11. "When they divided Purusha how many portions did they make? What do they call his mouth, his arms? What do they call his thighs and feet?" 12. "The Brahman was his mouth, of both his arms was the Rajanya made. His thighs became the Vaishya, from his feet the Shudra was produced." [Varna (Hinduism)- Wikipedia]

This *Purusha Sukta Varna* verse is now generally considered to have been inserted at a later date into the Vedic text, possibly as a myth. V. Nagarajan believes that it was a *"later interpolation"* to give *"divine sanction"* to an unequal division in society that was in existence at the time of its composition. He states: "The Vedic Hymns had been composed before the Varna scheme was implemented. The Vedic society was not organized on the basis of varnas. The Purusha Sukta might have been a later interpolation to secure Vedic sanction for that scheme."[15]

[16] James Massey, "Roots", in: *Concise History of Dalits*, (New Delhi 2004), 20. This may explain the enslaved condition of the *panchama* (the '*fifth*' group) added to the four castes (cf. **2.1. Dalits in Indian Caste Society** below).

[17] D. D. Kosambi, *Culture and Civilization of Ancient India* (London 1965), 1 [*italics* added].

[18] The very recent trends in certain quarters to brand some as "foreign religions" are being considered today by informed sections of India as strange as howls of wolves and jackals at mid-day.

[19] Cf. Ignacio Echaniz S.J., *Community Prayer Book*, (Anand 2006).

[20] Cf. "*Upayas*" (downloaded on 11-06-2019) for explanations.

[21] Acharya Sachidananda Bharathi, '*Bharatiya Dharma Rajya*' *Vision of 'Kingdom of God' in India* (Delhi 2018), 46. However, '*Dharma*' is used these days to refer to 'religious communities' (e.g., 'Hindu Dharma,' 'Sikh Dharma,' 'Christian Dharma,' etc.) (*ibid.*, 47).

[22] *Collected Writings* of George M. Soares-Prabhu, S.J., Vol. 3, ed. by Scaria Kuthirakkattel, (Pune 2003), 260. In classical Hinduism *dharma* is the first of the four *purusharthas* (goals of life: *dharma, artha, kama, moksa*).

[23] *The United Nations Development Programme (UNDP)*, 16.

[24] Cf. **1.4.** above and **2.1.** below.

[25] George Mlakuzhyil S.J., *IGL*, 208.

[26] D. D. Kosambi, *op. cit.*, viii.

[27] "Phantom" is described as "a ghost…; a form without substance or reality; a mental illusion (*The Concise Oxford Dictionary*, Ninth Edition).

[28] *Manusmriti* (10.51,52), quoted by James Massey, *History of Dalits*, (New Delhi, 2004), 23.

[29] At the bottom of the pyramidal social structure are the *panchamas*, the *Scheduled Castes* (*SCs*), who comprise 16.6% of the Indian population (according to 2011 census).

[30] "The term 'Dalit' is perhaps one of the most ancient words which have been used in some of the ancient languages. For example, Hebrew and Sanskrit share the same term 'Dalit', almost with the same root and sense. The Hebrew root is *dall* which means to hang down, to be languid, weakened, low and feeble. The Sanskrit root is *dal,* which means burst, split, broken, or split asunder, downtrodden, scattered, smashed, destroyed." (*The Church and Dalits*, 4).

[31] James Massey and Samson Prabhakar (editors), *Frontiers in Dalit Hermeneutics*, (Delhi 1999), 3 [*italics* added].

[32] It is said that, according to Buddha, "No one is an outcaste or a Brahmin by his birth but by his deeds."

[33] Prof. S. M. Michael (Director of Institute of Cultural Studies, Mumbai), *Frontiers in Dalit Hermeneutics* (Delhi 2005), 88. [*italics* added].

[34] Mari Marcel Thekekara, *Endless Filth: The Saga of the Bhangies* (Books for Change), (Bangalore 1999),126.

[35] V. Devasahayam, in: *A Reader in Dalit Theology*, ed. Arvind. P. Nirmal, (Madras, no year!), 2.

[36] "The terms like *tribes* and *scheduled tribes* are widely used in social science literature and State documents" (Nirmal Minj, *Rethinking Theology in India*, [Delhi 2013],122 [*italics* added]). Although the *tribes* are the nation's '*indigenous people*' (the earliest inhabitants), the *Government of India* has *not yet recognized* them as 'indigenous people'!

[37] Angami, Chakma, Dimasa, Kuki, Garo, Nagas, Khasi, Wancho are some of the tribes in the North Eastern States. Bhils, Dhamaria, Minas, Patelias are those in Rajasthan and Gujarat. Katkari, Warlis, Khond, etc. are in Maharashtra and Warli, Dubia, etc. in Goa. Santals, Oraons, Gonds, Asur, Kharia, Munda, Ho, Khuruk are among the tribes in Jharkhand and Bihar. Adiyan, Koraga, are in Karnataka. Sippi, Beda, Bakarwal, Churhas, Valmiki etc. are in Punjab, Jammu and Kashmir. Odisha has Khonds, Gadaba, Kharia, Munda, Kui and other tribes. (cf. *Wikipedia*, via Google, retrieved on 1 July 2020).

[38] Nirmal Minj, *Rethinking Theology in India*, 123.

[39] Agapit Tirkey, *Jharkhand Movement: A Study of Its Dynamics*, 8.

[40] Yangkahao Vashum, *The Tribal Worldview and Ecology*, 69-70 [*italics* added].

[41] Virginius Xaxa, "Tribes and Indian National Identity: Location of Exclusion and Marginality," *Brown Journal of World Affairs*, (Fall/Winter), Vol. xxiii (Issue I), 227 [*italics* added].

[42] *Ibid.*, 227 [*italics* added]. The main *heroic figures* in the *Sarna liberation movements/revolts* against the British and others were: (1) *Sidhu and Kannu* (2 Santal brothers), (2) *Birsa Munda* and (3) *Jatra*

(Oraon leader). (*Fr. Constance Lievens S.J.* managed to free Tribal land from landlords by filing cases against them in the courts.)

[43] Wati Longchar, "Tribal Identity and Theology," in: *Rethinking Theology in India: Christianity in the Twenty-first Century*, eds. James Massey & T. K. John, (Manohar, 2013), 107 [*italics* added].

[44] *Ibid.*, 107.

[45] *Ibid.*, 106.

[46] On the feast of "Mary, Mother of God" Pope Francis said during his homily that we celebrate a "nuptial union between God and humanity," inaugurated "in the womb of a woman." The Pope continued: "The rebirth of humanity began from a woman" and "Women are sources of life" and hence "every form of violence inflicted upon a woman is a blasphemy against God, who was born of a woman" (Vatican News, 01-01-2020). Pope Francis, however, is aware of the *disparity* between *preaching and practice* in the Church and is calling for radical changes regarding the status and role of women in the Church.

[47] *Empowerment of Women and Church in India* (a report of a survey conducted by CBCI Commission for Women), "Foreword," p. v.

[48] Here is a poser from a ninth class girl student about *female feticide*: "Now it is up to us to take a decision, whether we want to make 'mother's womb' an 'execution chamber' for girls or heaven from where humanity grows and propagate the ideas of love and peace" (Reba Varghese, IX C, Presentation School, Delhi, "The Voice of a Child in Favour of a Child", reported by Sr. Mary Scaria SCJM).

[49] Dr. Devaki Jain, "A Study on Legal and Political Impediments to Gender Equality in Governance," *The Times of India*, (April14, 2020) [*italics* added].

[50] Due to constraint of space, we have *not included* the *OBCs* (Other Backward Castes) in the *subaltern groups* and *Buddhists, Jains, Parsees*, etc. in the *religious groups*.

[51] Francis Gonsalves S.J., "Global Perspective: Theology outside the temple," *National Catholic Reporter* (22 Oct. 2003, Vol. 1, No. 30), 2.

[52] Cf. **2.1. "Dalits in Indian Caste Society"** above. According to 2011 census, *16.6%* of India's population are '*Scheduled Castes*' (*Dalits*).

[53] Cf. **2.1.2.** above.

[54] Strictly speaking, *Dalit Christology* must be done by the *Dalit Christians* in the light of their personal and communitarian faith in Jesus in view of the integral liberation of all the Dalits in our country. Even though we (the authors of this book) are not Dalits by birth, we feel deep solidarity with our Dalit brothers and sisters as a result of many decades of our close contact with them in their marginalized and oppressed situations, listening to their painful stories, reflecting with them and learning from them. Hope that our humble attempt at presenting a Dalit Christology would be meaningful for them and would help them to go beyond. Faith reflection on their own Dalit experiences will enable them to relate deeply to the *crucified-risen Dalit Jesus*, which, in turn, will inspire them to be engaged in the *prophetic and liberative praxis* of the Dalits.

[55] Cf. A. Maria Arul Raja, "Dialogue of Identities: Indian Dalits and Markan Jesus," in: *DBCNT*, 29-31.

[56] *Ibid.*, 29. "Scheduled Caste" (SC) is the term used by the Indian government.

[57] *Ibid.*, 30 [*italics* added].

[58] *Ibid.*, 165.

[59] Cf. *ibid.*, 163.

[60] *Ibid.*, 31.

[61] *DBCNT*, 25.

[62] *Ibid.*, 27 (*italics* in the original).

[63] Cf. James Massey, "Luke's Gospel: Relevance to the Dalits," in: *DBCNT*, 32-35.

[64] *DBCNT*, 33. All these groups are like the Dalits in India.

[65] *Ibid.*, 237 [*italics* added].

[66] *Ibid.*, 41 [*italics* added].

[67] Even though *Jesus' genealogy* (cf. Mt 1,1-17) contains the names of two *Gentile women* (*Rahab* and *Ruth*), who were married by Jewish men, and two *sinful women* (*Tamar* and *Bathsheba*), it does *not prove* that Jesus had '*impure blood*' (*mixed lineage*) because he was *not* the *natural son of Joseph* (but *only his legal adopted son*), since he was *born of the virgin Mary without sexual intercourse with Joseph* (cf. Mt 1,25). Hence Jesus was *not a Dalit by birth*.

[68] If Jesus were to be born in India today, he would be found in a deprived *Dalit's hut* outside the caste village or in a congested *shanty* in a city slum but not in a rich man's mansion or in a millionaire's villa house.

[69] *DBCNT*, 98.

[70] *Ibid.*, 171.

[71] *Ibid.*, 218 [*italics* added].

[72] *Ibid.*, 121. According to Luke: "*My mother and brothers* are those *hearing (akouontes) the word of God and doing (poiountes) it*" (Lk 8,21). It means that they are *constantly listening to God's word* and *always doing it* in their lives. In fact, this is what *Jesus' mother* did: "Behold the handmaid of the Lord; let it be to me according to your word" (Lk 1,38).

[73] *DBCNT*, 191-92 [*italics* added].

[74] *Ibid.*, 271-72 [*italics* added].

[75] *Ibid.*, 294.

[76] *Ibid.*

[77] *Ibid.*, 302.

[78] *Ibid.*, 175 [*italics* added].

[79] Cf. George Soares-Prabhu S.J., "The Table Fellowship of Jesus: Its Significance for *Dalit* Christians in India Today," in: *Collected Writings of George M. Soares-Prabhu S.J.*, Vol. 1, ed. by Isaac Padinjarekuttu (Pune 1999), 223-40.

[80] *DBCNT*, 283 [*italics* added]. This is what *Jesus told his disciples before healing the man born blind*: "*We must work* the works of him who sent me" (Jn 9,4).

Similarly, when Jesus saw a *hungry crowd* coming to him, he asked Philip: "*How are we to buy bread* so that *these people may eat?*" (Jn 6,5). "It is said that about twenty crores of people in India are forced to go to bed without one meal a day in spite of the sufficient and even surplus production of food grains. Unequal distribution, avaricious accumulation, and exploitative systems multiply hungry stomachs in our country." (*DBCNT*, 285). When will the Indian Christians (and governments) answer Jesus' challenging question about *feeding the hungry*? If they don't, even if they build grand cathedrals (as in Kerala) and magnificent temples (like the Ram Temple in Ayodhya), they will be told on the day of judgement: "Depart from me, you cursed, into the eternal fire…, for *I was hungry*, and *you gave me no food*" (Mt 24,41-42)!

[81] Like the *cured man with the withered hand* (Mk 3,1-5), the discriminated *Dalits* today have to be *empowered to stretch out their hands* to claim their legitimate constitutional rights in the rigid and hard-hearted caste-ridden Indian society.

[82] The *Dalits* must also learn from the *cured blind man* to *defend the giver of sight* (cf. Jn 9,8-38) and *not* be like the *healed paralytic* who *betrayed* his healer to the Jewish leaders who persecuted him (cf. 5,9-16). Sadly, there are some self-centred well-off Dalits (e.g., SC government officials) who *take bribes*, like Judas, and *betray* their benefactors and defeat the cause of Dalit liberation!!

[83] *DBCNT*, 128.

[84] *Ibid.*, 114.

[85] *Ibid.*, 142 [*italics* added].

[86] *DBCNT*, 257. But in many caste parishes in Tamilnadu there is *discrimination against the Dalit Christians* during the celebration of the Eucharist even today (e.g., they have to *sit behind* the caste Christians in the Church and the Dalits are given Holy Communion *last*)! Such *unchristian behaviour* of the caste Christians is a *betrayal* of *Jesus* present in the *Eucharist* and in the *Dalit Christians* (cf. Lk 22,21)!

[87] *DBCNT*, 297 [*italics* added].

[88] *Ibid.*, 301 [*italics* added].

[89] *Ibid.*, 306.

> [90] "The long episode of Jesus' trial in the various Roman courts [cf. Lk 23,1-25] and torture which he faced during the trials and afterwards, reveal how far a judicial system controlled by the dominants can miscarry justice without upholding the basic human rights of a person. This truth again brings home a fact very close to the situation of the Dalits of India, who every day face human rights violation from the hands of both judicial as well as the law implementing bodies like police and others" (*DBCNT*, 260).

[91] *Ibid.*, 159 [*italics* added].

[92] *Ibid.*, 201 [*italics* added].

[93] Like Mary Magdalene and the other Mary (Mt 28,1), the *Dalit Christian women* must *wake up the slumbering Church leaders* to form an *inclusive, casteless community of Christ's "brethren"* (28,10: brothers and sisters).

[94] *Ibid.*, 201.

[95] Like the crucified Jesus, *non-Dalits* can join the Dalit liberation movements, provided they are *ready to suffer in solidarity with the Dalits.*

[96] "Enthused and strengthened by the very presence of God who is active in history, the Dalits need to march forward hopefully even in the midst of disappointments, unfavourable and antagonistic situations so that Jesus' mission of being and giving life to all continues" (*DBCNT*, 309).

[97] Francis Minj S.J., "An Adivasi Quest for Jesus Christ", in: *Searching Christology through an Asian Optic*, ed. by P. R. John, John B. Mundu and Joseph Lobo (FSAJT, Vol. 1), (Delhi 2017), 139.

[98] Cf. **2.2. "Tribals in Ancient, Colonial and Modern India"** above.

[99] Boniface Tirkey S.J., *Oraon Symbols* (Delhi 1983), 28 [*italics* added].

[100] Cornelius Ekka S.J., *Salvific Significance of Jesus in the Tribal Context* [unpublished B.Th. Dissertation done under my guidance in Vidyajyoti College of Theology] (Delhi 2003), 14.

[101] *Ibid.*, 15-16.

[102] *Ibid.*, 17.

[103] This is illustrated in the Assur myth of *Khasra-Khusru*, as we shall see below.

[104] Boniface Tirkey S.J., *op. cit.*, 29.

[105] Cf. Cornelius Ekka S.J., *op. cit.*, 22-29; Boniface Tirkey, *Oraon Symbols* (Delhi 1983); John Lakra, "Genesis of Spirits: The Uraon Myth," *Sevartham* 11 (Research Annual, 1986), 45-58; Agapit Tirkey, "The Origin of Evil Spirits," *Sevartham* 18 (1993), 35-39. We will be dealing *only* with those *myths* which are *relevant for Tribal Christology.* (Therefore 'Creation Myths' ['Genesis Myth' and 'Fall Myth'] which reveal God as the Creator, are not included.)

[106] A '*metaphor*' manifests the *transferred quality* of one reality to another (e.g., "He has a *heart of stone*" means that his heart is as *hard as stone.*) Jesus tells his disciples: "You are the *salt* of the earth" (Mt 5,13) and "You are the *light* of the world" (Mt 5,14).

[107] Cornelius Ekka S.J., *op. cit.*, 27 [*italics* added].

[108] *Ibid.*, 36 [*italics* added].

[109] If *Dharmes* (God) is regarded as the *Grandfather* by the Tribals and if they are his *grandchildren*, they could be thought of as "children of the *Son* of God" (Jesus). In fact, many *Adivasi* Catholics (especially women), we are told, address Jesus as *Baba* (Father) and teach their children to call Jesus their *Jisu Baba* ("Father Jesus") (cf. Francis Minj S.J., *op. cit.*, 145).

[110] Boniface Tirkey S.J. calls Jesus, "the first ancestor" (cf. *Oraon Symbols,* [Delhi 1983], 75).

Yangkahao Vashum too regards *Jesus* as '*the Ancestor*' (cf. "Jesus Christ as the Ancestor and Elder Brother: Constructing a Relevant Indigenous/Tribal Christology of North East India," in *Tribal Theology: A Reader*, ed. Shimrengam Shimray (Jorhat, Assam 2008), 31-32.

Francis Minj S.J., however, prefers to refer to Jesus as "*Paramadivasi*" (Supreme Adivasi Ancestor):

> "Jesus is the supreme ancestor because Jesus comes from God, our origin. He embodies the qualities of ancestors and also supersedes them through his unique anteriority and mediatorship. He is not just the initiator of the tradition but is the tradition, the way, the truth and the life (Jn 14,6). He is *present* in the community and beckons the living members to follow him" (Francis Minj, *op. cit.*, 151).

[111] *Ibid.*, 150.

[112] Boniface Tirkey S.J., *op. cit.*, 75.

[113] Francis Minj S.J., *op. cit.*, 161 [*italics* added].

[114] *Ibid.*, 159. Cf. also Paulus Kullu S.J., "Figures of Christ in Kharia Religion," *Sevartham* 12 (1986), 110.

[115] Francis Minj S.J., *op. cit.*, 160.

[116] Y. Vashum presents to the Nagas *Jesus Christ* as 'the Rooster' (because of its sacrificial death for the life, welfare and harmony of the people) (cf. *op. cit.*, 21-22).

[117] S. C. Roy, *Oraon Religion and Customs* (Ranchi, 1968), 22.

[118] Francis Minj S.J., *op. cit.*, 178 [*italics* added].

[119] Cf. **2.3.** **"Women in Patriarchal India"** above, especially **2.3.2.** ***"Actual Place of Women in Indian Society."***

[120] Shalini Mulackal, "Who is Jesus for Indian Women? A Feminist Critical Enquiry," *VJTR* 80 (2016), 433-51; quotation from p. 435 [*italics* added].

[121] Cf. **2.3.1** and **2.3.2** above.

[122] Interpreting Mary's "keeping all things in her heart" (Lk 2,19.51), Pope Francis said during his homily on "Mary, Mother of God":

> "Women typically take life to heart... Women show us that the meaning of life is not found in making things but in taking things to heart. Only those who see with the heart see things properly, because they know how to 'look into' each person" (*Vatican News*, 01-01-2020).

[123] "This passage [Lk 8,1-3] must be read in conjunction with 23,49-24,12, which is another instance of a Lucan completing *analepsis* or "*flashback*" and shows that when readers read of "*disciples*" in 8,4-23,54 they should *include women* in that group. These *faithful women* are *witnesses* to what Jesus has done in Galilee, on the road to Jerusalem, and in Jerusalem, even at the Last Supper. They preach the gospel meaning of what they have witnessed (24,7-10) and receive the promised Holy Spirit (Acts 1-2)" (Robert J. Karris, *op. cit.*, in: *NJBC*, 697 [*italics* added]).

[124] George Mlakuzhyil S.J., *AL*, 53 [*italics* in the original text].

[125] Cf. *ibid.*, 53-54 for the reasons.

[126] *Ibid.*, 54 (*italics* in the original text).

[127] *Ibid.*, 275.

[128] Cf. George Mlakuzhyil S.J., *CLDS*, 659-60 for further explanation.

[129] *DBCNT*, 308 [*italics* added].

130 This is part of the title of the message "FALL IN LOVE, STAY IN LOVE" [with God] of Fr. Pedro Arrupe S.J. (former Superior General of the Jesuits).

131 All these so-called *male and female qualities* are *culturally conditioned* but *all* (men and women) must *integrate* them in order *to become fully human.*

132 *Jesus' birth* as a *male* child was a *historical fact* but *not an ontological/ theological necessity.* If this is true, one is surprised to read statements like the following related to the question of the *ordination of women*: "There *must be physical resemblance* between *Christ and the priest*" (Vatican declaration in 1976, *italics* added)! If so, must every priest be 'circumcised' in order to *'resemble'* Jesus *'physically'*, since the latter "was circumcised" (Lk 2,21)?

133 "In this episode we see the life affirming forces at a greater advantage than the forces of decay, destruction and death. The dead body was powerless to make Jesus unclean; on the contrary the *touch of Jesus* made the *dead girl rise to life*" (DBCNT, 113).

134 Jesus' calling the bleeding woman *"daughter"* indicates his tender love for her, and his words to her: *"your faith* has *made you well"* (Mk 5,34; Mt 9,22) underline *her unshakable faith.* She is an *inspiring example* to all women believers in Jesus.

135 Surekha Nelavala, "Christology of Mark: An Indian Feminist approach," (Draft Paper, 2003, pp. 1-15), (retrieved on 09-03-2020), 9 [*italics* added].

136 *Ibid.,* 12.

137 *DBCNT,* 282.

138 *Ibid.,* [*italics* added].

139 Shalini Mulackal, *art. cit.,* 447 [*italics* added].

140 *Ibid.,* 448 [*italics* added].

141 *Ibid.,* 450.

142 Cf. Lk 23,34 (cf. Is 53,12); Lk 24,25-27 (cf. Is 53); Jn 1,29 (cf. Is 53,7); Mt 27,46.

143 Jessica Richard, "Resisting Bodies" as a Hermeneutical Tool for a Critical Feminist Christology of Liberation and Transformation

(Master's Degree Dissertation, 2010), 86 [*italics* added] (retrieved on 09-03-2020).

[144] *Ibid.*, 70. This *ongoing struggle against injustice* is illustrated by the *naked protest of the "Manorama Mothers"* against the brutal rape and murder of Manorama by the Indian army on 10th July 2004: "All of the 30 naked Manipuri women [were angry and held banners saying, "Indian Army Rape Us!"].... This kind of "anger" is what Jesus too practiced when he drove the vendors and merchants from the temple…" (*ibid.*).

[145] Dianne L. Oliver, "Christ in the World" in Sarah Katherine Pinnock. ed., *The Theology of Dorothee Soelle*, (Harrisburg 2003), 294.

[146] Evangeline Anderson-Rajkumar, "Asian Feminist Christology", *In God's Image*, Vol. 22, No.4 (Kuala Lumpur 2003), 9.

[147] Cf. Sook Ja Chung, "Becoming Christ: A Woman's Vision", *In God's Image*, Vol. 22, No.4, (Kuala Lumpur 2003), 18.

[148] Once a mother in labour pain was told by her doctors that she had to be operated but they would not be able to save both her life and her child's life! She told them: "I am ready to die to save my child!"

[149] Shalini Mulackal, *art. cit.,* 451 [*italics* added].

[150] *Three sample Creeds by Indian Christian women* are given below: a) by an *individual,* b) by *a group of students* of Vidyajyoti College of Theology, written at the end of the Course on Christology, and c) by a small *group of Women Religious* at the end of their *sharing* after an eight-day *Retreat* at Navjivan Renewal Centre in Delhi. All these **"Indian Feminist Creeds"** highlight the *aspects* of the *person and mission of Jesus* which are *appealing and meaningful to Indian women.*

[151] It is to be noted that in John's Gospel *"apostle"* (*apostolos*) is used to refer to "anyone who is sent" ("Amen, amen I say to you, a servant is not greater than his master; nor is *he who is sent* [*apostolos*] greater than he who sent him": Jn 13,16). In fact, in the Gospel of John, Jesus is often referred to as *the one sent by God the Father* (cf. 3,34; 5,36; 6,57; 17,3.8.21.23), and on Easter Sunday evening the risen Jesus tells the disciples: "As the Father has sent me, I too send you" (20,21).

[152] Cf. above **3.1.1. Jesus' Option for and Identification with the Dalits**.

[153] In order to be *effective co-liberators*, they have to be *united* (like the branches) with *Jesus*, the *Neem Tree*, and they must be ready to be the *drum* in the hands of *Jesus, the Drummer*.

[154] Cf. **2.2.** *especially* **2.2.4.** above.

[155] Cf. **3.2.1**-**3.2.4** above.

[156] Cf. **3.2.5.** above for *explanation* of these Tribal images for Jesus.

[157] Paulose Kullu S.J. calls "Jesus the Total Liberator," in: *Phenomenon of Tribal Religion and Culture* [unpublished notes], (Ranchi), 116-119.

[158] This is similar to the "Vision - Mission statement of the Ranchi Jesuits": "to be the Companions of Jesus and to share in his Mission of love and service by participating in the struggle of the people, particularly the marginalized and the oppressed in Jharkhand." ("Ranchi Jesuits - Vision mission", p. 1), (retrieved on 01-03-2020).

[159] They are the *truths* of "*suffering*" (*dukkha*), "*cause*" of suffering (*samudāya*), "*end*" of suffering (*nirodha*) and "*path*" that leads to the "end" of suffering (*magga*).

[160] Mund. Up. 3.1.6.

[161] Vatican II, "Declaration of the Relation of the Church to Non-Christian Religions" (*Nostra aetate*), No. 2 (*Hinduism*) and No. 3 (*Islam*).

[162] Cf. V. D. Savarkar, *Hindutva: Who is a Hindu?* (Bombay, 1923).

[163] K. M. Panikkar, *Asia and Western Dominance: A Survey of the Vasco da Gama Epoch of Asian History, 1498-1945* (New York, 1954).

[164] The emphasis here is "*at any cost*", which would refer to aggressively "*apologetic*" *defence of one's position,* since "dialogue is not apologetics…" (cf. "*Fifth*" guideline in the quotation).

[165] *A Dictionary of Asian Christianity*, edited by Scott W. Sunquist, David Wu Chu Sing and John Chew Hiang Chea, (2001), 388.

[166] Pope Francis, *Fratelli Tutti* [Social Encyclical on "*Fraternity*"], # 271 [*italics* added]. Endnote [259] refers to *The Catholic Bishops' Conference of India* [CBCI], "Response of the Church in India to the Present-day Challenges," (9 March 2016).

[167] Pope Francis, *Fratelli Tutti*, # 279 [*italics* added].

[168] Br. Up. 1.3.28.

[169] *AL,* 19 [*italics* added].

[170] Cf. *Ibid.*, 46-93 for detailed explanation. Cf. also *CLDS*, 594-603.

[171] Cf. Jerome Sylvester, *Khristbhakta: Viswas ke hamsafar [Christ-devotees: Co-Pilgrims of Faith]*, (Varanasi 2017).

[172] Raimundo Panikkar, *The Unknown Christ of Hinduism* (London 1964) [published during Vatican II (1962-1965)].

The new insights of theologians like Raimundo Panikkar, Karl Rahner, etc. on inter-religious dialogue influenced several paragraphs of Conciliar Declarations (e.g., *Nostra aetate*, "Declaration on the Relation of the Church to Non-Christian Religions", nos. 2-3 on 'Hinduism' and 'Islam' respectively) that stand as departure from the traditional stand of Catholic theology on world religions (e.g., *extra ecclesiam nulla salus*, "outside the Church there is no salvation"). "Solidarity of the Church with the whole human family" is affirmed in *Gaudium et Spes* (Pastoral Constitution on the Church in the Modern World", nos. 1-3 & 92-93).

[173] Ishanand Vempeny S.J., *Krishna and Christ* (Anand,1988).

[174] Shashi Tharoor, *Why I Am a Hindu* (New Delhi 2018), 4.

[175] *Pope Speaks to India: All Addresses and Homilies of the Holy Father during His Ten-Day Visit to India* (St Paul Publications, 1986), 22.

[176] Robert Ernest Hume, *The Thirteen Principal Upanishads* (Translated from the Sanskrit, with an Outline of the Philosophy of the Upanishads and an Annotated Bibliography), 2nd Edition, Revised (Oxford University Press, 1877).

[177] In the following pages we will try to *combine* the **insights** from "**Multi-Religious Context**" (**1.6.**) and "**Integral Approach**".

[178] See below "*Avatara in Hinduism and Incarnation of Jesus*".

[179] It is to respond to this spiritual need of humans today that the Society of Jesus has chosen one of the "*Universal Apostolic Preferences*" (2019-2029) as: "Show the way to God through the spiritual exercises and discernment."

[180] Cf. *GNJCG*, **Chapter 3** for the detailed explanation of Lk 12,49.

[181] Cf. Henry de Lubac, *Catholicism: Christ and the Common Destiny of Man*, (England 1950).

[182] R. E. Hume, *The Thirteen Principal Upanishads*, 290.

[183] Cf. *GNJCG*, **Chapters 1-4** for detailed explanation of Jesus' progressive self-revelation in the Gospels.

[184] Dr. Rev. Praseed, *Sacrifice and Cosmos: Yajna and the Eucharist in Dialogue* (2009), XI.

[185] A. A. MacDonnell, *A Vedic Reader*, (Oxford University Press, London 1917), 195 [*italics* added].

[186] Louis Renou, *Religions of Ancient India, Hinduism,* (London 1968), 72.

[187] The 'exclusivity' (implied in "the only true God") may create a stumbling block for inter-faith dialogue, unless the dialogue-partners acknowledge that ultimately there is "only one God" even though there may be many manifestations of God. *Ekam Sat Vipra Bahudhā Vadanti* ("The Real is one, the learned speak of it variously") (Rig Veda, 164.46).

[188] Jesus Christ's *Jñana* is more like Ramanuja's *Vishitadvaita* than Sankara's *Advaita*.

[189] "This progressive self-revelation of *Bhagavan* (God) to the *Bhakta* (devotee) is very much stressed in the *Bhakti marga* ('the way of loving devotion') in the Hindu religious tradition" (*AL*, 362, n. 21).

[190] Collected Works of George M. Soares-Prabhu S.J., (Vol. 3), 3-12.

[191] On different occasions I have explained *Jesus' Prem marga* as an integration of the three *margas* and many Hindus have found it very meaningful to them.

[192] C. T. R. Hewer, *Short Guide to Understanding Islam* (2013), 3 (retrieved on 20-04-2020). Another important quote from the author is: "If you want to understand a religion, you need to learn to see it through the eyes of those who follow it." This is equally applicable to our understanding of the Quran and the Gospel. It is with this inner conviction that we enter into "empathetic" Muslim-Christian dialogue.

[193] After reading the first *draft* carefully, Victor Edwin sent me the following appreciative E-mail (on 6th June 2020):

> "In the Spirit of Vatican II, the *attitudinal change* expected in *our dialogue with Muslims* is one of *listening to and sharing with* (not talking at) *one another* the *gifts of our faith*. Pope John Paul II and Pope Francis reflect such attitude. Our dialogue

with Muslims happens in our sharing … in the *spirit of joy* and *not* in the *spirit of polemics*. The chapter [draft] … does reflect this *dialogical spirit*".

[194] See Geoffrey Parrinder, *Jesus in the Qur'an* (1995) (free download from "Internet Archive"), [retrieved on 24-04-2020], 10-12, for a *similar positive approach* to the study of Jesus in the Qur'an and in the Gospels.

[195] Irfan A. Omar, "Qur'an Upholds Plurality as the Will of God," in: *Seeking Communion: A Collection of Conversations*, ed. by Victor Edwin S.J. (2018), 5 [*italics* added].

[196] Victor Edwin, "Is Christ a Stranger to Muslims? Constructing a Contextual Christology Among Muslims," in: *Searching Christology through an Asian Optic*, edited by P.R. John, John B. Mundu, and Joseph Lobo (Delhi, 2017), 179.

[197] Cf. *GNJCG*, **0.1. Introduction**.

[198] "He [Jesus] is thus the most mentioned person [187 times] in the Qur'an by reference; 25 times by the name *Isa*, third-person 48 times, first-person 35 times, and the rest as titles and attributes" ("Jesus in Islam," *Wikipedia*) [retrieved on 26-04-2020].

[199] Geoffrey Parrinder, *op. cit.*, 16 (*italics* added).

[200] Cf. *ibid.*, 22-51 for the detailed explanation of these *titles of Jesus* in the Qur'an. Jesus is also referred to as a "*Sign*" (*aya*), an "*Example*" (*mathal*), a "*Witness*" (*shahid*), a "*Mercy*" (*rahma*), "*Eminent*" (*wajih*), "*Blessed*" (*mubarak*), "*one brought near*" (*min al-muqarrabin*), and "*one of the upright*" (*min al-salihin*) (cf. *ibid.*, 51-54 for brief explanation of these titles).

[201] See *GNJCG*, **Chapter 3** for the reasons why *katalyma* (Lk 2,7) is translated as "guest-*room*" and not as "inn".

[202] This title "*son of Mary*" occurs 23 times in the Qur'an (which highlights Jesus being *human*), whereas it is found only once in the Gospel (Mk 6,3).

[203] The classical Muslim exegetes translated the word *zakī* in 19:19 to mean 'pure of sin' (Rāzī, Ṭabarī, Ṭabrisī) and 'growing up in goodness' (Rāzī, Ṭabrisī)

[204] This is one of the *many titles of Jesus* mentioned in the *Qur'an* (e.g. 'Servant,' 'Prophet,' 'Messenger,' 'Word,' 'Spirit,' 'Sign,' 'Witness,'

'Mercy', 'Blessed', etc.) (cf. Geoffrey Parrinder, *op. cit.,* 30-54) and in the *Gospels* (cf. *GNJCG,* **Chapters 1-4**).

[205] Cf. Geoffrey Parrinder, *op. cit.,* 30.

[206] See *GNJCG,* **Chapters 1-4** for the explanation of the *various aspects* of *Jesus the Messiah* (*royal, prophetic, universal*) highlighted in the Gospels of Mk, Mt, Lk and Jn.

[207] Geoffrey Parrinder, *op. cit.,* 32 (cf. *GNJCG,* the end of **Chapters 1-4** for the various meanings of *Jesus' self-designation* as "*the Son of Man*" in the Gospels).

[208] Geoffrey Parrinder, *op. cit.,* 35.

[209] These **'disputed' issues** are discussed below in **4.2.2.**

[210] Geoffrey Parrinder, *op. cit.,* 151.

[211] See *GNJCG,* **Chapters 1-4**.

[212] "Take me and my mother as *two deities besides God*?" (Maulana Wahiduddin Khan's translation of 5:116).

[213] "*Do not say:* '*There are three* [*gods*]*.*'" (M. W. Khan's translation of Q 4:171). Christians never say that 'there are three [gods]'. Christians' faith in the "*Trinity*" does *not* mean that they believe in "*three gods*" but that the *one God* is a "*Triune Unity*".

[214] Victor Edwin S.J. interprets this *Quranic warning* against the *worship of 'three gods'* in the following words: [in a letter on 15-06-2010] as follows:

> The Qur'an warns against anyone who worships 'three gods' and affirms that God is one. Traditionally it is conceived and interpreted as a censure against Christians. As Christians are thoroughly and radically monotheists, Qur'an's stricture could be said not against mainstream Christians who never in history worshiped 'three gods'. This Qur'anic warning is against all who hide 'gods' of their own creation in their hearts that leads them to live in ungodly ways.

[215] A. Yusuf Ali comments on Q 19:34: "Begetting a son is a physical act depending on the needs of men's animal nature. Allah Most High is indepenent of all needs, and it is derogatory to Him to attribute such an act to Him. It is merely a relic of pagan and anthropomorphic materialist superstitions" (n. 5 on p. 267).

[216] *Samad* is translated by Maulana Wahiduddin Khan as '*the Self-sufficient One*'.

[217] Geoffrey Parrinder, *op. cit.*, 126.

[218] Cf. GNJCG, **Chapters 1-4**.

[219] "This is a confirmation of the previous messages and as such acknowledges the close relationship that exists between the Jewish, Christian and the Islamic messages" (Irfan A. Omar, *art. cit.*, 5).

[220] Abdullah Yusuf Ali comments on Q 4:157: "The Qur'anic teaching is that Christ was not crucified nor killed by the Jews, notwithstanding certain apparent circumstances which produced that illusion in the minds of some of his enemies" (*The Meaning of the Holy Qur'an: Complete Translation with Selected Explanatory Notes* (Birmingham, 2008), p. 83, n. 21).

Regarding the next verse (Q 4:158: "*Allah raised him up*") A. Yusuf Ali says: "There is difference of opinion as to the exact interpretation of this verse... One school holds that Jesus did not die the usual human death, but still lives in the body in heaven, which is the generally accepted Muslim view" (*Ibid.*, n. 22).

[221] "Towards an Islamic Christology II: The Death of Jesus, Reality or Delusion (A Study of the Death of Jesus in Tafsir Literature)", *The Muslim World*. 70 (2): 91–121 (April 1980), [*italics* added].

[222] Victor Edwin's letter to me (sent on 15-06-2010) [*italics* added].

[223] Geoffrey Parrinder, *op. cit.*, 100. Mark A. Gabriel comes to a similar conclusion: "these prophecies had their fulfilment outside of Muhammad" (*Jesus and Muhammad: Profound Differences and Surprising Similarities*, [2004], 233).

[224] The Christian mystery of "*three persons in one God*" was/is often misunderstood by many Muslims as "*tritheism*" (belief in "three gods")!

[225] The '*Most Beautiful Names*' of God (like 'Most Gracious', 'Most Merciful', etc.) in the Qur'an manifest God's multiple relationships with human beings.

[226] The *early Christian Creed* starts by affirming: "We believe in *one God...*" and then points to the mystery of the *Triune God*, indicating the roles of *the Father* as *Creator, the Son* as the *Saviour* and the *Holy Spirit* as the *Sanctifier* (Council of Nicea, 325 CE). Based on God's

revelation in the Qur'an, *Muslims* believe in '*one God*' and, based on God's revelation to Jesus Christ in the Gospels, *Christians* believe in '*one God*' who is '*Triune*' but '*not* three'.

[227] "The divinity of Christ" is not a "pre-conceived idea" for Christians but an *integral part of Christian faith*. As it has been explained in **4.2.2.** *a)* above, "Jesus, *the Son of God*" does *not* mean the *same* thing for Christians and Muslims. Muslims object to "Jesus being the Son of God" because it seems to go *against monotheism*, as though Jesus were a "*second God*"! Christians do *not* believe that "Jesus, the Son of God" is a "*second God*" but that he has a *filial relationship with God, the Father* (as revealed in the Gospels).

[228] Godwin Rajinder Singh, *Gur Parsad: Sikh Doctrine of Divine Grace (An Interfaith Perspective)*, (Hong Kong: The Christian Conference of Asia, 1992), 38.

[229] The reprints of the GGS follow a system of standardized page numbering. There are 1430 standard Pages in the GGS and the references to the GGS follow this standardized pagination.

[230] Kharak Singh, "Guru Nanak in the History of Religious Thought," in: *Recent Researches in Sikhism*, ed. Jasbir Singh Mann & Kharak Singh (Patiala, 1992), 77.